THE WELSH SPRINGER SPANIEL

THE WELSH
SPRINGER SPANIEL

History, Selection, Training and Care

William Pferd III

SOUTH BRUNSWICK AND NEW YORK: A. S. BARNES AND COMPANY
LONDON: THOMAS YOSELOFF LTD

A. S. Barnes and Co., Inc.
Cranbury, New Jersey 08512

Thomas Yoseloff Ltd
Magdalen House
136-148 Tooley Street
London SE1 2TT, England

Library of Congress Cataloging in Publication Data

Pferd III, William, 1922-
The Welsh Springer Spaniel.

Bibliography: p.
Includes index.
1. Welsh springer spaniel. I. Title.
SF429.W37P43 1976   636.7'52   75-38437
ISBN 0-498-01846-6

To My Family:

Jane
Sarah
Stephen
Jeffrey

And To My Welsh:

Holly
Jess

CONTENTS

PREFACE

What began as a search of the local bookstore shelves for information about our newly purchased Welsh Springer Spaniel puppy has grown into the book you are now reading, and which I hope you will find as interesting and enjoyable as it has been for me to author. My introduction to the Welsh occurred one spring day while on a trip to visit friends in a nearby state. Traveling with my wife, Jane, and daughter, Sarah, I was told that we would be stopping soon to look at a litter of spaniels, and, since I was not particularly interested in what appeared to be a waste of time or in acquiring another responsibility, only with great reluctance did I follow along into the home of Mrs. Bryon Maine to see my first Welsh Springers. After suitable introductions and discussion about things Welsh, such as their beauty, disposition, and rarity, we were permitted to see eleven delightful, rollicking, boisterous puppies, a sight that brought smiles and ahs to everyone, especially Jane and Sarah. What we saw was not entirely new to Jane since, in her thoroughly studious way, she had considered a great number of other breeds before narrowing the choice to three, with the Welsh Springer Spaniel at the top of the list. Interestingly, this decision was made without the benefit of ever seeing a Welsh and is an indication of the value and power of well-written material. The breed description in the AKC Complete Dog Book and an illustrated book by Robert V. Masters, which contains single-page descriptions of the different breeds, gave enough information to draw our attention.

Characteristics, such as size, coat, and color, and a disposition described as attentive, friendly, and accommodating, along with the note that the breed is rare and not overly cultivated, still a natural, ancient in type and manner, were the words that caused our search to begin for a Welsh Springer Spaniel. Now fortune played a hand because within two months of the decision to look at Welsh, an advertisement appeared in a major newspaper. So rare was the breed at this time, that this was the only litter advertised in the Northeastern states during a four-year period.

Since that spring day my interest and feeling for the breed has grown through study and experience. Moving steadily from a one to two-dog owner, to trainer, handler, and breeder, and more recently, to help organize the breed club, and finally author, has given both pleasure and friendship. I soon learned that there was very little written information available about the Welsh, yet many authors noted the dog's apparent ancient origins. Fleeting references were made to evidence of the dog during early times, yet no book was available that presented all available information that would be useful and of interest to the owner or fancier of a Welsh Springer Spaniel. It was natural to ask why this was so and, in gaining an answer to the question, to begin to see a web of interrelated facts and statements that seemed to be unique—to place the Welsh in a special category of the breeds—and to warrant serious documentation. With an aroused interest and some time available for research and writing due to convalescing from an illness, a project was born to "put it all together" for the Welsh Springer Spaniel in a book that would be devoted entirely to the breed in the form of a definitive history. Because of my training and natural skepticism, I have avoided repeating information that appeared in the typical dog books, but rather have obtained and studied the original texts and primary sources, and used direct quotes to present the evidence or viewpoint of an older or ancient source. This has been possible because of the accommodating attitude and service of the American Kennel Club Library, New York; the Morris County Library, Morristown, New Jersey; the Shakespeare Birth Trust Library, Stratford, England; and the National Library of Wales, Aberystwyth, Wales—where all requests for ancient and modern books were met with friendliness and imagination.

My research encounters were especially rewarding with the people at the front desk, in the stacks, and in the "back rooms" of the Morris County Library. Their willingness to accommodate, combined with civility and pleasure, is a model to emulate. The special help, which I received from Miss Janet E. Bone, Principle Librarian, Inter-library Loan Department, is appreciated. Her resourcefulness and energy is commendable. Also, Mrs. Margherita G. Sandelli, Circulation Assistant, was most kind and prompt in processing my loan books at the front desk.

The second major source of help in providing pictures and words about Welsh Springer Spaniels has been the many owners both in Great Britain and the United States. Only their love of the breed and in particular, for their own dogs and bitches, would cause them to send along the wealth of favorite pictures, pedigrees, and records, and to take the time in many cases to write long letters to describe their experiences and favorite pets, hunters, or showmen. In addition to the valuable information that I have received in response to my requests, I have gained many new associates whose friendship I hope to repay by the publication of this book. Their wishes of success, expressions of pleasure, and kindest regards have been a source of encouragement. It has been most gratifying to have gained a corresponding acquaintance with Miss D.H. Ellis, Mrs. D. Morriss, Mrs. E. Falconer, Mr. and Mrs. C.J. Kitchener, Dr. E. Rickards, Mr. and Mrs. H.C. Payne, Mr. E.H. Perkins, the late Mr. H. Pocock and Mr. and Mrs. H. Newman, all in Great Britain. In America, too, many new friends have helped in providing extra information, especially Mrs. Sylvia Foreacre and Mrs. Edna Randolph, and Mr. and Mrs. Jack L. Dumbleton and D. Lawrence Carswell. A special word of recognition must also be given to the Secretaries of the Welsh Springer Spaniel Clubs in America and Great Britain. Some of you know of the help that I received from Anne Walton, the British Club Secretary. Not only has she sent pictures and statements about her own dogs, but has performed extra tasks for me in Britain to encourage the Welsh owners there to send along special pictures and records. Similarly in America, Lori Hatz, the American Club Secretary during the period when this book was prepared, has helped by sending along her records of American champions in addition to pictures of her own dogs.

To Catherine Johns, Research Assistant, The British Museum; Ellis Waterhouse, National Gallery of Art, Washington; Maria H.S. Costa, Curator, Gulbenkian Museum, Portugal; R.M.R. Peers, Curator, Dorest County Museum; D. King, Keeper, Department of Textiles, Victoria and Albert Museum; Fred P. Hughes, Supervisor, Show Recording Division, and Beatrice E. Peterson, Librarian, American Kennel Club; J.A. Bateman, Keeper of Zoology, National Museum of Wales, Cardiff; Lt. Cdr. J.S. Williams, Secretary, The Kennel Club; Romain S. Somerville, Assistant director, Maryland Historical Society; Bryan J. Culliford, Metropolitan Police Forensic Science Laboratory, London; Alexander Marshack, Peabody Museum; Y. Rollondo, *Conservateur du Musee du Morbihan, Bretagne;* Dr. Juliet Jewell, Mammal Section, British Museum (Natural History); Rosamond Hurrell, Curatorial

Secretary, The Minneapolis Institute of Arts; Klas Borjesson, Gateborgs Arkeologiska Museum; Dr. R.B. Vallender, Hon. Manager, Salisbury Museum Replicas Ltd.; Madame Madeleine Jarry, *Inspecteur Principal du Mobilier National, Paris*; Howard L. Blackmore, Keeper of Firearms, The Armouries, H.M. Tower of London; George C. Reed, President, Reed Petigrees; Dr. Aled Rhys Wiliam, University of Salford, England; S.A. Asdell, Cornell University (now retired); Elizabeth Thomas, Estate Secretary, Blenheim Place; Dr. M.I. Williams, Keeper of Printed Books, and G.M. Griffiths, Keeper of Manuscripts and Records, the National Library of Wales; Mrs. F.J. de M. Vatcher, Curator, Alexander Keiller Museum—I am indebted for help and advice on many aspects of the records and pictures of ancient and modern Welsh Springer Spaniels.

With James A. Bateman, Keeper of Zoology, National Museum of Wales, correspondence has been particularly agreeable. Mr. Bateman's prompt attention to my questions and extra effort to trace references of the skeletal remains of prehistoric dogs is acknowledged. His detailed comments and those of a colleague, Dr. Hubert Savory, Keeper of Archaeology, on the manuscript of the chapter, "Prehistory of the Hunting Dog in the British Isles," have been considered respectively in preparing the final work. The section about tiles from Neath Abbey in the chapter, "Renaissance Springer Spaniels," reflects information provided by another colleague, John Lewis, Medieval historian at the Wales Museum. The cooperation of these three gentlemen I appreciate. Further, I acknowledge the kindness and courtesy shown to me by James Bateman during my visits to the Museums at Cardiff and Caerleon.

Finally, my special thanks are extended also to Mary E. Unangst for her good cheer, care, and efficiency in typing the manuscript and to my wife, Jane, for reading the original, making valuable suggestions, and waiting patiently for the end of this endeavor.

In formulating the plan for this book, three major objectives were noted and hopefully satisfied in this edition. One was to provide a complete record of Welsh Springer Spaniel Champions in Great Britain and America since the last war. This has resulted in the pictorial register of past champions. Two was to trace back in time all references to Welsh Springer Spaniels, no matter where or how far, using the work of authors, artists, and scientists over the years. This record is presented in the chapters that convey the historical perspectives. I should like to think that this portion of the book will be of interest to a wider audience than the owners or fanciers of Welsh Springer Spaniels. Since the facts have been collected and checked with care, the work has a scientific basis and thereby should appeal to students of history and persons interested in the origins of the spaniel-type dog. The result is a deductive treatment that hopefully will satisfy even the more serious writers and researchers of hunting dogs. Three was to provide valuable reference material for the owner of Welsh Springer Spaniels. Information about the selection, care, and training of puppies and dogs for hunting, show, and as pets is presented in an easy-to-use manner in the last chapter.

And so, as Geoffrey Chaucer, in his first work, "The Book of The Duchess," said,

> The master hunter, forthwith, with a great horn blew three notes at the unleasing of the dogs

William Pferd III
Vice-President, Welsh Springer
Spaniel Club of America

AN ODE TO THE WELSH SPRINGER SPANIEL
Raynor Jacobs

They asked me what a Welsh Springer was;
It's a working dog, I said,
A dog with chestnut, fox-bright coat
With Llanharron spot on head.
A dog with trimming brilliant white
And tail quite short, and merry,
A dog to love, and love me too
And bark when necessary.

With real Welsh fire in its ancient blood
And spirit in its breeding
No slouch or lapdog is the Welsh,
Nor fussy in its feeding!
So sweet and gentle they can be
Or so rebellious, some days
Changing like wind on the Welsh hills,
But like them lovely always.

(1973 W.S.S. Club Yearbook)

THE WELSH SPRINGER SPANIEL

And then he looked at the color of the pack, and of all the dogs he had seen in the world, he had seen no dogs the same color as these. The color that was on them was a brilliant shining white, and their ears red; and as the exceeding whiteness of the dogs glittered; so glittered the exceeding redness of their ears.

Pwyll Prince of Dyfed, a Welsh story
from the second half of the eleventh
century, preserved in the Red Book
of Hergest and the Mabinogion.

1
AN HISTORICAL OVERVIEW

This dog is of very ancient origin; he is probably the oldest of all the spaniel breeds now in Great Britain. The Welsh Springer Spaniel is a distinct variety, and differs from all other breeds in type and other respects; writings and pictures, dating back some hundreds of years, describe and depict this spaniel.

These words were penned by Mr. A.T. Williams, of Ynisygerwm, Wales, Great Britain, in a letter to the editor, Herbert Compton of the book, *The Twentieth Century Dog*, published in 1904. They were in response to Mr. Compton's request for information about the breed, which he had previously addressed to knowledgeable sportsmen and women of Wales as part of the effort to gain official Kennel Club recognition for the Welsh Springer Spaniel. Of all the people who came forward to explain and defend the breed, Mr. Williams was the most persuasive due to his family's long association with the Welsh Spaniel. He stated that this breed of spaniel existed at his family kennels since 1750, that his grandfather used to go shooting in the years 1805 to 1850 with a team of twelve to fourteen dogs trained by himself, and that his father carried on the sport from 1845 to 1894 working with eight dogs. This long family history with Welsh Springer Spaniels was accepted fully by friends and associates of Mr. Williams. Testimony such as this and old references and pictures of the breed settled the issue; in 1902 The Kennel Club of Great Britain gave the breed a distinct classification, followed by the American Kennel Club in 1906.

But beyond the testimony of Mr. Williams, what other evidence do we have to show the history and origin of this "starter" for the hunter, flashy showdog, or devoted family pet? Such an inquiry leads the researcher into many fields beyond the dog world and so, too, the reader will learn a bit about art and archaeology, law and literature, and the lore of history as they relate to the dog and his owner. The evidence is found in odd places and, at times, requires conjecture and logic to develop its full meaning. Once the search begins, it soon becomes clear that man and dog have been exceptionally close. Wherever there is a record of man, no matter how small or fragmentary, the delight comes in finding a surprisingly clear picture or reference to our friend the dog. How far back can one go in the search for evidence? Would the time of the discovery of America do? Can one find evidence of our Welsh canine companion with Harold of England prior to the Battle of Hastings in 1066? What about the Dark Ages? Where they dark for Welsh Springer Spaniels? And did the Romans in Britain have anything to do or say about our smallish hunter? What about during the Iron Age, Bronze Age, or Neolithic Period? Does the record ever end? Of course it does. We shall see that the record is continuous with that of man and ends with our understanding of the history of Western European man back through the Mesolithic Era. For the Welsh Springer Spaniel, the focus must be on Wales, the adjacent countries, and the places of origin for the different groups of people who first settled in Southwestern Britain and who later came from the east, north, or west as either friend or foe to the original Britains who settled in Wales.

But what should one look for in the record? Certainly the name of the dog is an important note. Any reference to Welsh Spaniels, spaniels in Wales, or finally, just the descriptive word "spaniel" would be significant. Also, the main variable characteristics of dogs controlled by the chromosomes can form the basis for accurate identification. Asdell of Cornell University in his book entitled, *Dog Breeding: Reproduction and Genetics,* has indicated these to be as follows:

1. Body skeleton
2. Limb Skeleton
3. Shape and set of head
4. Form of tail
5. Eye and skin pigmentation
6. Size and set of ears
7. Hair and color pattern of coat
8. Blood types
9. Behavior and hunting traits

The combinations and permutations between these various basic characteristics can account for all the differences seen today in domestic dogs. Surely they can be used advantageously to identify the Welsh Springer Spaniel type dog in historical settings.

Considering these genetic characteristics, we find the Welsh Springer Spaniel a dog standing about eighteen inches high, symmetrical, with a fairly deep chest. His skull is proportionate, of moderate length, slightly domed, and with a clearly defined "stop." His eyes are dark and his nose is flesh colored or dark. He has floppy ears and a very distinctive red and white coat. His behavior is very friendly to man and shows a natural inclination to hunt all types of small game.

Does the description of the Welsh Springer Spaniel set him apart from other types of spaniels and hunting dogs? In a few respects, yes, very decidedly. The body size, shape of the head and ears, and most importantly, the color of the coat are the distinguishing features. The appearance of these genetic characteristics can serve as the connecting link in the search for the ancestry of the spaniel type of hunting dog, which is the forerunner of the present Welsh Springer Spaniel.

There is, of course, considerable controversy among dog historians about the origin of certain breeds. While the record is surprisingly full, it is by no means so detailed as to remove all argument for certain classes and types of dogs. For sporting or gundogs which specialize in the finding and tracking of game, there are a number of subdivisions that include expertise in pointing, swimming, and retrieving game on land or in the water. Of the twenty-six breeds of gun or sporting dogs that are presently recognized by the American and British Kennel Clubs, many stand out as close relatives to the Welsh Springer Spaniel. As can be shown, most of the sporting breeds are manufactured dogs, bred and refined by dog trainers, gamekeepers, and members of the landed gentry of Great Britain and Europe, principally during the eighteenth and nineteenth centuries. Only a few claim origins back further than the year 1700. Most have been fixed in their present type and style during the recent past so that there are good authentic records of the names of the people who managed the breeding, and of the places where the first distinctive types appeared. By using the color of the coat as a distinguishing feature, most of the sporting dogs lose the contest for the oldest breed, since the known record of the color coat for sporting dogs prior to 1500 settles on white and red. Three dogs of ancient origin, in addition to the Welsh Springer Spaniel, have red and white coats either now or within recent past. These are the Irish Setter, the Pointer, and the Brittany Spaniel. It is of interest here to note that all except the Welsh Springer Spaniel have pointing instincts, a latter-day characteristic that appears to have been bred into dogs as a refinement after the thousands of years of using the dog for the chasing of game, both large and small.

The Irish Setter and the Pointer appear to be relatively earlier breeds from Ireland and Spain, respectively. The Irish Setter is larger today—all red or rich mahogany—and is hardly ever used for hunting. Coming out of Ireland, however, it can be imagined easily as a large version of a Welsh type spaniel but bred for special purposes by our Irish forefathers. The Pointer came out of Spain into Great Britain around the beginning of the 1600s, has the ticking so well known on Welsh Springers, has less hair and stands a little higher, but is documented to have been trained out of the hound to chase and point in Spain and France at even earlier times. Their place of origin, Spain and France, should not be forgotten in the relation of these breeds to the Welsh Spaniel.

The last of the four red and white sporting dogs is the Brittany Spaniel that looks most like a Welsh Springer Spaniel. Of course, such a statement is heresy to a true Welsh Springer Spaniel, or Brittany fancier for that matter. Each is at times mistaken for the other, even in the best of circumstances. Fanciers of both breeds can tell of the horrible times when at the most respected of dog shows, announcers of the best-of-breed contest described one or the other as its breed cousin. Of course, to a Welsh Springer or Brittany owner there is little if any similarity between the breeds, but on first appearances one is certainly taken with the common features. Except for the height and build, stiltiness, and air of tenseness of the Brittany breed, they are similar yet very different to the trained eye. Of course, the Brittany points, which is never characteristic of the Welsh Springer Spaniel.

The places of origin of these four red and white sporting dogs cannot be ignored. In fact, they represent a recurrent link in the travels, language, and customs of the people that inhabited these regions of Western Europe. Brittany, Spain, Ireland, and Wales have been visited and populated by nomadic and adventurous peoples of the Western seaways for thousands of years. Interestingly, these same people possessed and used to great advantage a common four-legged friend—the dog. It should not be surprising that links, such as color coat and dominant hunting characteristics, should be seen in viewing these breeds that are linked by the people. The claim for the oldest is naturally related to the evidence that can be brought forth to substantiate the claim. Of the four, the Welsh Springer Spaniel can be judged as most ancient, a true original in this age of modernity and change. Not a pointer, not a specialist in the field of sport and hunt, but equally at home in water or on the land, the Welsh Spaniel is willing to give chase to feather or fur, and is a dog that can be trained to retrieve. The Welsh Springer is of medium height, obviously not bred for either great or small size as are the Irish Setter or the American and English Cocker Spaniels.

What follows then is a conjectural history of the Welsh Springer Spaniel from the time of the earliest record of hunting dogs in Western Europe. This story can be gleaned from the works of many archaeologists, starting with the earliest writings of the Greek and Roman authors. What they have to say about the hunting dogs of Britain is made clearer by the record left in the remains of ruined Roman villas and military towns. The place of the dog in Wales during the first thousand years since the birth of Christ is presented in the writings in Welsh law and literature. These early letters are supported by references to spaniels in an increasing number of medieval writings, and culminates with the definitive book by the doctor to the Courts of King Edward VI and Queens Mary and Elizabeth, Johnnes Caius, who was born in 1510. During this period and up to the present, works of art as found in tapestries and paintings tell a vivid story of the history of the Welsh Springer Spaniel hunting dog.

Since the eighteenth century, published written material is available in a flood and is finally supported by a tremendous photographic record that gives a crystal clear picture of the Welsh Springer Spaniel in America and Great Britain today. From an overview, the history of the breed can be seen in three major divisions: (1) the Welsh Springer Spaniel prior to recognition by the Kennel Clubs of Great Britain and America, (2) the development of the breed in Great Britain during the twentieth Century, and (3) the cultivation of the Welsh Springer Spaniel in the United States since World War II. Each of these fields are of great interest to Welsh Springer Spaniel fanciers and dog people the world over, and form the basis for this study of the breed.

The modern Welsh Springer Spaniel is an attractive red and white dog, in size between the black and white English Springer Spaniel and the various types of Cockers. He is from thirty-five to fifty pounds in weight and is absolutely distinct in type and character in every way. No other hunting spaniel has its color and it never breeds away from that color. Its muzzle is not deep, and its ears, hanging close to the head, are of vine-leaf shape, being short, set low, and not profusely covered or fringed with hair. Although today, the Welsh Springers have dark noses and eyes, flesh-colored noses and hazel eyes were the original colors and are still seen at times and considered acceptable in the breed standard.

The Welsh Springer Spaniel is an excellent and willing worker, has perseverance, dash, and stamina. He has sharp vision and a keen nose, and uses both sighting and scent to advantage in hunting. His size is ideal, standing no more than nineteen inches high. Unlike some of the hunting breeds, he is a great "family dog", naturally friendly with a merry disposition toward his people and kennel mates. He is intensely interested in his surroundings and protective of his property, barking or not, depending on his training. He is a great sport, always willing to play, and is devoted to children.

The Welsh Springer has always been a dog of sound temperament and good health, no doubt because of his ancient lineage that has resulted in the elimination of undesirable physical and mental characteristics. From the earliest records of the breed it is noted that he was not a dog to be easily upset by outside influences. This handsome, medium-sized dog can withstand extremes of heat and cold better than most dogs due to his natural hardiness. He can be as good a retriever from water as in upland shooting; and he can live happily both in country or city due to his great desire to associate with people.

2

PREHISTORY OF THE HUNTING DOG IN THE BRITISH ISLES

Can you imagine a family group on a sunny afternoon seated around the entrance to a cave that opens to the southeast and overlooks the sea? Across the way and below an overhanging ledge is a crude but serviceable shelter of tree limbs and branches covered with skins. This is the sleeping hut of some of the members of the family. Tiny flint pieces, the remains of many attempts to shape stones into a form that could be used on a spear or harpoon, lay all about as do the remains of edible shellfish. One of the young boys is trying to sharpen the end of a bone dagger that broke during the last hunt as his father plunged it into the back of a fallen deer. There is little talk as each member is occupied with their tasks or thoughts.

The father and leader of the group is more removed than usual, for this is a time of crisis in the lives of the family. He is reflecting on the events of yesterday during the hunt and whether he had been wise in calling off his dog as he did or whether he should have let him try to kill the buck alone. Only he knows that it was just when he called the dog that the deer drove his antler into the dog's side. The cry of pain from the dog caused him to move too quickly, and he had even broken his dagger in his rush to kill the stag. Hunting would be much harder now. He would have to go back to tracking the wild animals. But first they must bury the dog. It seemed that he was alright last night, but this morning he was dead. They would dig a hole nearby in the kitchen refuse and cover him over. He was a good dog. They would all miss him. The leader let his eyes wander over the members of his family and then out to sea. This was a good place to live. The woods had plentiful game and fuel for the fire, and the sea out ahead gave its fish and shells for food. He'd have to get another dog though, and soon.

Events, such as these, can be easily imagined by reflecting on the remains of Mesolithic family sites that have been found along the Atlantic coastlines of Brittany, Cornwall, and facing the Irish Sea in Wales, Ireland, and Scotland. At least one hundred homesites have been identified by archaeologists, and over ten of these have yielded the skeletal remains of one or more dogs, clear evidence that the canine pet and hunting campanion has been a part of the family group since 7000 B.C. in Western Europe.

Even in earlier times than the Mesolithic Period, dog and man were companions. At various places during the Upper Paleolithic Era, primitive inhabitants developed contacts with the ancestral types of present day dogs. It is accepted by modern authorities that all present breeds are derived from four ancestral stocks — *Canus lupus* (European northern wolf), *Canus lupus pallipes* (Asian wolf or dingo), *Canus latrans* (American prairie wolf or coyote) and *Canis azarea* (South American azaras dog). A branch of the northern wolves, *Canus lupus chanco* (Tibetan Wolf), is judged to be the most likely candidate for the ancestor of the modern mastiff group from which the breeds of hunting spaniels, setters, pointers, retrievers, and hounds are derived. Somewhere in Central Europe man's first associations took place as evidenced by the discovery of the skeleton of domesticated dog in Russia, AS1, and at early lake settlements in Switzerland and Austria, BS2. The first pictures of wolves in Western Europe are found as cave paintings in Spain. Made at the end of the last glacial period, about 10,000 B.C., the paintings have been interpreted by the world famous expert of prehistoric cave art, Abbé Breuil. These paintings appear in caves in the north coast of Spain, as do paintings from about the same period on the walls of caves located in Southeastern Spain. The caves were occupied during the Magdelanean Era that just preceded the Mesolithic Period or Middle Stone Age. The sites of most recorded archaeological finds of paintings and the skeletal remains of dogs that have been dated by modern methods, such as Carbon 14 studies, are shown on the map of Europe in Figure 2. The location of the Spanish Cantabrian cave paintings is at AP1 on the map. A painting in small black figures located at Cueva del Polvorin, Puebla de Benifazá, Castellón, Spain, (AP2) represents possibly a hunting dog with a boar. Because of the size and crudity of the figures, there is not a unanimous view that dogs are represented in all pictures, some being possibly pictures of wolves. Some good evidence does exist to show that dogs were already domesticated before the Mesolithic in the Near East, so it is not unreasonable to state that it is the dog that appears in prehistoric Levantine art.

This is not to say that all groups of primitive man used dogs for hunting. It is the view of such naturalists as Fiennes and Lorenz that the various breeds of dogs descended from the wolf and dispersed along the migratory routes during late Paleolithic times, prior to 15,000 B.C., they were developed first into the family as aide's and protector's rather than for hunting reasons primarily because of the "affectionate" aspect of the relationship between man and dog. This running together or friendship is seen even today where wild dogs choose to live near man, feed on his garbage, and become the haphazard playmate of the young children in the area. There is other pictoral evidence in cave paintings in Algeria of dogs in the hunting role, but surprisingly they do not appear in the prehistoric caves of France. Could it be that the great abundance of game in the great valleys between the Pyrenees Mountains and the Massif Central of France made hunting with dogs unnecessary? Whatever the reason, no paintings of dogs exist such as those of the other wild animals of the period found in the famous Lascaux caves. From these archaeological finds it seems that the Spanish Levantine and the Cantabrian Mountains are the home of the earliest hunting dog in Western Europe, and as we shall see, the southwest Europe is considered also to be one area of origin of the Stone Age settlers who subsequently populated Brittany, Southwest England, Wales, and Ireland.

With the gradual change in climate to a more temperate sort and the gradual submergence of the Britain Peninsula to form the British Isles, immigrants from west-central Europe as well as south-west Europe settled all along the shores of the European continent. Mesolithic settlements have been identified from the north coast of Spain, in the Brittany area, Southwest Cornwall, and along the coast of Wales, Ireland, and Scotland that border the Irish Sea. The skeletal remains of dogs have been unearthed at a number of European sites, particularly in Denmark (BS1 on the map). These date from about 7000 B.C. and are associated with the presence of hunting people who settled the region. The greatest number of the remains of dogs are concentrated on the island of Zealand, and their presence is associated with the Maglemosian hunting people. Additional finds of dog skeletons have been uncovered from the lake settlements found in Switzerland, in Germany, and in Western France. The examination of the remains of dogs from these Mesolithic sites have indicated the presence of types of dogs that can be classed as either herding, hunting, or minature dogs. In 1852, Rutimeyer, who first discovered the remains of a dog at a Switzerland lake site (BS2), gave it the name *Canis familiaris palustris* — the peat dog. What did it look like? It was small sized, halfway between the jackal and the fox, it had a tapering but not long muzzle, a wide deep chest, and a slight skeleton and limbs, and about the size of a Terrier. In 1877, the bones of a medium-sized, stronger dog, with a more elongated head and powerful jaws with a pointed muzzle were discovered in the mountainous regions of Germany by Woldrich. This type dog, *Canis familiaris intermedius* was judged by Studer to be similar to the modern Setter and Spaniel.

Of particular interest in tracing the prehistoric relations of the Welsh Springer Spaniel is the find at the site in Western France, Téviec, Saint Pierre Quiberon, Morbihan (BS3), where the homesite of a Mesolithic hunting family was described in 1937. It may have been this family that sat around its cave entrance pondering the loss of their dog, for it was at the Téviec site that the jaw bones of another *Canis familiaris intermedius* was found. The site has been studied in great detail and forms the basis for the Tardenoisian culture, the first representative of over a hundred other sites located along the Atlantic seaboard and Irish Sea that were settled by similar people. At the Téviec site, located at a rocky islet to the west of the Quiberon peninsula in Brittany, archaeological studies have uncovered many items of daily life of these Mosolithic hunters. The dog, clearly domesticated, would have been of medium height with a tapering muzzle. It can be classed as a hunter that was domesticated in the late Mesolithic forest cultures of Scandinavia, Switzerland, and France. This prehistoric dog has been found by Dahr to have primitive cranial and mandibular features. Dahr considers the breed to be widely dispersed during Mesolithic and Neolithic times and to have originated in a Pleistocene species. While this dog has been identified at three archaeological sites on the European land mass, there is no evidence of its presence in the British Isles in pre-Neolithic times. While there are sites of earlier settlers along the eastern and western coasts of the Irish Sea, no remains of dogs have been found in Britain and Ireland that predate around 4000 B.C. Prior to this period, the coastlines of the British Isles changed to their present form. The Straights of Dover were opened and became navigable to more adventurous settlers. A northward migration of people using the northern searoute gradually occurred, resulting in the establishment of many new homes just inland from the coasts of Southwest England, Ireland, and Wales.

What is the evidence of Stone Age dogs in Wales? Just over one-hundred years ago, a then young graduate of Oxford and subsequently Curator of the Museum and Lecturer in Geology in the Owens College, Manchester, published a book that described the results of his research on the archaelogical evidence found in caves of Wales and England. This was a most important book and set down for the first time the fact that dogs were an accompaniment to the Neolithic cave-dwelling people of Britain. The Book, *Cave Hunting,* by W. Boyd Dawkins, published in 1874, places the dog in Wales at Pembrokeshire (BS4) and Denbighshire (BS5). The most remarkable of the sites that were investigated was a group of caves clustered at Perthi-Chwaren on a farm high up in the Welsh hills, about ten miles to the southeast of Ruthin, in Denbighshire. The investigation produced the bones of the ox, goat, horse, pig, and dog. Some will be disturbed by this classic observation by Dawkins: "The remains of the domestic dog were rather abundant, and the percentage of young puppies implies also that they, like other animals, had been used for food." Fractured dog leg-bones in another cave also indicated that the dog assuaged the appetite as well as obeyed the command of these early Welsh primitives. All but one of the six other caves in the Denbigh area yielded the bones of dogs.

Of equal interest is the conclusion from the study by Dawkins of the dimensions of the skulls of the people who inhabited the caves; that they are in size and shape comparable to the early stone-age type of man that prevailed throughout the Iberian Peninsula and Western France. It would be quite natural for family groups to move northward along the coast of Europe in small dugouts and to bring along their most-valued possessions. Certainly, the young children would demand that their playmate dog come along and young men of the tribe would insist that their best hunters had a safe place for the trip to the new land. Here is the first conclusive evidence of a link between dogs in the Brittany and Welsh countryside, and at what an early age!

By the Middle Neolithic Period, about 3000 b.c., considerable colonization of Wales and Southwest England had occurred. Archaeological studies show the climate to be warm and reasonably dry with forests of ash, oak, and lime trees in the low country. There was much open land in the south of England, useful for grazing and farming. Improved tools appeared—grinding and polishing stones, better stone axes for felling trees, and hoes for agricultural use. These tools are found widely dispersed over the areas that border the Irish Sea and southern England. Important stone factories existed in Cornwall, while actual factory sites have been found in Wales in the Presely Mountains, in Pembrokeshire, and at the Graig-Lwyd axe-factory, Penmaenmawr in Caernarvonshire, North Wales. The finds of implements at remote locations in England and Ireland, which were made from stone from these quarries, clearly demonstrate the considerable movement of people during this period and the transport of valuables from Wales to other parts of Britain. Surely included in the movement would be dogs who were no doubt considered prized possessions.

Generally during the one thousand years before 3000 B.C. or the start of the Neolithic Period, there must have been a steady rise in population of the lands bordering the Irish Sea and Southwest England as can be deduced from the relatively large number of burial sites of these stone-age people. The chambered and passage graves, comprised of large, flat, stone slabs levered or slid into position and then mounded over with dirt, became the final resting place of the more illustrious of the stone-age population. Fortunately, for the history of the dog, some of these early British settlers chose to have their favorite pets buried with them, for it is usual that at least a few of the many graves that have been studied yield the skeletal remains of one or more dogs. Generally, the graves and occupation sites are found in groupings that cover a region of the British Isles and comprise a culture that exhibits similarities in the shape of the graves and the objects that are uncovered during the excavations. Just such a rather small grouping of graves occurs to the east of the Graig-Lwyd axe-factory in Denbighshire, and not too distant from the caves that were explored by Dawkins. The Dyserth Castle site investigated by Glenn showed a prehistoric layer that contained a Graig-Lwyd axe, flint arrowheads, a grain rubber, bone beads, and the bones of horse, ox, sheep, pig, and dog.

Directly to the south at the other side of Wales, where the indenture of the Severn and Wye Rivers exits to the Bristol Channel after draining the eastern side of the Welsh highlands, there occurs a group of caves, graves, and occupation sites of the Severn-Cotswold culture of Neolithic people. Over sixty chambered tombs stretch along to the east and west side of the Bristol Channel with concentrations in Gloucester (CS1) and Brecknock (CS2). Of these, four contained the skeletons of dogs. It is reported by Bate that at the Nympsfield site it was possible to distinguish from leg bones two breeds of dog, one the size of a Scottish Deer-hound, and the other of a smaller Collie or Terrier.

Dogs in graves of the Clyde-Barlingford culture also occur with other domesticated animals. At Ballyalton (CS3) and in Scottish sites (CS4) the usual range of domesticated animals was found. Of quite different implications were the finds in North Scotland (CS5) and the Orkney Isles (CS6) where, to gratify the death wish of some old chieftains who were no doubt also great hunters, a curious burial ritual was enacted. In the tombs at Caithness and Orkney there were found carefully deposited dog skulls — seven at Burray and as many as twenty-four in the Maes Howe type tomb on Cuween Hill. In this region at various occupation sites skeletal remains of numerous red deer and the bones of wild birds were also found, evidence of a disposition toward hunting and fowling of the people of the Orkney-Cromarty group of Neolithic people. As reported by Piggot, Ibera-Hibernian art motifs, the skull formation of some of the buried individuals and the method of construction of some of the tombs might be regarded as substantiating a fairly direct link with Iberia far to the south; further evidence of the use of Western searoutes as the means of approach for colonists and a link between Spain, Brittany, and the dog remains at the various cultural areas in the British Isles. In Portugal, at one of the few sites in Spain, where detailed archaelogical study has taken place, our friend the dog again appears. At Vila Nova, located northeast of Lisbon on the Tagus River (CS7), the bones of dog, horse, and mule have been identified. This hilltop occupation site is dated about 2400 B.C., coincident with many of the Neolithic sites in the British Isles discussed earlier.

From a historical viewpoint, one dog in particular has great importance in the long history of the Welsh Springer Spaniel. In Southwest England the complete skeletons of ancient dogs were discovered in the early 1930s. At both the Maiden Castle and the Windmill Hill archaeological excavations near Avebury, England (CS8), the skeletal remains of Neolithic dogs were uncovered in an area estimated to have been laid down about 3000 B.C. The Windmill Hill dog stood about eighteen-inches high and, in form, resembled a retriever-pointer. As we have seen, the dog in Stone Age Britain was bred earlier to serve as a companion, in the hunt, and as a source of food. At Windmill Hill we see a new role for the dog — helping to herd and protect flocks from the wild animals living in the forest nearby, for these people were the first farmers of Britain. This dog has been thoroughly examined by R. and A. Fiennes and reported on in their book, *The Natural History of Dogs*. They report their work as follows:

> After death this dog was flung into a ditch without proper burial, and it is therefore unlikely to have been a favorite pet of the family. Nevertheless, it was evidently well fed and cared for; the skeleton shows no injuries which could be attributed to sticks or stones or kicks, although some time before death it seems to have suffered from a blow which caused separation of the two maxillae (jaws). Although the dog was not a special family pet, evidently it was highly regarded. It had good powers of scent, speed and probably endurance. We know that the owners kept numerous cattle, sheep and goats, and we may suppose that this was primarily a sheep or herd dog, possibly used also for hunting.

An examination of the skeleton at the Auebury Museum leads to some other important factors that cause one to consider this dog a prototype of the Welsh Springer Spaniel. The overall size both in height and length of the body is representative of a medium-sized animal. The skull is narrow and moderately long. It has a marked "stop," suggesting an animal of the mastiff group. The nasal openings are wide, indicating a scenting behavior. The feet are wide and splayed. This dog had many of the physical features to permit it to serve as the prototype of the retreiver/spaniel group of dogs and, therefore, a distant cousin to the modern Welsh Springer Spaniel.

Comparison between prehistoric and modern dogs can be given more credence when quantitative measures are employed. Three of the genetically variable characteristics of dogs indentified by Asdell—body skeleton, limb skeleton, and shape of skull — are subjects for precise measurement. By selecting important limbs and skull features, the relative size and shape of the dog can be discerned and reasonable judgments can be made regarding ancestral relationships. Such a comparison is presented in Table I for three prehistoric dogs and two modern ones — the Fox Terrier and the Welsh Springer Spaniel. The prehistoric dogs are the Windmill Hill and Swiss Lake Dwelling canines described previously, and the Easton Down dog from the later Bronze Age. Of these three, the Windmill Hill dog is the larger, standing about eighteen inches (45.7 cm) at the shoulder, with length of limbs and skull almost the exact size of the Welsh Springer Spaniel. The Swiss Lake Dwelling dog is the smaller, of a size similar to the Fox Terrier. The measurements of the Easton Down skeleton indicate a dog similar to a large Terrier. These measurements support the view of a continuous presence of the Welsh Springer Spaniel type of hunting dog in Britain from earliest times. The archaelogical finds of dog limbs both larger and smaller than those recorded in Table I indicate the existence of at least three different breeds — the Deerhound, the Terrier, and the retriever-pointer or Spaniel. These quantitative measures confirm that this old Welsh breed of dog has survived from a primitive form in the culturally isolated and mountainous regions of Britain.

The presence of dogs in the periods after the Neolithic Age is as difficult to trace as the specifics of the life of Bronze and Iron Age people. Unfortunately, great stone structures, save for Stonehenge, do not grace the Bronze or Iron Age countryside to serve as protectors of relics and the bones of the dead. The benefits of wood construction no doubt improved immeasurably the life-style of these predominantly farming folk. The well-known propensity for rain in the British Isles, however, has all but completely destroyed the chance for reconstruction or survival of the many homesites that must have dotted the landscape. Even the means of burial changed to cremation, and so there is a very meager history in which to view the fifteen-hundred years before the Roman invasion of Britain. A dog buried with his hunter-owner at Snail

Table I
Prehistoric and Modern Dog Bone
Measurements (mm.)

	Welsh Springer Spaniel	Windmill Hill	Easton Down[1]	Swiss Lake Dwelling[2]	Fox Terrier[3]
Femur	160	165	145	127-144	135
Tibia	150	140	148	144	138
Humerus	150	152	133	127-144	123
Radius		135	133	122-128	125
Ulna	170	172	160		145
Skull Length	185	170[4]	167		138
Zygomatic Width	98	97[4]	89		82
Breath over Canines	40	36[4]	35		30

[1] Jackson, J. W., F.G.S., Report on the Skeleton of the Dog from Ash Pit at Easton Down.

[2] Rutimeyer, Die Fauna der Ptahlbauten der Schweiz (1861) -

[3] Wagner, K., "Regente Hunderassen," Norske Vid. - Akad. I. Mat. - Nat. Kl. 1929, No. 9, 1930.

[4] Vatcher, F.J. de M.: Curator, Alexander Keiller Museum, Avebury, Wilts.

Down in Wiltshire (DS1) and a few finds of dogs that are clearly members of a family group are the chance finds in the many sites that have been examined. One of these was in the Easton Down Area (DS2) at one of the rare permanent settlements of the Beaker people of the region. At this site a most interesting find confirms the continued presence of the *Canis familiaris intermedius* in Southwest England. At the bottom of a circular pit filled with powdered bone ash under the floor of one of the huts, a dog had been carefully buried in an attitude of sleep. The dog is reported by Stone to have died about 1400 b.c., and is the same moderately sized breed of dog as those encountered at Windmill Hill and Maiden Castle.

Let us consider for a moment the circumstance that could have induced this Bronze Age family to prepare such a grave for a dog. Surely this dog must have been important to the adult members of the group for them to have taken such measures indicated by archaeological evidence. The disposal of the dead animal could have been as casual an act as that performed at Windmill Hill where a dead dog was thrown rudely into a drainage ditch. Alternately, he could have been buried as most dogs are today, with some sense of affection in a constructed grave a short distance from the home of the owners, as was the case in the disposal of the dead hunting dog of the Téviec family. This would be the more logical of the methods of burial since it avoids the presence of offensive odors that occupany the decay of the dead remains, yet ensures that the carcass is protected from being unearthed by scavengers of the field and forest to be dragged away for food.

But the Easton Down dog must have been a special sort since neither of the usual methods of burial occurred. The most distinguishing feature in the burial is location − inside the hut of the family group. Was this action taken through reverence or fear? Certainly it cannot be classed as an act of convenience. One would have a problem to dispose the dirt and chalk from the hole, aside from the disturbance it would cause. Nor is it logical to assign this unique burial as an act of love or religion. These considerations prompt an outdoor gathering for the final acts. But fear does afford a reasonable explanation. Clearly, this burial can be taken as an act of secrecy. Where better to hide something whose discovery would cause great harm than in the floor of one's home. Could this be the final resting place of a chieftain's dog that was killed or poisoned by one of the lesser families of the region in revenge or to end a nuisance? One can imagine this burial as primitive justice that was the forerunner of the many laws that regulate the relationships between the dogs of the chieftain or lord and his subject and, in more recent times, the dog's owner and his neighbor.

One must also consider in passing the clever technical aspect of this Easton Down dog burial. To avoid the smell in the hut of the decaying flesh, the dog was buried in powdered bone ash, a charred organic material that has odor-fixing properties. One can almost see the plot unfold with the clever solution for the question, "How shall we dispose of the body?" This archaeological find points to the burial of the dog in the hut to hide the evidence by covering it with the remains of the fire, the ashes, and partially burned debris that had to be carried out from time to time for disposal anyway. No one would ever know. And, in fact, no one did until the chance discovery of a modern investigator.

At almost the same time that the Beaker family, with some obvious care, buried this canine friend or nuisance, a primitive artist on a sunny slope in Hältane, Sweden was carving on a rock for posterity his recent feat of killing a boar or wolf with bow and arrow. This vivid scene shows ten dogs in states of excitement charging after the wounded beast, ears flying, tails up, all hard on the heals of the prey. This type of scene could just as easily have been made by one of those Neolithic Scottish hunter chieftains who was laid to rest with his twenty-four favorite and prized hunting dogs. The Hältane rock carving appears on a flat rock at ground level on a farm in the Kville parish of Bohuslän and measures about two by three feet. The figures are sharply made and appear to be a composition made all at one time during the Early Bronze Age or Late Stone Age.

These examples of care and pride in the long association of dog and man surely proceeded into the pre-Roman period, although there is little archaeological evidence at hand. Just as it proceeds in the millions of family groups that contain a canine member today, so it must have been as the incursion of Celtic people from Europe entered Britain and finally made their belated appearance in Wales. So, too, it must have proceeded as the next wave of Brythonic settlers that entered Britain from the east and eventually filtered to Wales. Up to the time of the invasion by Caesar, Wales was so positioned and forested to escape the radical intermixing and turmoil that occurred in Eastern Britain. It represented a backwater of early people and ways. Along with Ireland, Wales had the long peace to maintain ways of the past in both values and life-style. A tenacious people, they resisted the armed might of many an adventurer, secure in their hill forts and intense family ties. In this social framework, the early dogs of the prehistorical period of Wales surely survived, just as the people kept to themselves and survived to be able to meet the advancing legions of the Roman army a century after Caesar — the last to fall before the Roman Imperial might. The Irish and Welsh ties with the Spanish people in skull type and appearance held then; so much so that it was commented on by Roman writers and generals. Was the common dog of Wales also fixed in time during this long period of stability for the people? One can only guess, but logic would lead to a positive view.

ARCHAEOLOGICAL SITES OF ART WORK AND
SKELETAL REMAINS OF DOGS

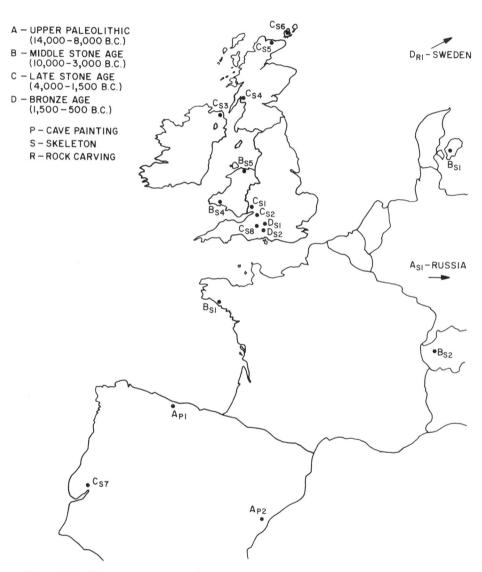

A – UPPER PALEOLITHIC
    (14,000 – 8,000 B.C.)
B – MIDDLE STONE AGE
    (10,000 – 3,000 B.C.)
C – LATE STONE AGE
    (4,000 – 1,500 B.C.)
D – BRONZE AGE
    (1,500 – 500 B.C.)

P – CAVE PAINTING
S – SKELETON
R – ROCK CARVING

Map of the Western seaways and surrounding European countries where archaeological sites have produced artworks and the skeletal remains of prehistoric dogs. (Pferd)

Early Bronze Age hunter with his dogs shown in a rock carving discovered in 1927 in Håltane, Bohuslan, Sweden. Note that this scene of ten dogs, all of a type, with longish bodies and large flappy ears, is the earliest record of a pack of dogs with common features. (Lars Krantz)

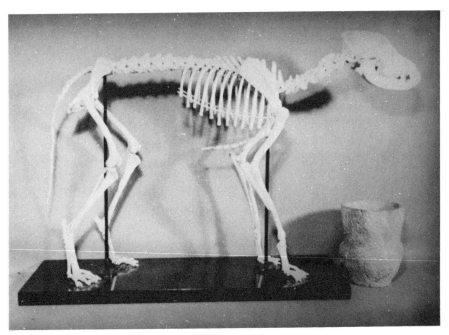

Complete skeleton of a dog, standing fifteen inches high, from the early Bronze Age encampment on Easton Downs, Wiltshire. This is a smaller specimen than the dog uncovered at the Windmill Hill archaeological site. (Salisbury Museum)

3

ROMANO-BRITISH AND WELSH TRIBAL DOGS

With the rise of the Roman civilization and its expansion to include the British Isles, a literary record appeared that now serves to show many aspects of the economic, military, and social relationships in Western Europe during the first centuries after the birth of Christ. The meager archaeological finds of the prehistoric period are supplemented by a considerable amount of written material by Greek and Roman authors. The literary talents of the Romans were applied to books, poems, and papers to present viewpoints and facts about almost all subjects. Included were works on natural history, zoology, and hunting; subjects that cover the activities and characteristics of dogs. The real founder of scientific zoology is Aristotle who completed his great work before 322 B.C. For over fifteen-hundred years this served as the major source of information about the animal world, and succeeding authors hardly did more than copy or translate his works. This is not surprising when one considers that Aristotle wrote a total of twenty books on animals, which include their history, parts, generation, and locomotion. Unfortunately, Aristotle wrote before the discovery of Britain and therefore offers no view of the dog in the British Isles during Roman times.

Our written information on British dogs during the Roman period must be found elsewhere and fortunately it exists in the works on hunting and geography. The first of these to be considered is by Xenaphon who wrote shortly before Aristotle, prior to 354 B.C. While he too wrote before the discovery of Britain, his comments on the hunting of the hare provide our first documented glance of the relationship between man and dog in the field. He writes of hare hunting as follows:

> Against the Hare, because he feeds in the night and hides in the day, you reared dogs which should find him by scent. And because, when found, he fled swiftly, you had other dogs fitted to take him by speed of foot.

Xenaphon devoted several pages in his book to Cretan and Laconian dogs and gave his views on conformation and hunting style. One can assume that these descriptions were simply a statement of conditions well known at that time and fully developed. It is clear that we are seeing but one of the descriptions from possibly many of a similar and earlier sort that did not survive the destructive effects of two thousand years of violence and natural catastrophy. When one considers that it was not until the 1500s that full awareness of the existence of these early documents occurred, it is truly fortuitous that so much is available. In fact, there are five chief references to British dogs in the Roman literature, each with something of interest relative to the origins of the Welsh spaniel-type hunting dog.

The earliest of these was written by Strabo about forty years after Caesar's return from his invasion of Britain. The *Geography of Strabo* is far more than mere geography, being an encyclopedia of information concerning the various countries of the civilized world as known at the beginning of the Christian era, including social and historical comment. Of Britain, he has four pages that describe the boundaries of the Isles, means of access from the continent, Caesar's experience in 45 B.C., and, of greatest interest to the history of dogs, the description of activities of the tribes that inhabited the country at that time. Strabo's most quoted statement is as follows:

> Most of the island is flat and overgrown with forests, although many of its districts are hilly. It bears grain, cattle, gold, silver and iron. These things, accordingly, are exported from the island, as also hides, and slaves, and dogs that are by nature suited to the purposes of the chase.

One can surmise from this description the important role in the British tribal community played by the hunting dog. It is ranked with gold and slaves, and its very nature is of such interest and value that it is clearly described in what is otherwise rather tersely written material. Strabo also states that it was distinctly different from the "native dog" that was no doubt large and trained to be vicious. From the bones of dogs found at numerous Iron Age farming settlements in England there were also types used as scavengers and as herd dogs. Claudian, another Roman writer, describes a fifth type of Briton dog that "could break the back of mighty bulls."

Some two hundred years later a young Roman, Oppian of Apamea, provided additional information about hunting and dogs in his poem "Cynegetica" or "The Chase." Whether other writers of the preceding years wrote about dogs, we do not know, since the search by many authorities of all remaining works show that the subject is not covered. Fortunately, the writings of Oppian have much to offer of interest, and considering the summary nature of the work, he must have used a library of other sources on hunting and dogs. His list of twenty-two differently named dogs, which "are the most excellent and greatly possess the mind of the hunter," contains one of special interest since it is singled out for detailed comment. Oppian's words about this British dog are as follows:

> There is one valiant breed of tracking dog, small indeed but as worthy as large dogs to be the theme of song; bred by the wild tribes of the painted Britons and called by the name of Agassaeus. Their size is that of the weak and greedy domestic table dog: round, very lean, shaggy of hair, dull of eye, it has its feet armed with grievous claws and its mouth sharp with close-set venomous tusks With its nose especially the Agassian dog is most excellent and in tracking it is best of all; for it is very clever at finding the track of things that walk the earth but skillful too to mark the airy scent.

Now a careful reading of the description by Oppian of the Agassian dog shows a significant number of characteristics that are similar to those of Welsh Spaniels, while others are obscure or seemingly overstated. In the latter case, grevious claws and venomous tusks are at first glance inappropriate. But are they? Certainly the nails of hunting dogs, including Welsh, have a natural inclination toward length if not maintained by cutting or removal. Where the conditions of the ground are soft so that there is little abrasion, the nails of the dogs grow naturally to curved ends similar to those of the rabbit or hare. It is quite clear that this was the case during Roman times since tools for grooming dogs, obviously, did not exist among the primitive tribes of Britain. As for venomous tusks, this comment could relate to the disease-bearing tendency of animals and problems experienced with wounds inflicted by dogs, especially after carrying field game in their mouths. In this respect, Oppian had these additional words of interest about how the Agassian dog went about his business:

> So the dog . . . rushes this way and that and searches every stone in turn and every knoll and every path and trees . . . But if thou were to array him

against the hare difficult to capture, stealthily he draws nigh, planting step-on-step . . . But when he approaches the covert of the hare, swiftly he springs, like an arrow from the bow. So the dog gives tongue and springs; and if he hits his quarry, easily he will overcome him with his sharp claws and take his great load in his mouth and go to meet his master . . . swiftly he carries his burden but laboring and heavy-laden he draws near . . . and the swift hunter meets him joyfully . . .

What a vivid description of a hunting spaniel! The instinctive actions are described clearly. Most of the attributes of a qualified field dog are included in this ancient Greek text written about A.D. 200. We see the dog hunting-eager, silent, and with drive, never tiring and willingly facing all types of cover of bushes and woods. He is able to track and work the wind to mark the presence of scent. He draws up on approaching game and springs the game to make the catch. Here we see a difference compared to the modern spaniel who has been trained to stop to game and shot automatically. But, of course, this was long before the invention of the fowling piece or shotgun, and the taking of game was by direct action of the dog or by the use of lance, net, or bow by the hunter. Oppian was so impressed with the final action of the dog that twice he noted the "springing" of the dog and game. We see that the use of this descriptive word, which is fixed to most spaniels, has a truly ancient origin. Oppian also wrote of the acts of retrieving and delivering the game to the hand of the trainer that many Welsh do with a natural willingness that must come from an ancient heritage. Praise for the dog from the hunter for a good carry is also understood by this ancient author. To show further the relationship between the hunter and dog as cultivated during this period there are the writings of Claudius Aelian who described the final actions of the chase:

> But if the dog tracks out some beast and comes upon some scent, then it halts. And the huntsman approaches while the dog overjoyed at its good luck fawns upon its master, licks his feet, and resumes its original quest, advancing step-by-step until it comes upon the lair; further it does not go. So then the huntsman understands and with a low call gives the signal to the men with the nets. And they set the nets in a ring. Thereupon the dog barks. The intention of its baying just then is to provoke the boar to rise in order that he may emerge and as he flees may be caught in the nets . . . This is what dogs do in dealing with boars and stags.

Aelian was a Roman author and teacher who, in *De Natura Animalium,* wrote in Greek his curious stories of animal life, frequently with moral lessons. In over seventeen sections of his work, *On Animals,* he provided a wide range of comment, fact, and legend about dogs, their love of masters, and their habits as companion and hunter. In this last category, Aelian added the final touch to the picture of a hunting dog, one that stops to game and responds to commands and barks to arouse the game for capture. This last trait would be unacceptable today, but one must consider again the weapons of the hunter of the Roman period. It is often noted that the prime reason for spaniels stopping to game and shot is to provide a safe position for the dog during discharge of the guns. The means of catching or killing the game among the ancient Britons obviously did not require this type behavior.

We can look to Oppian again in his "Cynegetica" for a statement about the weapons of the glorious chase:

> The stalwart hunters should carry to hill and wood, these: purse-nets and long sweep-nets and net-props and grievous feltering nooses, three-pronged spear, broad-headed hunting lance, hare-stick and stakes and swift winged arrows, swords and axes and hare-slaying trident, bent hooks and lead-bound crooks, cord of twisted broom and the well-woven foot-trap, and ropes and net-stays and the many-meshed seine.

It would seem that such a load of weapons would break the back of any hunter, even a stalwart one. No doubt Oppian was simply cataloguing all the useful weapons to catch hare, boar, or hart. While the long sweep-nets might lead to the view that the bird, too, was hunted with the dog, earlier passages in the "Cynegetica" by Oppian describe the actions of the fowler and his gear; but without dog or net. Oppian deemed the fowler to have had a easy time, for he did not need to carry "sword nor bill nor brazen spear." He speaks of the fowler attendant only with the hawk when he traveled to the woods and used "long cords and the clammy yellow birdline and the reek that tread any airy path."

So it is evident that the Agassian hunting dog, the prototype of the present-day Welsh Springer Spaniel, managed by instinct and training to perform nearly all of the accomplishments that we see performed in the field today by the best hunting spaniels. Two exceptions stand out: giving tongue to spring the game, and not being used to raise birds, which can be readily explained by the need of the hunter to snare, catch, or kill outright the game and where the swift flight of the bird gave no such chance. With valuable accomplishments as these to help provide food for the table, it is not surprising that the hunting dog from the Britons was a prized export from earliest time.

When Oppian of Apamea and Claudius Aelian wrote about hunting, the Romans were settled in England and Wales for over one hundred and fifty years. Many years before, in A.D., 50 the last of the British chieftains, Caratacus, led the Silures of Gwent and Glamorgan against the Romans. So troublesome were these early Welsh that they were the last to be subjugated of the many British tribes and caused the Romans to construct, at Gloucester and Caerleon, military camps as protection against further uprisings of the native Britains. South Wales was fully occupied by Roman troops. The period was not easy for tribe or legion. Cohorts and regiments recruited by the Romans from their previously conquered lands made up the garrisons. The Second Cohort from Spain was stationed for a time at Llanio in Dyfed, while a cavalry regiment of Spanish Vittonians served for a time in the fort at Brecon. Cohorts from France and Germany were also in the Welsh countryside. Caerleon was the major base of operations, the home of the Second Augusta Legion and a military base and trading center for several hundred years. It was a thriving city and a center of commerce during the period when Oppian wrote his descriptions of the British hunting dog. The long Roman peace had come to Britain and the other regions of the Roman Empire. The roots of a fully developed society in England were evident everywhere. The remains today of Roman buildings in the cities of Britain and the foundations of villas that dotted the countryside are proof of an advanced society that would have time to develop the interests of a leisurely life. The training of dogs and their use in the field and woods by officers of the legions and the landed gentry who lived on the large farms would be a natural development.

Studies of villa sites have been a rich source of information about the secular life of Romanized Britain. The exposure of lower courses of the farm buildings by archaeologists have revealed the methods of construction, size of buildings, their purpose, heating systems, and decorations. Such facts can be helpful in devising a credible scene of villa life. During the latter part of the third century, mosaic pavements, a new style in home adornment, were introduced first in the Bristol area and subsequently over a wide region extending principally across Southern England and Southeastern Wales. During the next one hundred years, in an increasingly elaborate manner, many prosperous villa owners and their wives made the decision to purchase and have installed a mosaic floor of their favorite design. They ranged from geometric patterns, to human figures, floral scenes, and animal figures. Over four hundred mosaics have been uncovered to date, but for the history of the spaniel-type dog, one in particular stands out. In 1963, at the village of Hinton St. Mary in Northern Dorset, the chance digging of postholes for a new building brought forth residue that was identified as of Roman origin. The site was cleared by members of the Dorset Natural History and Archaeological Society and revealed a large rectangular room of a villa measuring twenty-eight feet by twenty feet and covered by an elaborate mosaic. Two features set this pavement apart from all others disclosed at the other villa sites in Britain. One of the two large circle mosaics is a picture of a man with the Chi-Rho monogram beneath his head. This is recognized as the earliest-known portrayal of Christ in a floor-mosaic. The second feature is the presence of two rectangular areas and three roundels that all contain a similar scene of a hunting dog chasing a stag. Of the six hundred possible examples of Roman villas uncovered in Britain only a few are paved with mosaics that are comprised of scenes of nature or the hunt. Of these, only the Dorset pavement is done with great style and completeness. The figures of the dogs and stags are sharp and detailed. They convey a sense of fear and vitaility in the stags, and aggressiveness and dash in the dogs. The colors of the mosaic are muted and consist of two shades of yellowish buff, black, and a lighter and a darker dull red. The dogs are outlined in black to set them off from the buff color of the background area of the pavement. Red tiles are used to color the inner lines of the dogs across the back, and on the top of the heads, while the color shifts to dark buff and light buff toward the bellies. Details such as the shoulder line and the ribs are accentuated by the use of red and black, and the tails are a simple black line.

Considering the limitations inherent in mosaic artistry, the dogs in the Hinton St. Mary pavement are a surprisingly reasonable likeness of the Agassian dog described by Oppian. While this mosaic was made over one hundred years after Oppian prepared his text, the dogs and their actions in pictorial form can be seen as an extension of his views of the British dog. Additionally, the conformation is of great interest to the history of the hunting spaniel-type dog. These photographiclike reproductions are the most complete and earliest available for study. The long ears, squarish jaw, and fairly well-defined "stop" are clearly evident. The color used is also worthy of special emphasis, being red and buff. Was this a casual choice made by the artist to accentuate the form of the dogs, or to match in color the natural dull red coat of the stags? We can only guess, but a more tolerant view would accept the choice of color as an attempt to represent accurately the natural color coat of this early hunting dog as red and white.

In size, the dog stands about eighteen inches at the shoulders as seen by its relationship to the stags of this early period, which were small compared to present-day animals. The claws and teeth are well defined in the scene. Are these the "grievous claws and the close-set venomous tusks" described by Oppian? The length of the ears and their gradual narrowing toward the tips are similar to the vine shape of the ears of a typical Welsh Springer Spaniel of today. Only the shape of the tail is an obvious departure from spaniel characteristics.

The photograph contained in the text is the scene in one of the roundels, reproduced from a plate taken shortly after the pavement was first exposed to view at the Dorset site. While no doubt, extreme care was given to the task of brushing and cleaning the mosaic pieces, the result is less than was possible with the elaborate methods employed during reassembly and placing of the pavement in the British Museum. There the mosaic has a magnificent appearance as it did originally on the floor of the main room of a large country villa, obviously owned by a patron of the arts and adherent to the Christian faith who also had an appreciation, if not commitment, of the hunt and the raising of dogs. Could this villa be one of those that raised hunting dogs for export to other parts of the Roman Empire as is known through the writings of Strabo and Oppian? These farmers and stockbreeders no doubt used the working dog on the villas and pastures, while the wealthy owners and managers regularly went to the fields and forests with their hunting packs to chase the boar and deer. While considered a delight to break the day with the business of hunting, the effort was no doubt a vital one in providing meat for the family and slaves of the estate, and the city folk, soldiers, and families at the military garrison communities. The large forests that covered the northern and western portions of Britain served particularly well in this way and are long associated with the wild activities of tribal life and the hunt.

The need to rely on the game in countryside and forest surely reached the level of a necessity after the exodus from Britain of the protecting Roman legions. Their withdrawal to Gaul between A.D. 410 and 450 paralleled a breakdown and failure of central government dedicated to the preservation of basic liberties and the protection of the individual and group from destructive forces. Under the conditions of the following centuries, the civil period typified by the villa and cities was replaced by a darkness over the greater portion of Britain. In the southwestern portion, particularly from the Dorchester region, a large group of Britains, speaking the Cymic dialect migrated to Brittany because of fear and the unsettled conditions.

To the west in South Wales, the partially Romanized Cymic peoples of the Demetae and Silurean tribes were impacted by a movement of Scoti from Ireland, while in north Wales the Ordovicean folk were joined by provincial Britains from the north as they moved south before the Angles from the east. The migration of this Northern Cymric population to Wales brought about a gathering of tribal groups that gained the Anglo-Saxon name of Welsh, or foreigners. They have left to history a rich body of poetry, prose, and law to illuminate this western portion of Britain during the Dark Ages. The outstanding fact in Welsh history is that Wales is a mountainous country to the west of the English Plain and therefore has been exposed time after time to wave after wave of invaders. All movements of invading groups from the continent reached their climax in Wales and ultimately were absorbed. In order, the Neolithic families, the "Beaker-folk," two waves of

Bythonic Celts, the Romans, and the Romano-British from Southeast Britain, each moved westward for gain or refuge to the Welsh highlands of the west. In Wales, therefore, there survives not only old language, but old customs, habits, and letters. The mountain reaches and pastoral regions have not only prevented the domination by outside influences, but have served as a shield to preserve older ways. In this setting it is natural to accept the notion of continuity for all things Cymric or Welsh—the language, the people, and their life-style—including their dogs.

The traditions of the hunt and dogs appear often in the early Welsh literature. Five major works remain for study that are collections of poetry and prose preserved by copyists in the monasteries during the thirteenth and fourteenth centuries. Prose tales and poetry are contained in two of the Welsh collections—the *White Book of Rhydderch* and the *Red Book of Hergest*—while poems are recorded principally in the *Black Book of Caemarthen,* the *Book of Aneirin,* and the *Book of Taliesin.* The stories from the White and Red books were first published with an English translation by Lady Charlotte Guest in 1849 and also occur in a modern form under the title, *The Mabinogion,* by G. and T. Jones. These translators consider the work to have been first prepared early in the second half of the eleventh century with some portions in the tenth. The poetry was written at even an earlier date. Based on a study of the form of the poetry and language, as well as the subject matter, Sir Ifor Williams contends that the "Y Gododdin" by the poet Aneirin was composed near the end of the sixth century, as was twelve historical poems by Taliesin that describe events in Northern Britain during the same period. In these early poems, Taliesin praises Urien, king of Reged, and his son, Owain, both in battle and at home. The poet, in his terse bare style, conveys striking pictures of the attitudes of the leaders and their surroundings.

In Taliesin's poems, which contain allusions to events prior to A.D. 560, there are numerous references that, by inference, show the position filled by the dog among the Britons during this period—a position of regard and close association hardly different from what is common today. From the *Book of Taliesin* as translated by Skene, the lines,

> "His dogs raised their backs at his presence,
> They protected, and believed in his kindness."

while referring to the members of an alien warring group, show, by similitude, familiar characteristics of the dog. Selected lines such as the following add to our understanding of the place of the dog in Welsh tribal society:

"Monks congregate like dogs in a kennel."
"A horseman resorts to the city, with his white dogs."
and
"Handsome my dog and round-bodied,
and truly the best of dogs;
Dormach was he, which belonged to Maelgwn.
Dormach with the ruddy nose!
What a gazer thou art upon me."

In the *Red Book of Hergest,* lines in a poem by Taliesin relating to Urien Reged, give a glimpse of hunting roles:

"He was the chaser with the dogs with the men of Reged"
and
"Many a hunting-dog and fine grown hawk
Have been trained on its flow,"

These few words, composed before A.D. 700 as part of a long historical verse, provide a basis for imagery and conjecture. They permit hunting to be viewed clearly as an organized effort with various roles to fulfill and dogs carefully trained to the chase. One can see the chieftain and his men on fast, long-maned stallions riding behind the dogs, the pack in full cry, and chasers on foot driving in the outrunning dogs and coming in to draw off the dogs from the stag or boar and make the kill with their staffs and long swords. Or we can imagine a more leisurely hunting scene of the chief and his dam poised on a rise looking skyward at the hawk that has just been released, while their trained dog awaits a command to fetch from the brush, the bird downed by the slash of the diving hawk. This reference to the hawk trained-to-hunt is especially interesting since it is the earliest sure record of hawking in Briton or Wales. The statement by Oppian, some five-hundred years earlier, in his "Cynegetica" about the fowler, implies only that the hawk, in a generic sense, is their attendant, something to be caught in their birdlines. As noted earlier, no dog accompanies the fowler in Oppian's description of fowling. This is not the case for the people of Wales and Briton during the Dark Ages, for there is a second reference to hawking, but from a later date than the Taliesin poem. In the first chapter of the *Four Branches of the Mabinogi* where Pwyll prince of Dyfed is portrayed returning to his domain, it is related that from that time forth there was peace and the leaders exchanged horses, greyhounds, and hawks. This tale is traced to the middle of the eleventh century and, as will be noted later, hawking was by this time a fully developed sport both in Wales and among the English.

Tucked within the lines of the Gododdin in the *Book of Aneirin,* and having no connection with the narrative poem, or apparently the author, is a delightful song in Welsh, which is dated from the ninth century. Thought by I. Williams to have been placed there by one of the copyists, it is known by the title *Peis Dinogad,* "Dinagod's Petticoat," and is fascinating as both a social statement and evidence of spaniel-type behavior for the Welsh dog. It is a lullaby that heralds some of our present-day nursery rhymes where the mother sings to her child of the father's deeds as a hunter and returning home with his "rabbit-skin" for the child. This poem is the earliest in recorded verse from Briton on hunting and gives a surprisingly detailed account. The Welsh from I. Williams and English translation from G. Williams follows:

Peis Dinogat

Peis dinogat e vreith vreith
o grwyn baloat ban wreith
chwit chwit chwidogeith
gochanwn gochenyn wythgeith
pan elei dy dat ty e helya
llath ar y ysgwyd llory eny law
ef gelwi gwn gogyhwc
giff gaff dhaly dhaly dhwg dhwg
ef lledi bysc yng corwc
mal ban llad llew llywywc
pan elei dy dat ty e vynyd
dydygei ef penn ywrch penn gwythwch pen hyd
penn grugyar vreith o venyd
penn pysc o rayadyr derwennyd
or sawl yt gyrhaedei dy dat ty ae giewein
o wythwch a llewyn a llwyuein
nyt anghei oll ny uei oradein.

Dinogad's Petticoat

Dinogad's speckled petticoat
is made of skins of speckled stoat;
whip whip whipalong
eight times we'll sing the song,
When your father hunted the land
spear on shoulder, club in hand,
thus his speedy dogs he'd teach, call
Giff, Gaff, catch her, catch her, fetch, fetch!
In his coracle he'd slay
fish as a lion does its prey.
When your father went to the moor,
he'd bring back heads of stag, fawn, boar,
the speckled grouse's head from the mountain,
fishes' heads from the falls of Oak Fountain.

Whatever your father struck with his spear,
wild pig, wild cat, fox from his lair,
unless it had wings it would never get clear.

The key words for the history of the Welsh tracking dog are "call,"
"catch her, catch her" and "fetch fetch." An earlier translation by
Thomas Stephens in 1886 of the poem employs the words, "well-
trained dogs" and "bring, bring." Of importance here is the use of
terms that are associated with spaniel behavior by a simple folk in a
modest family setting. The details of the rhyme and the warm
relationship described indicates a commonness in the role of hunter-
father with his dogs—trackers, retrievers, well trained, family pets, and
an everyday scene in the Welsh countryside.

Fortunately for the history of the Welsh Spaniel, there are the old
Welsh laws that provide an additional authoritative source for study.
Known as the *Laws of Hywel Dda,* the extant manuscripts were written
in Latin and Welsh near the end of the twelfth century, but refer to
their codification during the tenth. Hywel Dda was a king in Wales
during the period between 918 and 950, when, after hundreds of years
of survival as a number of strong but small kingdoms, often very hostile
to one another and continually on the defensive against Irish, Viking,
and English raiders, he gave strong leadership, first as the King of Dyfed
and later to all of the remaining ancient British tribes. During his career
he developed close relations with the Count of England, and in 927, at
a meeting in Hereford with Athelstan, king of Wessex, Hywel offered
tribute of gold, silver, cattle, hunting dogs and hawks, and fixed the
boundaries of Wales along the Wye river. Sometimes after 942 when
Hywel Dda became King of all Wales, Welsh law was codified and it can
be assumed that Hywel Dda had some role in this singular achievement
of the Welsh people. These laws were, in their day, among the finest in
Europe and permit a close look at important social and economic
factors in Welsh society.

Wales during this period was essentially a pastoral and mountainous
country with a little agriculture carried on in the more favored regions.
The raising of cattle, sheep, and pigs, along with hunting, were the chief
occupations. The majority of the people were free men, who according
to law were required to be of pure Welsh descent. The Welsh freeman
could own land, move wherever he liked, hunt, fish or hawk, practice
religion, engage in any craft, and have the right to life. Men of
substance were expected to offer shelter and food to all travelers and
these signs of hospitality are traditional even today among the Welsh.
These relationships and many others are depicted in the laws found in
the *Book of Blegyweyd,* which is referred to as the "Dimetian" code,
and the *Llyfr Iorwerth,* considered a "Venedotian" version. These

documents in Medieval Welsh were transcribed in the 1300s from earlier manuscripts that were first written after 950. Richards and Wiliam consider them to be much like the original documents. They serve as an invaluable legacy from these early times and provide specific information about dogs of the period and their relationships within the community of pre-Norman Britain and Wales.

In the laws, there are numerous references to the huntsman and falconer of the king and nobles, the various types of dogs and their worth, and the duties and fines associated with dogs in the field, home and on the farm. The rearing, training, and hunting with staghounds and greyhounds appears as the major responsibility of the chief huntsman. There must have been many huntsmen since each nobleman appeared to have at least one in his group of retainers. To the chief huntsman and his aides went such things as lodging in the king's kiln-house, a kennel for the dogs, a warm place in the hall opposite the king, food and lodging for their families, portions of mead, and a share from all the game. Clearly, a huntsman lived well, almost the best of all the numbers of the court. Of course, if he could not find game for the king and his retinue, he was speedily replaced by another huntsman.

As for the breeds in medieval Wales, study of the laws shows them to be seven in number. There were the staghound, *(gellgi)*, the spaniel *(colwyn)*, the greyhound *(milgi)*, the sheep or herddog *(bugeilgi)*, the tracker *(olread)*, the housedog *(costog)*, and the watchdog *(ci callawed)*. More accurately these should be classed as types of dogs since all their names except the spaniel relate to the functions that they performed in the community as domesticated animals. The name *colwyn (kolen* in Breton; *cuilen* in Irish) although not found in the *Book of Blegyward*, appears in the "Venedotian" version and the "Gwentian" code. *Colwyn* was first translated as "spaniel" by Aneurin Owen, the great nineteenth -century scholar of ancient Welsh law. Interestingly, today *colwyn* is translated from modern Welsh to English as "puppy." The Welsh dogs were great in number, and were essential to the welfare of the court and farm. Their relative value can be judged by comparing the legal worth set upon them in the laws. The king's trained staghound and spaniel *(colwyn)* were each valued at one pound, the same as a perfect stallion. At the other end of the scale, a bondsman's housedog was worth but one penny. The trackers' leash, valued at eight pence and more than any other, can be explained by the need for a special design with strength to restrain the dog.

The manner of the chase, as regulated by the *Laws of Hywel Dda,* is shown in the prose of the *Mabinogion* as translated from the *Red Book of Hergest* and the *White Book of Rhydderch.* In the opening of the first chapter, which describes the exploits of Pwyll Prince of Dyfed, a typical eleventh-century hunting scene in Wales is described in the translation by Gwyn and Thomas Jones:

> Pwyll prince of Dyfed was lord over the seven cantrefs of Dyfed; . . . In the young of the day he arose and came (on his stallion) to Glyn Cuch to loose his dogs into the wood. And he sounded his horn and began to muster the hunt ; . . . and whilst he was listening to the cry of the pack, he could hear the cry of another pack, but they were not of the same cry . . .
>
> And he could see a clearing in the wood, . . . and as his pack reached the edge of the clearing, he could see a stag in front of the other pack, . . . And then he looked at the color of the (other) pack; . . . and of all the hounds he had seen in the world, he had seen no dogs the same color as these. The color that was on them was a brilliant shining white, and their ears red; and as the exceeding whiteness of the dogs glittered, so glittered the exceeding redness of their ears.

Not only do these lines give a vivid picture of the chase but also they bring to mind the scene in the mosaic pavement in the villa at Hinton St. Mary, even to a reference to dogs with red and white coloring. These Welsh prose are the earliest extant that provide as a narrative the events of a stag hunt, predating by at least three hundred years the writings of the chase by the French and English authors, Gaston de Foix and dame Juliana Berners. Certainly one can appreciate the significance of this passage from the *Mabinogion* with the striking description of the glimming red ears and white coat of the dogs, and thereby accept the presence of tracking dogs in Wales at this early date. This is also the earliest recorded reference to red and white colored dogs in any of the literature out of Western Europe, since color is not mentioned by any of the five Roman authors who comment in anyway about British dogs.

During the period credited with the writing of the *Mabinogion,* a new Welsh national resurgence was being led by Gruffydd ap Llywelyn who ruled the greater part of Wales from 1039 to 1063 up to his defeat by the forces of Harold of England. During these last years Harold ravaged the Welsh countryside, first in the northeast, and in 1063 he sailed around the coast of South and West Wales to Anglesey for the final battles with the Welsh, taking spoil and demanding allegiance to his rule. It was but two years later that Harold left the English court traveling on horseback to the coast and subsequently embarking for a hunting trip in France. This journey and the subsequent events with Duke William of Normandy that led up to and which occurred during the Battle of Hastings in 1066 are portrayed in the famous *Bayeux Tapestry.* Commissioned by Bishop Odo, half-brother to William, this 231-foot long embroidered band of linen was completed in 1092, supposedly for Mathilde, wife of William, to show the principal incidents between Harold and William the Conqueror. It is of great interest as a work of art and as evidence for the history of the conquest.

The tapestry also contributes to our knowledge of military weapons and tactics, and also to the role of dogs, horses, and the hunt as practiced by the nobility. Embroidered in the edging are small scenes of over twenty-three dogs in various hunting poses and, of special interest to the history of the Welsh spaniel type of hunting dog, there appears in a main scene, five dogs running ahead of Harold on horseback as he makes his way to the coast on his journey to France. The scene shows three large hounds with chock collars and two smaller dogs. The presence of the dogs indicate a mission of peace and were probably of a special sort to be gifts to William along with the hawk that Harold is carrying in his left hand. The next scene on the tapestry shows two of Harold's retainers, each carrying a dog across the shallow water to the boat. The dog's size in relation to the men is about that of a Welsh Springer Spaniel and one is of a yellow hue while the other is red. The three larger dogs are shown light brown, beige, and tan. The ears of the smaller dogs, while small, are shown bent over and laying flat against the head, and bands around their necks shown for collars are different than those on the larger dogs. Later scenes show Harold and William in France hunting together with the hounds. Once again dogs from Britain are being exported, as is shown clearly in the tapestry, to France, home of many a reknowned type of hound and spaniel.

Although one thousand years apart, the scene in the *Bayeux Tapestry* of Harold taking a red-coated hunting-type dog to France, and the statements by Strabo and Oppian about the exporting of Agassian dogs from Britain have a common theme. Both are evidence of the long and continous presence of the Welsh spaniel-type dog in England and Wales. The color red and white for the coat is confirmed as early as A.D. 300 by the mosaic at Hinton St. Mary in the floor of the Roman Villa, which was only recently discovered. The mosaic scene also supports the views about size since the villa hunting dogs are about the same height as the dogs being carried to France by Harold and, also, the Welsh Springer Spaniel of today. The ears and shape of the head all agree and, most importantly, they are all shown or described as great hunting dogs, either giving chase or retrieving game with exceptional tracking ability. Seven of the nine basic characteristics defined by Asdell as genetically controlling the overall appearance and manner of a dog are common in the Roman and Welsh descriptions. The only aspect that changes with time is the type of game hunted and the weapons used in the chase.

Up until the time when hawks were trained to aide the hunter in his pursuit of birds, the dog was only used to track game or give chase to and to run the wild four-footed beast to cover or into nets. The hunter's job, either on foot or on horseback, was to follow and aide the dogs at killing the game. Fowling, or more properly, bird catching, was a Greek and Roman sport that combined the skills of the hunter in throwing a line or setting nets to snare the bird. It is in early Welsh literature that we find the first reference to dogs being used during the hunting of birds, and then in a reference with hawks to first flush and then retrieve the downed bird from some distant brush. The transition of the Welsh spaniel-type dog from one that tracked the boar, deer, and hare, to one that also retrieved birds would be natural as the change in hunting style occurred. A well-trained dog used every day, just as Giff and Gaff of the Welsh nursery rhyme, can easily master the commands of hunting fur or feathered game. During the thousand years that the Romano and Welsh tribal dogs went into field and wood with the hunter, the one new weapon that required a change in the relationship between man and dog was the hawk. To fill its new role, the dog was trained to retrieve over land and water the fallen birds. He was given quite naturally the name bird-dog to describe this new role, and no doubt began to develop as a special type joining the other dogs with special talents such as the stagdog, watchdog, and herd-dog. By the time of the war between England and Wales in 1060, the bird-dog was sufficiently well known and useful in Britain to have become a prize to be taken from a defeated enemy and a gift to be given to a friendly king. If he had a name during this time, the dog that worked with the hawk had to be called *colwyn* which is the ancient Welsh word for "spaniel." Somewhere in early Welsh history, the transition occurred. Did it have anything to do with the Roman legions, with recruits and officers from Spain who occuppied portions of Wales and England up to A.D. 400? Our only sources for the answer to this question must be the further study of the Welsh laws and literature of the post-Roman period, and the work of the archaeologists who are continuing to uncover and explain the past.

One of the five scenes of a hunting dog chasing a stag from the floor mosaic discovered in 1963 at the site of a fourth century Roman villa in Hinton St. Mary, Dorset. The dog would stand about eighteen inches high at the shoulders. (The British Museum)

4

RENAISSANCE SPRINGER SPANIELS

Any dog fancier who spends time reading in his dog book library about the history of sporting dogs will soon come upon the most quoted author from English Renaissance literature. I refer to Johannes Caius, Doctor of Medicine at the University of Cambridge who composed in Latin in about 1555 the reknowned dog book, *Of English Dogges, the Diversities; the Names, the Nature and the Properties.* This famous book is not the first one written in England about dogs during the Renaissance, but it surely is the most interesting and contains the most significant statements of the history of the Welsh Spaniel. Caius was born in 1510 at Norwich and was a student at Cambridge where he studied divinity. At the age of twenty-three he studied medicine in Italy and toured Europe before settling down to practice in London. After a successful career he endowed substantially his old college and was rewarded by having it named Caius College. Two years later he became its master while continuing to administer to the sicknesses of royalty. He was physician to King Edward VI and later to Queens Mary and Elizabeth. Well travelled and able to write in Greek, Latin, and English, he was a friend of other learned physicians of his age in England and Europe. One of his friends in particular is of interest in our study of the origins of the Welsh Springer Spaniel because he was the source of inspiration for Caius' writing about English dogs and an author of a much greater book than Caius,' entitled, *The History of Four-Footed Beasts and Serpents and Insects*. The author was Conrad Gesner, who was born in Zurich in 1516, and studied law and medicine, gaining his doctoral degree from Basel in 1541. Since he was not too interested in practicing medicine, he set himself the task of writing a new book on the history of animals, the first since Claudius Aelianus some fifteen-hundred years before. He asked his fellow doctor, Johannes Caius, to write a section on dogs of England. The work was part of a very large four-volume manuscript containing over three thousand pages, taking Gesner twenty years to write, all in Latin. This huge work was subsequently published in shorter versions by a number of authors in Europe, and one book from the *Four-Footed Beasts* volume of Gesner was published in England in 1607 by Edward Topsell of Sevenoaks, Kent, who also was a Cambridge graduate. Prior to the appearance of the Topsell work, which was translated into middle English from the Latin, Abraham Fleming translated and had printed in London an English edition in 1576 of Johannes Caius' earlier work. Topsell appears to have used this English translation also in his 1607 edition.

These men, Caius, Gesner, Fleming, and Topsell, were obviously of a special sort, educated at the best universities and able to write in at least three languages. By their attention to the subject they show the importance placed during this period in the emerging development of varieties of dogs. We can accept as accurate what they have to say since they were bringing considerable ability to bear on the subject. One can assume with confidence that what they say must be true. In fact, these manuscripts were the source of information about dogs and animals for at least the next two hundred years.

While the Caius work is important for what it says about hunting dogs of the sixteenth century in England, Gesner's and Topsell's works are equally important because of the illustrations that are included in addition to the descriptions of the dogs. Gesner's block prints are the first to show the great variety in the conformation and coats of the dogs of this period. The dogs are listed by name with some descriptive comment. The names indicate each dog's usage and habits. From *The History of the Four-Foot Beasts* and *Of Englishe Dogges* the following groups of dogs can be identified. The first kind were called *Venatici*, hound-dogs that excelled in smelling the beast and giving chase. The second group, *Aucupatori*, were dogs that sought the bird and showed its flight by pursuit. The third were dogs that served necessary uses and were called as a group, *Rustici*. The fourth group, called *Delicatus*, included one toy dog, the Spaniel Gentle or Comforter. This last was a very small spaniel sought to satisfy the desires of "dainty dames" and was carried about for pleasure.

SIXTEENTH CENTURY ENGLISHE DOGGE GROUPS

Venatici	*Aucupatorii*	*Rustici*
Harier	Land Spaniel	Mastive
Terrar	Setter	Shepherd
Blood-Hound	Water Spaniel	Butchers
Gase-hound		Mooner
Gray-hound	*Delicatus (Toy)*	Water-drawer
Leviner	Spaniel Gentle	Defending
Tumbler		Warner
Con dog		Turnspit
Rache		Dancer

While it is commonly thought that the term spaniel was first used by Caius and Gesner to describe types of bird-dogs, it probably has its origins back at least another three or four hundred years to the time of the Norman occupation of England after the defeat of Harold at the Battle of Hastings. The earliest recorded usage of the word spaniel is in the fourteenth century in the "Prologue to the Wife of Bath's Tale," in the *Canterbury Tales,* by Geoffrey Chaucer where, in describing the actions of a woman in love, he states in Middle English:

> For as a spaynel she wol on him lepe,
> In modern English this becomes:
> For she will leap on him as a spaniel.

Few English writers have been as honored by their associates as Geoffrey Chaucer. He is considered, along with William Shakespeare and Edmund Spenser who wrote two hundred years later, as the most engaging of the English poets. His humor, intelligence, and compassion in his assessment of fourteenth century English society makes his tales interesting reading even today.

The line above, penned in 1387, conveys a sense of commonness in judging the name and friendly behavior of the spaniel-type dog as if both its manner and title would be well known to everyone. Chaucer's words also imply a dog of medium size that would neither overwhelm the man if large, nor fawn at his feet if small. This medium-sized bird-dog, which was called spaynel by Chaucer, was used with the hawks for hunting and retrieving for at least five hundred years as is indicated by the scene in the *Bayeux Tapestry* of Harold with his dogs and hawk, and as stated in the Welsh laws and poetry. The training of bird-dogs similar to those of the Welsh was surely common in England during the time of Chaucer. The origin of the word spaniel must have occurred somewhere before the first usage by Chaucer as an everyday word in Renaissance England, and after the post-Roman times of Wales among the Cymric people. Of course it is possible that the word could have developed out of comment by the French during their long reign in England after the Norman Conquest, since the word espaignol means 'Spanish dog' in Old French, and could have been used to describe the Welsh and English bird-dog because of some similarities that were observed.

The next use of the word appears in the *Master of Game* written in 1410 as a translation of the treatise on the chase by Gaston, Compte de Foix. This work by Edward, Second Duke of York, is rated as the first book in English on the sport of hunting and, while basically of French venery, contains five new chapters dealing with hunting in England. Now the book by Count Gaston de Foix, entitled *Livre de Chasse,* was written in 1387 in Old French, the same year that Chaucer penned his "Wife of Bath Tale," and dealt entirely with French hunting customs. The Duke and the Count were kinsman and no doubt hunted together over the French countryside of Southern France and Northern Spain, which was under the reign of de Foix. That the full-time endeavor of royalty was riding to hounds, the Duke makes clear in the Prologue to his translation where he states:

"This book treateth of what in every season of the year is most durable, and to my thinking to every gentle heart most disportful of all games, that is to say hunting."

It should be kept in mind that hunting or venery in this period was defined as a "chasse" with hound-dogs and men after wild hare, deer, and boar. This was the noblest of sports and the best to the Duke as we see from the next lines in his Prologue to the *Master of Game.*

"For though it be that hawking with gentle hounds and hawks for the heron and the river be noble and comendable, it lasteth seldom at the most more than half a year" . . . as the hawks would be mewing and unable to fly. So we see that hawking with gentle hounds, that is to say spaniels, is of lesser interest to those who ruled, rode, and wrote. This point is demonstrated also by the fact that only one small chapter is included about our favorite bird-dog by the Count and not mentioned at all in the five new chapters by the Duke.

While Gaston de Foix and the Duke of York thought most highly of hunting with hounds, Frederick II of Hohenstaufen was the earliest and most brilliant exponent of the art of educating birds for the chase. This Holy Roman Emperor and King of Sicily and Jerusalem, wrote his *De Arte Venandicum Avibus (The Art of Falconry)* between 1244 and 1250. This lengthy work is more than a treatise on falconry since Frederick includes an account of the anatomy and habits of hunting birds, descriptions of the variety of hunting falcons and hawks, and their training methods and equipment; all in six, beautifully illustrated volumes. Despite the constant demands made on him by administrative, political, and military duties, Frederick always found time to engage in his most absorbing recreation, even to the extent that on one occasion he failed disastrously in a military undertaking because he spent a day of sport with his birds instead of attacking a fortress that he had under siege. This was a wise choice by the standards of a sportsman, since his writings on falconry are held today in far greater esteem than his other more wordly exploits. Out of five hundred pages in his famous book, Frederick devotes four to "On Hounds Used in Falconry." These contain the earliest detailed instructions about the training of dogs to work with hunting birds. The information is so clear in meaning and so sound in judgment that it can be used even today if one has the urge to train a dog to assist the falcon. But this is not our interest here; rather, our interest is in what Frederick II has to say about the types of hunting dogs. Writing in Latin he employs the words *Leporarius,* a hare-hound or harrier, and *Veltres,* a kind of greyhound to identify the kind that he recommends. He states:

> There are, in fact, breeds of dogs that are more decidedly useful . . . than any other variety. These strains are called harriers or greyhounds, and they should be used, mainly because of their speed, in assisting falcons.

In considering this statement we must imagine the vast semiarid terrain of Southern Italy and Sicily stretching into the distance: rolling hills that are almost treeless; King Frederick on horseback with his aides, and the hawks and dogs some distance away. This is quite a different setting than the British countryside with the fowlers walking slowly over the wet lush hills and dales. Other differences were noted by Frederick in his book when he comments that:

> Those who live in Britain and are called Anglians do not use the lure in the manner just described because they never lure on horseback, nor do they call out while luring. Instead they go on foot and toss the lure high in the air.

We can conclude that for this type of hunting, in England and Wales, a slower moving dog, like the spaniel, would be best—certainly not a greyhound or harrier. Frederick also describes the best kind of dog as follows: "It is well also, if they can be procured, to use that special breed that has been trained for generations to assist in the chase (of birds), and whose natural qualifications have been thereby augmented." He also states that the dog should be of medium height, big enough to get over long grass and shrubs, but not so large that its weight is a hindrance to effective work. He should have a good coat of hair so as to endure hard work and resist the cold, and be agile and prompt in executing his tasks. All of these are characteristics of a good spaniel-type dog. Frederick had ample opportunity to call this "special breed" by name or give its place of origin, yet there is no mention of Spain or spaniels in his book. Clearly, the breed existed, and, in fact, was sought after, but was called only "dog for the falcon" or "bird-dog" throughout most of Europe up to the fourteenth century.

La Chasse by Gaston de Foix is also of great interest for the history of the dog in Western Europe because of the exquisite illuminations in the original manuscripts. Unfortunately, those which appear in the English translation by Edward are much interior, but the French originals are advantageous in the study of hounds used in the chase. These paintings, in beautiful colors, are clearly some of the finest handiwork of French miniaturists of the period and give valuable detailed information about the noble art of venery as practiced in France. There is much of interest about "hounds" but, unfortunately, no picture of fowling with a "bird-dog." The closest to a likeness of the Land Spaniel of the period appears on a tile found at the site of an abbey in Neath, Wales. The tile measures fifteen by four inches and is dated from the early 1300s, about fifty years earlier than the Gaston work. The location in the Neath Valley of southwest Wales is intriguing. It was from the Vale of Neath that a movement arose in the late 1900s to recognize the Welsh Springer Spaniel by the Kennel Club and it is the ancestral home of the Williams who had known the breed for generations past. The Neath Abbey tile contains a white print of a hunting scene in three parts. A huntsman is blowing a large curved horn while a pack of nine dogs are in chase of a stag. In size and shape, the dogs are similar to Welsh—even the ears are the correct shape and length. Since the Cistercian Order of South Wales were aligned closely during this period with Europe, it is possible that this tile could have been made in France and brought to the Neath Abbey. In any event, here is evidence of a medium-sized hunter in use in Wales at early times.

A look at the Old French version of *Livre de Chasse* by the Count de Foix written in 1387 provides the first insight into the origin of the word spaniel and the types of bird-dogs that were used in France and Spain during this period. In the chapter entitled, "Of Spaniels and of Their Nature," we find the following lines:

> Another kind of hound there is that we called hounds for the hawk and spaniels, for their kind cometh from Spain, notwithstanding that there are many in other countries ... A fair hound for the hawk should have a great head, a great body and be of fair hue, white or tawny, for they be the fairest, and of such they be commonly best. A good spaniel should not be rough, but his tail should be rough ... They love well their masters and follow them without losing ... and commonly they go before their master, running and

wagging their tail, and raise or start fowl and wild beasts. Also they can be taught to be crouchers to aide in netting the partridge and quail. And also they be good when they are taught to swim and to take fowl from the river.

First we see that the count's spaniels came from Spain and were white or tawny coated and, if we except his description, rather large, "great" in head and body. These characteristics are certainly not in accord with those of an ancestor of the Welsh Springer Spaniel. What is agreeable then? Certainly the manner of the dog, his hunting style, and his love of master are familiar signs of a Welsh. There is also the interesting comment that "there are many in other countries" as if to say that the "spaynel" in Chaucer's verse in 1387 was developed in Wales and England and is not of Spanish origin. It is clear that during this time, bird-dogs called "spaniels" had frolicked across the country-sides of Wales, England, France, and Spain for at least four centuries, for there was such continual communication between these countries that the gentler sport of hawking was surely universally enjoyed and discussed along with the dogs, which made it successful.

The use of the word spaniel appears next in the writings of a sportswoman in 1487, just one hundred years after it first appeared in print. It is unique to read the words of a lady of this period, but in her manuscript entitled, *The Boke of St. Albans,* information is presented about hawking, hunting, and heraldry. She is generally accepted as Dame Juliana Berners, who lived at the beginning of the fifteenth century and probably compiled the book from earlier manuscripts for her young son. The most interesting portion of her writing for the history of the Welsh Springer Spaniel occurs when she names the dogs that were known during the time in which she lived. Using Old English words, she identifies fourteen dogs under the title "hounds," and even includes a Spanyell.

THE NAMIS OF DIVERSE MANER HOUNDIS
(THE NAMES OF DIVERSE MANNER OF HOUNDS)

This is the namis of hounds. First there is a Greyhound, a Bastard, a Mengrell, a Mastife, a Lemor, a Spanyell, Rachis, Kenellis, Terouas, Bocheris hounds, Myddying dogges, Trinkltails, and Pukherd curis and small ladies popies that beere away the flees.

In another section of her book she lists as types of dogs: "A coupull of spaynellis."

It is interesting to compare the list of different dogs compiled by Dame Berners in 1487 with the list given by Caius and Gesner one hundred years later, and with the different types noted in the old Welsh

Laws of Hywel Dda prepared some four hundred years before. The Welsh laws gave the names of seven different dogs. By Dam Berners time there were fourteen, and by 1550 the number worthy of identification had grown to over twenty-two counting some of the more inferior working types noted by Gesner. By this date, distinct groupings are accepted in describing the various breeds, and a clear separation exists between the hound group, the working group, and the sporting or gundog group. This last group, however, contained a small number of breeds, only three, no doubt because of their then recent acceptance as being worthy of special usage with the gun for fowling. The evolution of the role of the dog, from hunting companion, to working assistant, and finally to an aide for the net, hawk, or gun as a bird-dog, grew as specialization occurred in each class. We know today that the same forces continued to act between man and dog during the next four hundred years to produce the succeeding groups of terrier, nonsporting or utility and toy breeds, and ultimately the over one hundred and fifty distinctly different breeds of dogs known today.

Of the twenty-two dogs identified by Johannes Caius at the end of the sixteenth century, the land spaniel must have been especially attractive to the eye for it was singled out for special note. The dogs of the chase, the Venatici group, and working dogs, the Rustici, were described in many ways. Of their coat, however, only a general note was given by Gesner and Caius to the effect that they "are sometimes red, sanded, black, white, spotted, but most commonly brown and red." For the land spaniel, the description of the coat was given in a manner that conveys a unique condition, as if the appearance of this dog was truly different from all others. For the history of the Welsh Springer Spaniel, the description has special significance. Caius says that "their skins are white and if marked with any spots they are commonly red, and somewhat great therewithall." This is obviously a perfectly good description of the present-day Welsh Springer Spaniel's coat coloring. When associated with Caius' description of the behavior patterns of the land spaniel dog it is clear that Caius is describing a direct ancester of the present Welsh. Gesner says that these land spaniels were used by the French and called "Dogs of the Quails," and by the Germans who called them, "Vegel-hound," a fowl-hound. Interestingly though, there is no record of their use in Spain for fowling at this time even though they had a Spanish-sounding name. Accepting the words of Gesner and Caius, one can glean the beginnings of the color coats of other modern spaniel breeds, especially the present-day English Springer Spaniel. They noted that "othersome of the land spaniels be red and black" and also that recently out of France there was a new sort of dog that was "speckled all over with white and black." Caius tells us that these others were of a spaniel type since they were presented in the text with the land spaniel, but that "of these sorts there be but a very few." It is clear that the red and white color combination was dominant, of long standing, and that the spaniels bred true to type just as they must have during the eleventh century when the Welsh tale of the *Mabinogion* was being penned (which includes a description of a pack of gleaming white and red dogs) and during Roman times when red and white dogs, as shown on the floor mosaic at Hinton St. Mary, were being exported to European countries.

The descriptions by Gesner and Caius for the sporting group of dogs, Canes Aucupatorii, which were so prized both in England and abroad during this period, permit a comparison of hunting style, conformation, and manner for this group at that time:

CANES AUCUPATORII
(BIRD-DOGS OF THE 16TH CENTURY)
AFTER J. CAIUS AND C. GESNER

Land Spaniel

These dogs serve for fowling and are of a gentle kind. They delight on the land, play their parts either by swiftness of foot, or by often questing to search out and to spring the bird for further hope of advantage or else by some secret sign or privy token betray the place where they fall. They serve the hawk and have no names assigned unto them, save only that they be called after the bird which by natural appointment he is alotted to take: for which consideration some he called Dogs for the Falcon, the Pheasant, the Partridge and such like. The common sort of people call them by one general word, namely Spaniels.

The most part of their skins are white and if they be marked with any spots they are commonly red, and somewhat great therewithall, the hairs not growing in such thickness but that the mixture of them may easily be perceived. Othersome of them be reddish and blackish, but of that sort there be but a very few. The dogs are taught by Falconers to retrieve and raise Partridges and other birds, for they first take them into the fields, and show them Partridges, whom after they have favored twice or thrice, by custom they remember, and being uncoupled, will bestir themselves into all corners to find them, being after awhile very proud of employment and very understanding in their game.

Land Spaniel (Topsell)

The Water Spaniel

These smelling Dogs seek for things that are lost and also take water-fowl and hunt Otters and Beavers. They watch the strobe of a Gun when the fowler shooteth, and instantly run into the water for the dead fowl, which they bring to their Master. Their hinder parts are sheared so they may be the less annoyed in swimming. With these dogs also we fetch out of the water such fowl as be stung to death by any venemous worm. We use them also to bring us our bolts and arrows out of the water, missing our mark, which otherwise we should hardly recover, and oftentimes they restore to us our shafts which we though never to see or touch again.

Water Spaniel (Topsell)

This sort of Dog is serviceable for fowling, making no noise either with foot or with tongue, whites they follow the game. They attend diligently upon their master and frame their condition to such becks, motions and gestures as it shall please him to make, either going forward, drawing backward, inclining to the right hand, or yielding to the left. When he hath found the bird, he keepeth sure and fast silence, he stayeth his steps and will proceed no further and with a close, covert, watching eye, layeth his belly to the ground and so creepeth forward like a worm. When he approacheth near to the place where the bird is, he lies down, and with a mark of his paws betrayeth the place of the birds last abode. The place being known by the means of the Dog, the fowler, immediately openeth and spreadeth his net, intending to take them; which being done, the Dog at a sign from the Master rises and draweth nearer to the fowl that they might fly up and be entangled in the prepared net.

Words, of course, do not make a dog, and for convincing proof of the appearance and style there is no substitute for seeing the dog perform. When this is not possible one must resort to pictures. By the 1500s the craft of printing had expanded considerably and, in addition to varieties in type of print, the block picture process was introduced to give form and a sense of substance to many of the scenes with dogs that were described previously with words and phrases. The first hunting scenes were sketches, hand painted and inserted along the border or into the hand-written manuscripts as pictures. Because of the thousands of hours required to prepare just one of these books, they are very rare, and the subjects described are only of the greatest importance to the royalty and clergy who could afford to commission or purchase these documents. There are very few hunting scenes but one is the first to record the use of bow and arrow hunting. The scene shows a fourteenth century peasant aiming a rough-hewn bow with a blunt arrow at a large duck. The fowling scene appears in the manuscript by Walter de Milemete, *De Nobilitatibus Sapientiis*. While no dogs are in this picture, some two hundred years later a block print appeared in a book by Magnus that shows a dog retrieving arrows that were shot by a hunter using a crossbow. Since three oversized birds also appear in the scene, one can assume that the dog and archer were fowling. This skill of dogs retrieving arrows was recorded by Lady Lisle of Calais who wrote to a friend in 1540:

> I will send to England for a spaniel for I can get none in this town, except one, which I sent to your son. He is very good at retrieving the head or bolt of a crossbow both in water and on land.

During this same period there emerged a sharp conflict in the art of fowling as the "hande gonne" and the "fowling piece" became common and were used for hunting along with those who still used the bow and arrow, or the hawk. For all three weapons, game was downed some distance from the hunter and, therefore, a retrieving dog was desirable if not necessary when the bird fell into deep covert or in water. In 1582 there appeared a scene in the *Venatus et Ancupium* of two hunters with long guns about to shoot a sitting heron. Crouched and ready for action is a long-eared spaniel-type dog with a shortened tail. This type of hunting most certainly was attractive compared to the earlier methods, and permitted the taking of birds as was never possible before. A veritable slaughter must have occurred, evidenced by the scene from the book by G. Franco, *Habiti d'huomini,* written in 1609, which shows duck hunting near Venice. Each boat appears to have one or more long-eared, short-tailed retrieving dogs with typical spaniel conformation and head shapes. Both bow and arrows and fowling pieces are being used in the picture, and obviously with great success—the boats are full of geese. Even ladies, who appear to be having great conversations, have gone along for the entertainment.

Such easy sport was in sharp contrast to the older forms of fowling with net, bow, and hawk. There was no real competition between these three methods of hunting birds since it was not considered objectionable to carry a bow when hawking to shoot birds that stayed in their tree-top perch, thereby escaping the hovering hawk. But with gunners in the neighborhood, the fowler and his dog had little success since most game was driven away by the noise and smell of guns. Falconers were most disturbed and took pen in hand to voice their complaint to the authorities as noted in this letter written during Caius' lifetime from Sir Edmund Bedlington to the Earl of Bath:

> Persons dayly do shoote in handegonnes, and beat at the fowles in rivers . . . a man disposed to have a flight with hawkes may seek ten miles ere he find one coople of fowls to fly at, where in all yeres past there shulde have been founde in the same place five hundred coople of fowls . . .

While the protests increased, so did guns and the need for specially trained dogs for both shooting and hawking.

At the same time that Johannes Caius was writing his book about Englishe Dogges, hunting with hawks and the ills of the spaniels were being described by George Turbervile in the *Booke of Faulconrie or Hawking,* which this English gentleman wrote in 1575. A few years later, in 1619, Edmund Bert, in his *Treatise of Hawks and Hawking,* described in even greater detail the position of the land spaniel in this sport. But first let us look at what the writer and poet Tubervile has to

Painting by Thomas Gainsborough in 1767 of the *2nd Lord George Vernon* with his Welsh Springer Spaniel. Note the flesh-colored nose, light feathering, docked tail, ears, and coat coloring of the dog, all features that establish the presence of the breed during this period in England and Wales. (Southampton Art Gallery)

Harold of England in 1065 on his way to France carrying his hawk and a red-coated bird dog into the waiting boat as shown in the *Bayeux Tapestry*. (Maison Combier)

The *Offering of the Heart Tapestry* from Arras completed in the early 1400s, shows a hawk and a fawn-colored spaniel out of Spain as described by Count Gaston de Foix in his book, *Livre de Chasse*. The dog is similar in shape and color of coat to the hawking spaniel in the *French Falconry Tapestrys*, of the Devonshire Hunting Collection. (Musee des Arts Decoratifs)

say about our Welsh Springer type bird-dog. The author was a government official who lived in the time of Queen Elizabeth and was an intimate friend of the poet Edmund Spenser. Writing for the "pleasure of all Nobleman and Gentlemen," Tubervile prepared his book as a compilation of the best works of English, French, and Italian authors who wrote of falconry. This extensive work of over three hundred pages was a companion piece to Tubervile's other book on hunting entitled, *The Noble Art of Venerie or Hunting.* The clear distinction in the types of dogs used in the two sports of "Faulconrie and Venerie," that is hawking and hunting, is shown in Tubervile's book on the latter sport, published just one year after the first. The characteristics of numerous hound-dogs are described, however, not one word appears about the Land Spaniel. In this book the word "hound" is used in place of "dog" and denotes canines used for the hunt or chasing of game. In Tubervile's equally long book on hawking, he reserves the last chapter, only nine pages, for words by Master Francesco Sforzina Vicentino, a master falconer. The section is entitled "A Treatise and briefe discourse, of the Cure of Spanels, when they be anyway overheated." The introduction gives praise to the spaniel as follows:

> How necessary a thing a Spanell is to falconrie, and for those that use that pastime, keeping hawkes for their pleasure and recreation, I deem no man doubteth, as well to spring and retrieve a fowle being hoven to the marke, as also divers other ways to assiste and aide falcons and goshawks.

Tubervile quoting Vicentino, then proceeds to "describe their harmes, with cures due to the same," and spends most of the nine pages telling about "unguentes" that can be rubbed on the Spanell to cure "mangie"; how to cure swelling of the throat; how to "woorme a Spanell"; and how to take care of bites and wounds suffered by the "dogge." None of these remedies seem worthy of attention today, except the latter that is still often employed. Vicentino gives some useful advice when he states:

"When a Spanell is hurte, as long as he can come to licke the wounde with his tongue, he needes no other remedie. His tongue is his surgeon." Of course, all dogs lick their wounds, even sometimes to the owner's despair, when, after the dog has been to the veterinarian, he proceeds to lick away all the expensive medication recently applied with great clinical care.

The last portion of the chapter on Spaniels in the Tubervile book presents the first written record of instructions about docking the tail to aide in the dog's questing for game. With the heading "To cut off the tip of a Spanels tayle or sterne," the Italian Vicentino gives some interesting reasons why this should be done and how to perform the task.

> It is necessary to cutte off a little of the Spanels tayle, when it is a whelpe for sundry occasions: for in so doing, you shall deliver him, and be a means that no kind of woorme or other mischief shall greatly offende that parte of your Spanel. Which, if it not be cutte a little at the very point and toppe, is subject to many evils and inconveniences, and will be a cause that the dogge will not date to pierce overhastily into the covert after his game. Besides the benefit of it, the Dogge becomes more beautiful by cutting toppe of his sterne: for then will it bush out very gallantly, as experience will teach you.

Tubervile and Vicento also recommend worming the whelpes at one month, but this method seems cruel, horrid, and utterly worthless by today's standards.

The two acts of docking and worming, present today as tasks performed on all Welsh Springer Spaniel litters, were conceived over five hundred years ago and the reasons for doing these acts are as valid today as they were then. For hunting in deep cover and bracken, a short tail avoids being caught or torn, enhances the beauty of the dog, and permits gallant wagging. Ensuring the continued health of the pup through worming and attending to all sicknesses promptly should be the duty and obligation of every owner. As Tubervile says at the very end of his *Book of Falconrie,*

> whereas it shall not be amiss for a good falconer, always to breed and keep of the best kind of Spanels that he may come by, and so to respect them, . . . for a good Spanell is a great jewel and a good Spanell maketh a good hawk.

This hunting with hawk and the spaniel was described also in 1619 by Edmund Bert in his *Treatise of Hawks and Hawking.* In this work the place of the land spaniel is amply covered. It is clear that the sport required a dog to beat the cover and spring the game up into the air so the hawk could hit the bird while in flight. The dog followed this contest and was quick to enter the bush to retrieve the game. The close working relationship between hawk and dog was both a goal to be sought by training the team, and a hazard if not controlled by the fowler. These words by Bert show the need for care:

> Now you understant how I make my hawke fly to the field, and if you will now suppose her to be truely flying, and that she will tend upon the Dogs for a retrieve; for nature will quickly teach her to know what good service the Spaniell doth here . . . she would fall better in love with my Dogges than with me, for they answer her attendance with springing a Partridge unto her, and after a few times so served . . . she will expect it with such desire, as that she will neglect my calling her, and so in the end prove an ill commer.

The kind of spaniel employed to hunt with either the bow, hawk, or gun during the sixteenth century was the Land-Spaynel described by Caius and Gesner. The pictures contained in the Gesner, *History of Four-Footed Beasts,* and the Turbevile, *Book of Faulconrie or Hawking* give an opportunity to examine the physical features of this dog and to compare it to modern Welsh Springer Spaniels. It is already established that the colors and markings on the coat are the same, but what other genetic characteristics are in accord with the Welsh of today? We can only judge overall size by comparing the height and length of the dog to others shown in the books. Fortunately, the spaniels are pictured by Turbevile as members of a group of dogs and gentlemen so relative height or length can be established. One must assume however, that each sketch is drawn to scale, and with this standard it is apparent that the Caius-Gesner Land Spaniel and Turbevile bird-dogs are of moderate size and a bit longer than the height at the shoulders, which appears to be about eighteen or nineteen inches. He has a relatively straight or flat coat with just a little waviness toward the hindquarters. He is lightly feathered on the chest, on the back of the forelegs and hindlegs, and under the chest. His ears are comparatively small and gradually narrow toward the tip. They set close to the head and are shown covered with light feathering. The neck is stocky and the tail is long and lightly feathered, obviously faults for a modern Welsh. The feet are shown round and catlike and his head is slightly domed, with a reasonable stop, proportionate, and of moderate length. He appears to be a compact, fast mover built for endurance and hard work. On practically all accounts he is in accord with the present breed standard for the modern Welsh Springer Spaniel. It is fair to say that in four hundred years there has been little change in this first of the English Land Spaniels.

During the same year that Caius was writing about British Dogs, a twenty-five-year-old future poet, Edmund Spenser, was completing his studies at Pembroke Hall, Cambridge. Known as the "prince of poets in his time" Spenser was well acquainted with the English, Welsh, and Irish countryside because of shuttling between his castle at Kilcolman, County Cork, Ireland and the court in London. Spenser frequently used the dog as a simile in the "Faery Queene," published in 1590—his greatest poem of knightly romance and a statement of morals and manners. The breeds of dogs to which he alludes are the mastiff, banddog, hound, limehound, and spaniel. The use of the spaniel in hawking, as described by Turbevile, is confirmed by Spenser in the following lines from Books 3 and 5 of the "Fairy Queene":

Herselfe not saved yet from danger dredd
She thought, changed from one to other feare:
Like as a fearful partridge, that is fledd
From the sharpe hawke which her attached neare,
And falls to ground to seeke for succor there,
Whereas the hungry spaniells she does spye;
With greedy jawes her ready for to teare;
In such distress and sad perplexity
Was Florimell, when Proteus she did see thereby.

and

"Like a spaniel waiting carefully"

In these lines we can see a Land Spaniel in keeping with the role of a vigorous, intelligent bird-dog.

At the same time that Spenser was writing his lines about the hunting manner of the spaniel, the other great poet of the sixteenth century, William Shakespeare, was conveying quite a different sort of behavior in the spaniel and, by inference, the men in the verse. Whether the references are justified is a question any person knowledgeable in spaniel behavior would answer with a sharp no. While Shakespeare wrote of many types of dogs, here are the five ways he involved the spaniel:

From *Midsummer Night's Dream,* Helena says:
I am your spaniel; and, Demetrius,
The more you beat me, I will fawn on you.
Use me but as your spaniel, spurne me, strike me,
Neglect me, lose me; only give me leave,
Unworthy as I am, to follow you.

From *Two Gentlemen from Verona,* Act III:
Yet, Spaniel like, the more she spurnes my love,
The more it growes, and fawneth on her still.

From *King Henry VIII,* Act V:
You play the Spaniel,
And think with wagging of your tongue to win me.

From *Julius Caesar,* Act III:
With that which melteth Fools; I mean, sweet words,
Low-crooked curt'sies, and base Spaniell fawning.

From *Antony and Cleopatra,* Act IV:
The hearts, That spaniell'd me at heeles.

These all seem unworthy associations. For certainly the rough and ready Land Spaniel of Caius, Gesner, and Tubervile could not be compared to these dogs. It is more likely that Shakespeare was referring to the small Spaniel Gentle called the Comforter, carried by ladies of the court as "instruments of folly for them to play and dally withal" as noted by Caius. But even these provided a love that was unselfish, constant, and devoted, rather than the servile, cringing, habits of the fearing creature in the verses of Shakespeare. One can only feel sorrow that William obviously missed the pleasure of a self-confident, wise, and energetic red and white Land Spaniel of the times so that he could have portrayed him in more representative ways.

There is another field of inquiry to aid in the study of the history of the Welsh Spaniel. For the rich lord of the Renaissance, an attractive form of self-praise and display of wealth was to have made in his likeness a tapestry to show life in his court. Some remain in museums today, providing an opportunity to gain some insight into the Middle-Age society, and to witness, through the scenes depicted on the tapestries, details of action and physical form of the people and things that drew their interest. Two centers of the craft of tapestry-making existed—one in Flanders and the other in France. Of the many tapestries manufactured by the craftsman of Paris, Arras, Tournai, and Hainault, only a very few show the theme of hunting, yet some of this limited group are among the most famous. Hunting is shown either as a chase or as hawking. The tapestries give considerable information about the hound group of dogs. This is to be expected when one remembers the much-greater attention given to packhunting on horseback by royalty compared to the more solitary and gentile aspects of hunting with the net or hawk. Despite the fact that hunting of all types was the favorite sport of the wealthy gothic lord, there remains only four tapestries with the theme of hunting, and only a few others that contain dogs as incidental features of the pictorial composition. All sorts of hound-dogs are shown in the tapestries—the *Hunt of the Unicorn* (Metropolitan Museum of Art, N.Y.) and *Boar-Hunting* (Glasgow Museum). In the *Falconry Tapestry* of the Devonshire Hunting Collection and in the *Offering of the Hearts* tapestry, both of which completed in the late fifteenth century, smallish spaniels are depicted. These spaniels, and the one in the hawking scene of the *Departure for the Hunt* tapestry (Minneapolis Museum), are the only dogs of the sporting group, *Aucupatorii,* which are available to compare with the spaniels shown in the various prints that appeared in books some one hundred years later.

In judging these spaniels, one must accept the limitations inherent in creating exact likenesses in weaving; that these works were made in France or Flanders by European craftsmen; and that the "cartoons," which were fixed behind the loom as guides for the weavers, were drawn by French artists. The spaniel in the *Offering of the Heart,* is shown with a lady holding a hawk and is the size of a cocker spaniel. The artist had the opportunity to show color in the coat of the dog since many colors are used in various portions of the scene, but the dog appears with a solid whitish coat. It is clearly a small spaniel with a long tail and could be conceivably a large version of the Spaniel Gentle noted by Caius and Gesner as adored by the ladies of the court during the Middle Ages. The spaniel in the center of the Devonshire *Falconery* tapestry is larger, more representative of a Welsh, and is shown in a more logical hunting pose with two hawks overhead and a trainer with a hawk leash in his left hand observing the pair. A second handler in the scene is carrying a hawk and leading another type of dog that resembles a greyhound. The lady with her knight escort in the upper right corner of the scene carries a small dog against her right forearm and is stroking the dog's head. This toy, with its upstanding ears, full-feathered front, and very small size, can be taken to be a Maltese, which was brought to Tudor, England to join the *Delicatus* group during the fifteenth century.

Of course it is the larger spaniel in the Devonshire tapestry that is worthy of detailed attention. Although a French creation, the conformation of the dog is of interest; the head, body, and lay of the coat are true to spaniel type. Only the color of the coat causes one to question the relation of the dog to the English Land Spaniel, yet even here Caius' words may permit this dog to enter the class. He depicted the Land Spaynel as having "the most of their skins white and if they be marked with any spots they are commonly red" so that an all-white dog would be judged in the breed. The spaniel in the Devonshire tapestry is worked in white and fawn, with darker brown outlines for the legs to give sharpness to the scene. His bushtail and total lack of red would fault him in any Welsh Spaniel show ring today, but this conformation and hunting stance *do* cause him to be classed as a spaniel ancestor. This dog in the Devonshire tapestry, while small with a setterlike tail, is definitely looking upward at ducks that appear to have been just sprung from cover. Even so, this French dog is considered by many authorities, including William Arkwright, noted English dog historian and breeder, to be the forerunner of the Setter described by Caius, and to have come to France out of Spain as stated by de Foix in his chapter "Of Spaniels and of Their Nature" in his book *Livre de Chasse,* penned in 1387. Somewhere before the time of de Foix in France a distinction was first made between the setting or crouching habit of the Setter and the springing or flushing style of the Spaniel since both types of behavior are covered in de Foix's chapter on Spaniels. Here, also, de Foix makes the definite statement that French "hounds for the hawk come out of Spain." Yet it is also firmly established that bird-dogs used with the hawk were common in Wales before the tenth century, and were actually brought to France by Harold of England as a gift to the French court in the eleventh century.

While tapestries are the only source of pictorial evidence in color for bird-dogs during the fifteenth and sixteenth centuries, the work of the artist, painting in oils during the seventeenth and eighteenth centuries, provides a rich new body of fact about the dogs of commoner and king. It was also during this later period that the cultivation of specialized breeds of sporting dogs occurred in England among the landed and royalty, which was prompted by and grew on the wealth of written material. The role of the gamekeeper and husbandryman was identified as a vital force in the full development of the large land-holdings, and many a lord of the manner took a fancy to the breeding of dogs. It was then basically a gentleman's endeavor as seen by the shift in the titles of many of the books on hunting and dogs written during the 1600s and 1700s. They start very practically with *Hunger's Prevention* by Gervase Markham in 1620; led to *Gentleman's Recreation* by Richard Bloome in 1686; shifted to *The Whole Art of Husbandry* by John Mortimer in 1701; then to the *Art of Shoot Flying* by T. Page in 1767; and finally to *Instructions for the Management of Horses and Dogs* by Thomas Watson in 1785. These books are not to be thought of in and by themselves, but rather as representatives of the change in the subject matter in the over fifty books on all phases of hunting with dogs and dog-breeding published in Britain during the two hundred years before 1800.

As companion to the work of the writer, artists were also recording the faces, forms, and settings of the educated peoples who were buying and reading the type of books noted above. It was considered complimentary for the artist to include the favorite pet in his painting of an individual or family group. These scenes provide firm evidence in judging the existence of breeds of dogs and their conformations and styles. Many different types of dogs are represented, but of special note is the frequency of appearance of the red and white-coated Welsh Springer Spaniel in the paintings by Thomas Gainsborough and others. Painting portraits during the mid 1700s at Bath, England, of the rich and haughty landowning dukes, earls, and their wives, Gainsborough succeeded in bringing a touch of warmth and liveliness to these otherwise cool subjects often by including a good likeness of a canine companion. In his paintings, dogs are found such as the Pointer, Foxhound, Samoyed, Deerhound, Clumber, and Welsh. In addition, the painters Hogarth, Reynolds, and Romney, whose lives spanned the years 1697 to 1802, often used dogs as supporting elements in their paintings and included as subjects such breeds as the Pug, Cairn Terrier, Poodle, Greyhound, King Charles Spaniel, Harrier, and the Welsh Springer Spaniel.

The most striking figure of the red and white-coated spaniel of this period is in the painting of *George, 2nd Lord Vernon* by Gainsborough, which is reproduced for the frontispiece of this book. The stance of the Welsh in the painting is very characteristic of the breed, one of friendship, showing a desire to please and to be noticed. The color and texture of the coat, the head shape, and the ears are all true to type. Probably a young dog that filled out as it matured, it was definitely built for running long hours in the fields with its master. Another reasonably well-formed Welsh Spaniel appears in the painting of Mrs. Loundes-Stone completed by Gainsborough in 1747. The flesh nose, dark eyes, coat color, and general appearance are acceptable features of the breed. Of considerable interest in tracing the origins of other modern-day spaniels is the painting, *The Fourth Duke and Duchess with Their Family* completed in 1778 by Sir Joshua Reynolds, which shows three dogs, a greyhound, and two spaniels. One of the spaniels is Welsh with a full bushtail, typical color, markings, and head, which is in profile, while the other spaniel appears with black and red patches. Do we see here the beginnings of the black-patched-on-white English Springer Spaniel, which is associated with the Norfolk name? How different is this dog from the spaniels shown in the painting of *Thomas William Coke of Norfolk* by Pompeo G. Batoni? Not very different, even to the upturned head and shape of the smallish black nose. It would be an excellent likeness except for the patched coat of the William Coke dogs, which are the unusual red and white of the common Land Spaniel of the period.

Today, of course, we recognize these spaniels as ancesteral to the modern Welsh Springer Spaniel. Also, we know that the serious breeding of dogs began in earnest about this time, no doubt, fostered by the appearance of the writings of Charles Darwin, the great English naturalist who originated the theory of evolution. Controlled selection in the matings was practiced with a new eye, and distinctive types within a breed emerged. A true scientific basis for breed development was added during the mid-1800s after Gregor Johann Mendel, the Austrian monk and botanist, founded the field of genetics.

Beginning in 1800, a new type of book about dogs appeared, which was paralleled by the appearance of the ever-more refined examples of the different breeds. Books about the history of dogs, covered as breeds, groups, or classes, were published increasingly. Starting with *Cynographia Britannica* by Edward Sydenham in 1800, similar but more complete books followed such as the *Natural History of the Dog,* by D.P. Blaine in 1840, *The Dog by Stonehenge* in 1859, *British Dogs* by Hugh Dalziel in 1879, and finally, *Modern Dogs* by Raudon Lee in 1896, all worth looking at and reading for a view of the breeding art and interest in dogdom during the nineteenth century.

Now for the breeding in Britain of new spaniel types of dogs, the base stock had to be the predominantly red and white Land Spaniel. This is the spaniel first described by Caius in 1576, and which subsequently appears in the colored paintings of the British masters after 1700. By its frequency of appearance in prose and pictures this spaniel was surely one of Britain's most popular dogs. Yet by the end of the 1800s, it had been replaced by a variety of other types and, except for the continued use of the red and white spaniel by the gentry in the outlying regions of the country, it had completely disappeared as a dog worthy of attention or comment by the experts. Color also had a new fashion role to play in the development of new breeds, and lively discussions appear in the literature about whether black and white, red and white, or liver and white, or solids of either color without any spots is a sign of the better bird-dog. The art and then the science of genetics had given a new toy to the breeder, and the color of the coat was so obvious a mark of difference and achievement for the husbandryman that he and the hunters were fascinated by their handywork. By the early 1800s the varieties we know now as Clumber, English, Welsh, Field, Cocker, Norfolk, and Sussex, with all their different colors, were well along in development and were all being used to spring the game across the fields and woods of England and Wales. Distinct strains were appearing through very careful breeding, and stud records were conceived as a necessary means to keep track of events and the results of the matings. By the middle of the nineteenth century, the prosperous and leisure classes of Victorian England took to a new craze of exhibition at Town Halls and palaces across the country. These "instructive entertainments" were capped in 1851 by the Great Exhibition at the Crystal Palace, and shortly thereafter the first dog show was held where breeders could be entertained and encouraged to acquire a distinctive pet or hunter.

It was during this period that the dog in society gained an additional role to hunting companion, work dog, or family protector. I refer to the role of an adornment for the lady or man, as an object to show or with which to be seen in public. It was because of this need to exhibit that a controlling body, ultimately known as the Kennel Club, was formed in 1873 in London. One of the club's first undertakings was the preparation of a Stub Book that contained the records of early shows and the names of the entries. This group of interested Victorians, encouraged by numbers of royalty, particularly the Prince of Wales, soon became the leading and final judge of all questions about dogs, including whether a breed of dog was, in fact, distinctive and could be entered in a "licensed" show. This well-meaning and enthusiastic forum, for many years, made no separation between certain working-type spaniels, and grouped together for judging any breed of spaniel, requiring only that they be classed according to size, such as, "Over 50 pounds," "Medium sized dogs and bitches," and "Under 25 pounds." Our friend the Welsh, if he was shown at all, appeared as a medium-sized dog along with spaniels of all colors and types. It was in 1902 that the Secretary of the Kennel Club was finally instructed to register into the Sporting division such dogs as the English Springers (other than Clumber, Sussex and Field) and the Welsh Springers (Red and White). After many years of relative obscurity during the 1800s, this red and white spaniel of most ancient origin was finally recognized by this body of sportsman as a distinctive type, and thereby, sanctioned a condition that was obvious to most people who lived with and used springer spaniels as a way of life outside of the sphere of the show world.

To summarize the history of the Welsh Spaniel from Renaissance to Victorian times, there is no doubt that we have an authentic record of red and white Spaniels in the British Isles for at least four hundred years and for many years previous of the spaniel or bird-dog trained for work with the hawks. In the year 1570, Dr. Caius, at the request of Conrad Gesner, the German naturalist, prepared his book on *Englishe Dogges,* and was particular to comment on the color coat of the then English Land Spaniel: "The most part of their skynnes are white and if they be marked with any spottes they are commonly red." It is apparent that Dr. Caius took special pains here to set this dog off from all others as worthy of some special comment. There can be little doubt that this red and white spaniel was very well-distributed throughout Britain at one time, but their place was entirely usurped by the liver or black and white colored spaniels in England itself during the eighteenth and nineteenth centuries. Nevertheless, there is no reason why the breed should not have been maintained in the then-remote locality of South Wales. The Neath Valley seems to have been the principal home of the breed for many years, and we have the statements of shooting over Welsh Spaniels for at least back to the midseventeen hundreds by members of the family of Mr. A.T. Williams of Ynisygerwn, Neath. There is no question as to the uniform type of the Welsh Spaniel; although they may vary somewhat in the shade of color of the coat, they always breed true to the red color and type, the same that appears many times in old pictures in which the Spaniel is portrayed.

Shooting birds with a blunt arrow and the stout wild elm bow commonly used by Welsh and English peasants up to the fourteenth century as shown in a 1326 manuscript, *De Nobilitatiubs, Sapientiis et Prudentiis Regum.* (Blackmore)

Printed tile with hunting scene, including a huntsman, stag, and dogs from the early fourteenth century. Found at the ruins of the Neath Abbey in the Vale of Neath, Wales. (Courtesy of the National Museum of Wales.)

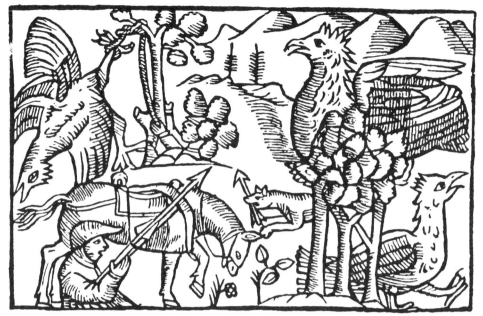

A dog retrieving crossbow bolts shot by a hunter after birds as presented by Claus Magnus in his *Historia de Gentibus* of 1555. (Blackmore)

Elizabethan Gentlemen with their hawk and spaniels as depicted in a woodcut from *The Book of Faulconrie and Hawking* by George Turbervile, 1575. The thick coats, long ears, and medium height of the dogs are similar to the Land Spaniel described by Caius and Gesner of the same period. (Pferd)

A portion of the *Falconry* fourth panel from the Devonshire Hunting Collection, which were woven at Tournai, France in the fifteenth century, shows three distinctly different types of dogs—a Maltese, a Greyhound, and a Land Spaniel. (Victoria and Albert Museum)

Hunters with a spaniel type dog after ducks and heron. While Count de Foix noted that the tails of hawking spaniels "shulde be rough," the tail of the spaniel is first shown docked in this woodcut from *Venatus et Aucupium* published in 1582. (Blackmore)

Painting of the *Fourth Duke and Duchess of Marlborough with Their Family and Pets* by Sir Joshua Reynolds in 1778. On the left is a Welsh Springer Spaniel with a good head, although cow-hocked as shown. On the right is a smaller spaniel with red and black patches on white as first described by Caius two hundred years earlier. (Duke of Marlborough)

Shooting from boats at flying birds near Venice with gun and bow. No less than twelve spaniel-type dogs are engaged in retrieving in this first illustration of wing shooting from the book *Habiti d'huomini*, written in 1609 by G. Franco. (Blackmore)

5

TWENTIETH-CENTURY BREEDERS IN BRITAIN

The emergence of the Welsh Springer Spaniel from obscurity in the hills of Wales to the winner's position at Cruft's is really the story of a few dedicated sportsmen who put forth the Welsh at the turn of the twentieth century as a distinct breed and one of very ancient lineage that deserved recognition. Why this acceptance of the Welsh Spaniel occurred at the Kennel Club General Committee meeting on 4 March 1902 in the face of considerable opposition is best told in the following interesting extract from an article by Baron Jaubert that appeared in the *Illustrated Kennel News* some months later.

> There are many valuable strains of dogs in England which never appear at shows, and are consequently ignored. Their owners — true sportsmen — preserve their dogs with care, and despise perpetual changes and fashions. Welsh spaniels, dogs intended for sport, and not prepared like modern dogs, would not have the least chance at a show of beating the inordinately long and low new type of spaniel which had been in favour for some time. Therefore the Welsh owners did not show them.
>
> The Sporting Spaniel Society (which was founded to bring back spaniels from the "dogs of fancy," into which dog shows had gradually transformed them, to a type more suitable to a working dog) succeeded in obtaining at exhibitions a special class for "working type spaniels." And then a Welsh dog was brought out at Birmingham in December 1899, which made a sensation. This was Corrin, belonging to Mr. A.T. Williams, a magnificent red and white dog. Mr. Purcell-Llewellin gave him first in a class of twenty-four; the dog

afterwards won at many other of the very first shows, including a championship at the Crystal Palace.

All this time ink was flowing freely. The pillars of the ordinary breeds of spaniels would not admit the Welsh; the dog could not, ought not, to exist. Endless letters appeared in the newspapers, but the last word has been said by the Kennel Club, which has recognised the Welsh spaniel as a separate breed. He comes victorious out of the struggle; not only does he exist, but he is of perfectly pure blood and more ancient breed than certain other spaniel strains.

There are a few kennels that have kept the pure strain of Welsh spaniels for over a hundred and fifty years; I will mention those of Mr. Jones of Pontneath, Sir John Llewelyn of Penllergaer, Colonel Lewis of Greenmeadow, and Mr. A.T. Williams of Ynisygerwm. The breed of spaniels has existed at the latter kennels since 1750. The grandfather of Mr. Williams used to go shooting in the years from 1805 to 1850 with a team of twelve to fourteen dogs trained by himself. Mr. Williams' father carried on the sport from 1845 to 1894, working with eight dogs, also trained by himself. Now Mr. Williams uses teams of from three to eight dogs, trained by a keeper. Two guns walk about 32 yeards to the right and left of the keeper, who directs the dogs.

Colonel Lewis and Mr. David of Neath also keep these dogs, and their kennels confirmed my impression that they were a distinct variety, very consistent in type, very uniform, and sharply defined by shape and coat. The latter is of a warm brick-red colour, though orange is allowable, sometimes inclining to wine-colour, a specially distinctive shade. The ear is rather small, though quite long enougth for a sporting dog; the body well off the ground, but not so much that the dog can be called "leggy." It is obvious that a dog built like this could gallop and jump as could none of the "long and low" show dogs, wittily defined, in the course of the recent polemics, as "living drain-pipes," for whom "vast halls and long corridors" are necessary. The Welsh "starters" — a term more frequently employed in Wales than "springers" — show amongst themselves similar differences of height and weight to those seen amongst pointers, where members of the same litter may be classed, some as large and others as small pointers. The scale of points indicates a sufficiently wide margin, ranging from 30 to 43 lbs. Below 30 lbs. we find the Welsh cocker, which is entered in the ordinary cocker class at dog shows, but proves its Welsh origin by its red markings.

We had an opportunity of seeing these spaniels hunt the steep slopes of the Neath valley. The ground was a bed of matted bracken, which hid completely the fallen stones, and made waling very difficult. In a country like this thc two teams we saw at the field trails worked for six consecutive hours. The dogs swarmed round their men as lightly and gaily as if in a stubble-field; they showed as much energy at the close of the day as they had done at the beginning. They proved themselves to possess excellent noses and great keenness. They reconciled — a necessary point in teams — the greatest activity with perfect immobility at the flushing of game or the sound of a gun. The sixty-six head of game to four guns certainly gave us more pleasure than 400 head would at a battue. We began the day with the before-mentioned prize-winner Corrin, who, despite his ten years, showed an energy and a dash as great as those of the puppies - a proof that the breed is sound.

It is obvious from the above article that early in 1901 special attention was being given to the Welsh Springer Spaniel, "starter" or "springer." Natives of Wales urged its claim to be accepted by the Kennel Club as authentic, while other spaniel enthusiasts wrote in opposition. In the end the Welsh dog won, supported most effectively in the effort by Mr. A.T. Williams and Mr. W.H. David from Wales, and by Mr. William Arkwright, noted sportsman and author of the classic, *The Pointer and His Predecessors,* which had been published some few years before and provided a credible historical base from which to judge the Welsh Spaniel type of hunting dog.

But of all the people who came forth to present and defend the Welsh Springer Spaniel, the name of Mr. A.T. Williams desires very special attention, and of all the early famous Welsh dogs, Corrin, owned by Mr. Williams, has the greatest of reputations. Both were most active in furthering the breed, one with his pen and as a breeder, and the other as a consistent winning dog in the working-type spaniel group and an exceptional leader in the hunt. When Corrin was first introduced into the show ring he was listed as a Welsh Cocker and did much winning, but after the Kennel Club recognition he became a Welsh Springer and went on winning! He was considered the best-looking sporting spaniel in Britain during the early part of his show career. He was exhibited at Birmingham in 1899, at Manchester and the Crystal Palace in 1900, at Brecon in 1901 and after. A view of Corrin's activities in show competition is related in the following excerpt from *The Kennel Gazette,* October 1900, which covered the Working-Type Spaniel event at the Crystal Palace under Mr. William Arkwright.

> In the medium-sized dogs, a very good class, Corrin, 1st, just won. He is a beautiful red and white Welsh Spaniel, strong and active, well balanced, and brimming over with Spaniel action and character, but he shows age a little. (He was seven years having been whelped in June, 1893.) Compton Frisk, 2nd, a first-rate black and white, was very close to Corrin. He has the better head and jaw, and is as truly made in body and limbs; but he is not nearly as good in dense, bright Spaniel coat, nor has he got the winner's superabundant bustle and push in his movements.

It is odd to read that a Welsh and an English Springer were competing in the same ring, but one must remember that this show occurred before their split by the Kennel Club into different classifications. At that time, the differences in conformation were slight, only color of coat being the clearly distinguishing characteristic. For the Welsh fancier, it is fun to read that the red and white went to the top. But just to even the score, at this same show, but in the medium-sized bitches class, Mena of Gerwn, the other Welsh in the head-study by Maud Earl, gained a second, being topped by a liver and white English named Stylish Wasp.

In February 1903, the *Kennel Gazette* reported, under the banner "Welsh Spaniels," the last show appearance of Corrin, at Brecon, when he was ten-years-old. His win was reported as follows:

The Welsh section was well filled; and most of the entries were a typical workmanlike lot. Mr. A. T. Williams, the modern father of the breed, again showed his old dog, Corrin, which won in the Open Class for Dogs. He ought to be allowed to retire now. He very nearly lost 1st prize to his son, Corrin of Gerwn, for he is falling off in his hind quarters, and his eye is glazing and assuming that vacant expression characteristic of old age. 2nd and 3rd, Corrin of Gerwn and Prince of Gerwn are both very typical, and looked like real workers.

While Corrin was being awarded C.C.s in the show ring, Mr. Williams was writing inspiring messages about the Welsh as indicated by the following piece published originally in the Kennel Gazette of January 1903. It is a statement that is timeless and should serve even today as a worthy message to all Welsh Springer Spaniel fanciers.

WELSH SPRINGERS
A.T. WILLIAMS

Since the Kennel Club gave this Spaniel a place, as a distinct breed, in their Stud Book, and accordingly included him in their "List of Breeds," comparatively few months have elapsed, but it is not too much to say that during that time greater interest has been taken, outside of Wales, in this splendid working Spaniel than has ever been the case before. More studious care also has already been taken in mating and breeding, and, although it is yet a good deal too soon to see the results, it may be taken for granted that in future we shall see a more uniform type than has been the case hitherto.

The standard of points having been settled, breeders have an authoritative guide before them, and it is to be hoped judges will have due regard to that standard and not encourage such exaggerations as have been permitted in other breeds, so that shows may not have the effect of spoiling this dog for work. The highest and first object should be to protect and preserve his working qualities and abilities. Up to the present time, and for hundreds of years past, he has been bred purely and exclusively for work, and it would be the greatest disaster to the dog and to sport if he were to be allowed to sink into a creature that cannot work.

As he is, there is no better, nor more amiable, and trustworthy, companion and friend, so that there can be no excuse, on that score, for altering his disposition. At the same time, he stands out as a pre-eminent worker, and all that is required is to breed in accordance with the Kennel Club's standard of points for this dog, without exaggerating it in any respect. Of course, uniformity is desirable, and this is the thing to be attained.

Present owners of this Spaniel are in some cases gentlemen, who have never exhibited, and who do not attend dog shows, and it be understood that it is most difficult to induce them to do so. There are others, however, who are now taking up the breed, and it is to be hoped they will exhibit a little more public spirit, in the interest of sport generally. At the same time, the latter gentlemen must be allowed time, because in some cases they owned other Spaniels. They are, gradually, giving the other up, so that they may replace them with the Welsh Springer. This is so, not only in Wales, but also in England. This should lead to one result, viz., – that in future we shall have a larger number of beautiful Welsh Spaniels than we have ever had before.

Some owners, from past experience of the influence of the bency upon other breeds, are anxious, and perhaps nervous, as to the influence it may exercise upon the working properties of this dog, and it will be for the show judges to maintain the position, and to satisfy owners that the effect of the bench will be to preserve the breed, and not to spoil it.

Now that Field Trials for Spaniels have been started, and it is to be hoped established, this should assist the judges in maintaining a hard working type, with all the necessary sporting qualities, and Field Trial Winners should be encouraged, in every shape and form, on the bench. With a sporting dog, "handsome is that that handsome does," but in saying this, there should be no desire to disparage appearances and good looks, but on the contrary, to encourage them. At the same time, the standard of beauty should be the structure and make that can best accomplish the object for which the dog exists.

Fortunately for the history and typing of the breed, during 1902 Miss Maud Earl included Welsh representatives in her group of oil paintings of hounds and gundogs that were first exhibited at the Grave's Gallery, London. The hit of the show was the painting of the Welsh Spaniels, which was subsequently offered in a limited number of photographic reproductions. A copy of a portion of one of these early prints appears in this book. In viewing the original at the showing, Mr. Williams stated,

the picture was most opportune, and will be of great value in the future in assisting to represent what these Spaniels were like in the year 1902, when they were first admitted as a distinct breed into the Stud Book, and which is therefore perhaps the most memorable year in their history.

Of the five head-studies of Welsh Spaniels in this 1902 Maud Earl, two are in fine profile and of size that permits close attention to details. Models for the picture were all from the A.T. Williams' Gerwn kennel and included as the larger figures, "Corrin of Gerwn," sired by Corrin, and "Mena of Gerwn." The small studies of the three heads looking from the rear were of "Brush," "Dash" and "Belle," all of Gerwn. In addition to these head-studies of early members of the breed, are the two Springers, Ch. Longmynd Colon Fach and Ch. Longmynd Megan, owned by Mrs. H.D. Greene and used as models for the full-length painting by Maud Earl in 1906. Here are beautiful Welsh, although somewhat artfully presented, which show their coat and feathering in stylish manner. The picture is reproduced in this book by permission of the kennel Club so that one can judge why this painting is considered to be the best ever portrayed of Welsh Springer Spaniels.

But what is the "ideal" Welsh Springer Spaniel? No less an authority than Mr. A.T. Wiliams answered the question when posed by Herbert Compton, editor of *The Twentieth Century Dog* who compiled expert opinion about all the breeds back in 1904. Mr. Williams' description was included as follows:

Mr. A.T. Williams' Ideal Welsh Spaniel

The old Welsh breed is not affected by shows, but has been bred and kept by shooting sportsmen for its working properties. A spaniel full of intelligence, and that, with the mere sight of a gun, instantly brims over with delight. His greatest pleasure is to set to work immediately, and force out for the gun whatever there may be in the shape of game or rabbits.

The ideal Welsh Spaniel must be exceedingly active and strong, able to negotiate the most difficult as well as the thickest places, and to last out the longest day. His colour must always be red and white, the red deepening with age. His head fairly long and strong, but not settery type. Ears should be small, offering a minimum of resistance and opportunity to gorse and briars; eyes dark and full of spaniel expression; body very muscular, not long on any account, with thick coat, not curly; stern down, never above the line of his back, with plenty of movement; legs medium length, with plenty of bone and good round feed. And for disposition he must possess utter devotion to his master, high courage, and not afraid of a fight if imposed upon him, but not quarrelsome.

A careful reading of Mr. Williams' comment about his "ideal" Welsh brings forth an image somewhat in variance with the Welsh picture in the 1906 Earl painting. These champions have a longish look, and the hindquarters of Megan, the bitch on the right, have a slight uphill run, yet Mr. Williams states, "body. . . not long on any account." Do we see here the edge of some past conflict in conformation between the dogs of Mr. Williams and those of Mrs. H.D. Green, of the Grove Kennel, which became in a few years the leading champions? The Longmynd dogs of Mrs. Green are certainly longer in the Maud Earl painting than the Williams description of an "ideal" Welsh would allow. As for the loin of Corrin, the photograph taken in his tenth year shows more excessive arch, due to the stance of his hind legs, than would occur in a more natural position. A photograph of the Grove Kennel bitch, Champion Longmynd Colon Fach, which appeared as the frontispiece of the 1934 *Yearbook of the Welsh Springer Spaniel Club of Great Britain,* and is reproduced in this book, seems to settle the question. This bitch, bred by Mrs. Green, was considered one of her best champions and in every way a typical Welsh. She is of the same type as Corrin, in length, head, and loin. Yet for all the comparisons, the Maud Earl painting is still a pleasure to look at and the best available of two Welsh on canvas.

An official-looking-standard for the Welsh Springer appeared in 1906 in the book *The Sporting Spaniel* by C.A. Phillips and R. Claude Cane. Mr. Cane, in 1902, was a member of the Kennel Club General Committee, which recommended breed recognition for the Welsh and English Springer. We therefore, may judge his "Points for the Welsh Springer" that appear in his book as authentic. They are the earliest that this author has been able to date and, in many respects, contain words and phrases that appear in the Williams description prepared prior to 1904. The 1906 Phillips and Cane Standard for the breed follows. It is also interesting to compare this first standard with those recognized as official today by the American Kennel Club and the Kennel Club of Britain, as given in Appendices F and G, and to notice how few changes and additions have been made over the last seventy-five years.

POINTS OF THE WELSH SPRINGER
(from *The Sporting Spaniel*)

The "Welsh Spaniel" or "Springer" is also known and referred to in Wales as a "Starter." He is of very ancient and pure origin, and is a distinct variety which has been bred and preserved purely for working purposes.

Head. – The skull proportionate, of moderate length, slightly domed, clearly-defined stop, well-chiselled below the eyes.

Muzzle. – Medium length, straight, fairly square; the nostrils well developed and flesh-coloured or dark.

Jaw. – Strong, neither under nor overshot.

Eyes. – Hazel or dark, medium size, not prominent, not sunken, nor showing haw.

Ears. – Set moderately low, and hanging close to the cheeks, comparatively small, and gradually narrowing towards the tip. A short chubby head is objectionable.

Neck and Shoulders. – Long and muscular, clean in throat, neatly set into long and sloping shoulders.

Fore-Legs. – Medium length, straight well-boned, moderately feathered.

Body. – Not long; strong and muscular with deep brisket, well-sprung ribs; length of body should be proportionate to length of leg, and very well balanced; with muscular loin.

Loin. – Slightly arched and well coupled up.

Quarters. – Strong and muscular, wide and fully developed with deep second thighs.

Hind Lets. – Hocks well let down; stifles moderately bent (neither twisted in nor out), moderately feathered.

Feet. – Round with thick pads.

Stern. – Well set on and low, never carried above the level of the back; lightly feathered and with lively action.

Coat. – Straight or flat and thick, of a nice silky texture, never wiry; wavy. A curly coat is most objectionable.

Colour. – Dark, rich red, and white.

General Appearance. – A symmetrical, compact, strong, merry, very active dog; not stilty, obviously built for endurance and activity, and from 33 to 40 lbs. in weight.

While numerical points have never been a part of the official standards, apparently the issue was discussed shortly after recognition of the breed by the Kennel Club since there appears just such a proposal in the chapter on "The Welsh Springer" in the 1906 book *A History and Description of the Modern Dogs of Great Britain and Ireland* by Rawdon B. Lee, then editor of *The Field.* The idea of a point system did not gain support, since this is the only one that has been identified with the breed and none is in use today.

NUMERICAL POINTS FOR A WELSH SPRINGER
(from R. B. Lee, 1906)

POSITIVE		NEGATIVE	
Head and expression (including eyes)	15	Light-coloured eyes (undesirable)	15
Ears	10	Curled ears (very undesirable)	20
Neck	5		
Body and loins	15	Coat (curly, woolly, or wiry, and bad colour)	20
Legs and feet	15		
Stern and its carriage	10	Carriage of stern (crooked or twisted)	25
Coat and colour	15	Top-knot (fatal)	20
General appearance	15		
Total	100	Total	100

Another description of the Welsh Springer, different in a few ways both from that which was given earlier and from the present official standards, is contained in *The Complete Dog Book,* published in 1921, by Dr. William R. Bruette, then editor of the American magazine, *Forest and Streams.* He provides the following as an description formulated by the Welsh members of the Sporting Spaniel Society. One can assume that this is an early American version of the "official" standard.

DESCRIPTION OF THE WELSH SPRINGER
(from Dr. W.A. Burette, 1921)

Skull. – Fairly long and fairly broad, slightly rounded, with a stop at the eyes.

Jaws. – Medium length, narrow (when looked at downwards), straight, fairly square, the nostrils well developed, and flesh-colored or dark. A short, chubby head is objectionable.

Eyes. – Hazel or dark brown, medium size, intelligent, not prominent nor sunken nor showing haw.

Ears. – Comparatively small, covered with feather not longer than the ear, set moderately low, and hanging close to the cheeks.

Neck. – Strong, muscular, clean in throat.

Shoulders. – Long and sloping.

Forelegs. – Medium length, straight, good bone, moderately feathered.

Body. – Strong, fairly deep, not long, well-sprung ribs. Length of body should be proportionate to that of leg.

Loin. – Muscular and strong, slightly arched, well coupled up and knit together.

Hindquarters and Legs. – Strong; hocks well let down; stifles moderately bent (not twisted in or out), not feathered below the hock on the leg.

Feet. – Round, with thick pads.

Stern. – Low, never carried above the level of the back, feathered, and with a lively motion.

Coat. – Straight or flat, and thick.

Color. – Red or orange-and-white (red preferable).

General Appearance. – Symmetrical, compact, strong, merry, active, not stilty, built for endurance and activity.

Weight. – Between 30 and 42 pounds.

We find in the above description two phrases about the jaw of the Welsh not found in the earlier British standard – "narrow (when looked at downward)" and "a short, chubby head is objectionable." The first is certainly a distinguishing feature of many Welsh today, yet the present official standards omit this identification entirely. The latter comment about the objectionable "chubby head" is retained in both the present British and American official standard and is certainly a feature to be shunned in the Welsh. The 1921 Burette description permitted an orange and white coat, although red was indicated as "preferable," and the weight range was extended by five pounds over the earlier Phillips and Cane standard, increasing the maximum to forty-two pounds with the minimum at thirty. Of course, all these points have been omitted in recent years with only "rich red and white" and "dark rich red and white" (American) allowed for coat color and no guidance given for the weight range of the dog or bitch.

For many years the British and American standards were virtually identical, but during the last year, the British added a height restriction that, in effect, limited the size of dogs and bitches somewhat in accordance to the older weight restriction. The latest British standard has size limitations as follows: A dog not to exceed nineteen inches in height at shoulder and a bitch eighteen inches, approximately. It should be noted that with modern nutrition, the tendency will be to grow healthier and somewhat larger dogs over the long term, which might pose some interesting judging issues in the future. Another recent addition to the British standard called for feet to be "firm and cat-like, not too large or spreading." This may be desirable to gain a stylish appearance but one wonders what adverse effect this shape of feet might have on the dog's swimming ability over long distances. One reason the Welsh has always had a reputation as a credible water spaniel is its ease of swimming to make a water retrieve. Without the natural broad-webbed foot to move, his action in water would be seriously altered. As the American standard states in the introduction, the Welsh "has been bred and preserved purely for working purposes" and this has included work in the water as well as on land. Of course, most of the "points" of standards deal with appearance factors and one must rely on field tests to identify the truly endowed hunters.

Through the pioneering efforts of Mr. A.T. Williams and others who exhibited with great success at the same time, notably Major H. Jones and Mr. W.H. Davies, interest in the breed extended and grew. They were soon joined by Mrs. H.D. Greene who took up the breed a short time later and, up until the outbreak of World War I, possessed what was undoubtedly the strongest kennel of its day having at one time, eight champions. Her favorites were Champion Cinila Dash and the Longmynd dogs of the famous Maud Earl painting. In the course of time puppies from the new kennels found their way into the possession of keen breeders in different parts of South Wales; the classification for Welsh Springers became common at local shows, and the level of interest grew to warrant the formation of the first Welsh Spaniel Club. Mrs. Green, as Secretary, was the mainstay of the group that functioned until World War I. This was a cruel time for dogs as well as men, and especially for the Welsh Springers, as most selective breeding came to an end and some kennels terminated altogether. In particular, Mrs. Green felt the war most keenly and, fearing that she would not be able to obtain sufficient food for feeding her large kennel, she had every dog killed. This great loss to the breed was most unfortunate since she owned some of the most typical Welsh Springers in the country.

After World War I, breeding and shows started again in Britain, and in 1922 the Welsh Springer Spaniel Club was reactivated through the leadership of Colonel J.H.R. Downes-Powell, with assistance from the old club in providing literature, minute books, and membership lists. At the first meeting in 1923, chaired by the Colonel, among those present were Messrs. T. Williams, F. Morris, L. Morgan, G.W. Herne, D. Neale, D. Hazzleby, Major H. Gunn, and Dr. T.W. Risely. After further meetings, the Kennel Club permitted registration of the Welsh Springer Spaniel Club, which has continued to function in Britain ever since, except for the break from 1939 to 1946 due to the war. In the first year, the club held field trials at Ruperra Park with six entries and followed this event the next year with trials at Margam Park, the home of the then club president, Capt. A. Talbot Fletcher, where events followed for some years afterward. Some of the great dogs that made their mark in the early field trials and shows between 1923 and 1929 were: Ch. Barglam Bang, Ch. Merglam Band. Topsy of Shill, Tawney Patch, Legacy Lex, Ch. Shoto'r Baili, and Ch. Good Sport; and among the bitches, Ch. Felcourt Flapper, Tess of Shill, Lass of Tolworth, Ch. Talybont Princess, and Ch. Felcourt What's Wanted.

Dogs for field performance during this period were dominated by the breeding get of Ch. Merglam Bang and Goitre Lass. This combination produced half of the previously mentioned top champion dogs, as well as many others not listed on the working side. Goitre Lass matings with Ch. Merglam Bang were important also as an influence on the facial appearance of all modern Welsh. The puppies from these matings were always true to color of coat, but some had a dark color in the eye and nose. This attractive combination has always been recognized as worth preserving and has now all but replaced the flesh-colored nose and hazel eye often seen in the original type. Why this shift in color occurred can only be surmized, although it is alleged by Dorothy M. Hopper in her book, *The Springer Spaniel* that Goitre Lass had some English Springer blood in her lineage. This of course would not be surprising since the history of the spaniel during the latter part of the nineteenth century was sufficiently obscure to have permitted such breeding. As stated earlier, color of coat did not separate in show competition before 1903 the various types of spaniels that are known today as Cocker, English, and Welsh. While Goitre Lass seems to be credited with distinctive coloring for her puppies, it is equally important to note that the breed standards have allowed a flesh or dark nostril and hazel or dark eyes since shortly before the recognition of the breed by the Kennel Club. This fact leads to the view that such coloring occurred in litters from much earlier periods and, certainly, long before the Goitre Lass matings in the 1920s. As an example, we see a black nose on the Welsh in the 1778 painting of the Marlborough family by Reynolds. At the most, one might say that the number of Goitre Lass puppies so marked was great, and that they had a solid brown to black nose and deep brown eyes. It was no doubt the activity on the show side that caused the shift in attention away from the originally dominant hazel eye and flesh-colored muzzle, although even today one sees now and then a spot of flesh tone on the muzzle of a show champion and, of course, the present standard still allows for both light and dark tones to nose and eye. Even so, there is no denying that the dark points with the rich deep red and white coat add materially to the Welsh Springer's good looks, and that essentially all breeding presently has dark points as an objective. The flesh nose as seen in the frontispiece painting by Gainsborough of the Lord Vernon Welsh Spaniel is definitely a thing of the past, yet in this same picture we see a dark eye, a distinctly modern note.

In the late 1920s and early 1930s, other well-known winners were Ch. Marksman O'Matherne, Ch. Mair-o'r-Cwm, Ch. Musketeer O'Matherne, Marigold O'Matherne, Serenade O'Silian, Ch. Dere Mhlaen, Lad of Tolworth, Master Gun, Gunner of Tolworth, Judith of Knaphill, High Game, Pat of Merrymount, Shot of Canonmoor and Rockhill Rock, all Challenge Certificate winners and/or field trial winners. The Tolworth dogs were bred by Mrs. Llewellyn Hughes, her finest bitch being Lass of Tolworth, daughter of Tafolog Lad and Quar Lady. A Best of Breed winner at Crufts in 1934 was Judith of Knaphill, bred by Mrs. M.E. Groombridge. She also took first at Cardiff in 1934, then the headquarters of the breed with its naturally strong showing. A winner at Crufts in 1933 was High Game, bred by Mr. W. Turford and exhibited by Mr. G. W. Herne. The Rev. D. Stewart of Rumburgh Vicarage, Halesworth, Suffolk was during this period a great enthusiast and promoter of the breed. He owned Pat of Merrymount who was bred by Lady Mercia Miles by Ch. Shot O'r Baili out of Judy Bang. Pat sired such notable dogs as Ch. Serenade O'Silian and Symphony O'Silian. A sterling dog on the show bench and in the field was Col. J. Downes-Powell's Ch. Marksman O'Matherne, while another dog with great intelligence on the working side was Legacy Lex. The latter dog was owned by Mr. R.H. Sprake, and was sired by Tawney Pippin out of Tawney Pansy. Legacy Lex won, in the same year, the Open and Puppy Stakes at Margam in 1931 and the Open Stakes at the Eastern Counties Trials for all varieties of spaniel's. This was an impressive win against many of the finest English Springers and was the first time that a Welsh had won a stake at an Open field trial in England.

The fortunes of the Welsh Springer Spaniel during the years between the great wars were intimately tied to the activities of Col. Downes-Powell. He advanced his favorite breed on the show and working side as well as being a judge, breeder, and handler. He guided the affairs of the Welsh Springer Spaniel Club in one office or another for over thirty-five years, and was honored in 1948 at the Annual General Meeting by accepting an illuminated address to show the appreciation of the members for all the Colonel had done for the breed during his twenty-five years as Honorary Secretary. Of all the dogs known to Col. Downes-Powell, he rated his Ch. Musketeer O'Matherne as the best. He was sired by Ch. Marksman of Matherne out of Merrymaid O'Matherne. An exceptionally good gundog who ran at field trials with distinction, he had firsts and seconds at Welsh Springer Stakes, and Reserve and Certificate of Merits at Open Stakes. Musketeer won three C.C.s under Judges J. Jones, D.E.R. Griffiths, and C. Houlker. It is not surprising then when we see that Col. Downes-Powell listed Musketeer as best of the breed he had ever seen. In 1938 there appeared in the *New Book of the Dog,* by Edward C. Ash, the following judgments by Col. Downes-Powell about the three dogs and bitches he liked best in the previous ten years.

Name	They Excelled In:	Their faults were:
Ch. Musketeer O'Matherne	Type, movement, color, and symmetry (I think him the best of this breed I have ever seen). His balance is wonderful.	A mere fraction short of foreface.
Ch. Marksman O'Matherne	Type, substance, movement.	As a dog, might be a shade shorter coupled.
Ch. Shot o'r Baili	Type, substance and expression, a great spaniel.	His ears are too pendulous. Rather a sluggish mover, but a great dog.
Ch. Felcourt Flapper	Substance, type and movement, a very great bitch, her color was perfect.	Always a trifle short in coat and feather.
Ch. Mair o'r Cwm	Substance, type and coloring.	Rather sluggish in movement, and a shade short in neck
Marigold O'Matherne	Type, color. Movement and substance. Won 3 C.C. before she was 18 months.	As a bitch she might have been a shade longer in body. Her expression too, was affected by nerves — apt to frown.

These comments show the work of an experienced judge of Welsh Springers and the need for attention to fine details to separate the top-rate from the best.

While the effort to enlarge the group at championship shows was an important issue for the club during the late twenties, the more vital discussions centered on the performance of dogs in the field. This followed the main interests of many of the more active members since it was the basis for their initial effort to gain recognition for the breed and start the Welsh Springer Spaniel Club. By 1924 and running through the mid-1930s, Challenge Cups for field trial wins were presented to the best Puppy at the Club Field Trial and to the best Welsh Springer at the Meeting. The first was donated by Capt. A. Talbot Fletcher of Margam, and the second by John Davies, Esquire, of Neath. Trials and awards were made regularly for the years up to 1937 but with a waning interest, which resulted in the suspension of Welsh Springer field meets until they were finally resumed after World War II, eleven years later in 1948. The list of winners at these field trials follows and contains many familiar and famous names.

The Talbot-Fletcher Challenge Cup (1925) Winners for best Puppy at the Field Trials. To be won three times before becoming the property of the winner (presented by Capt. Talbot Fletcher).
    1925, Mrs. S. Horsfield's "Rosamund."
    1926, Mr. E.F. Fieldhouse's "Susie of Sol."
    1927, Lt.-Col. and Mrs. Horsfield's "Tawney Muffin."
    1928, Capt. D.J. Griffiths' "Questa of Coegnant."
    1929, Lt.-Col. J. Downes-Powell's "Marksman o' Mathern."
    1930, Mr. G. W. Herne's "Handy Gester."
    1931, Mrs. M. Mayall's "Rockhill Rock."
    1932, Lt.-Col. J. Downes-Powell's "Marionette o' Mathern."
    1933, Mr. R. James' "Shot of Canonmoor."
    1934, Mr. R. James' "Shot of Canonmoor."
    1935, Mr. C.F. Chard's "Llanwern Advent."
    1936, Capt. N.W. Tredinnick's "Newburie Valerie."
    1937, Capt. N.W. Tredinnick's "Ginger Lad."

The "John Davies" Challenge Cup (1924), for best Welsh Springer at the Meeting. To be won three times before becoming the property of the winner (presented by John Davies, Esq.)
    1924, Mrs. S. Horsfield's "Tawney Patch."
    1925, Mr. W. Rickards' "Topsy of Shill."
    1926, Mr. W. Rickards' "Tess of Shill."
    1927, Mrs. S. Horsfield's "Tawney Patch."
    1928, Mr. G.W. Herne's "Handy Gunner."
    1929, Capt. D.J. Griffiths' "Questa of Coegnant."
    1930, Lt.-Col. and Mrs. R. M. Horsfield's "Tawney Pippin."
    1931, Mr. R. H. Sprake's "Legacy Lex."

1932, Capt. W. H. C. Llewellyn's "Ronna."

1933, Lt.-Col. J. Downes-Powell's "Musketeer o' Mathern."

1934, Lt.-Col. J. Downes-Powell's "Musketeer o' Mathern."

1935, Mr. R. James' "Shot of Cononmoor."

1936, Mr. R. James' "Shot of Canonmoor."

The "Grove" Challenge Cup (1935) (perpetual), for best Dog or Bitch in Show at W.E.L.K.S. (presented by Mrs. M. Mayall)

Winners —

1935, Lt. Col. J. Downes-Powell's Ch. Musketeer o'Mathern.

1936, Mr. A.J. Dyke's Marglam Marquis.

1937, Mr. A.J. Dyke's Marglam Marquis.

1938, Mr. J. Feddersen's Lady of Moile.

1939, Mr. J. Turford's Chief of Mons.

1940-45. No Award.

1946, Mr. H. Newman's Dewi Sant.

1947, Mr. T.H. Morgan's Dere Damsel.

1948, Mr. T.H. Morgan's Deer Damsel.

1949, Mr. L.J. Kemp's Tals Maid.

1950, Mr. G. Taylor's Taliesin Yr Ail,

1951, Mr. H. Newman's Denethorp Dido.

1952, Mr. H. Newman's Denethorp Dido.

1953, Mrs. J.A. Foster's Broadweir Bracken.

1954, Mrs. M.B. King's Kim of Kenswick.

1955, Mrs. M. Mayall's Ch. Rockhill Rhiwderin.

1956, Mrs. M.B. King's Legacy of Kenswick.

1957, Mr. H.J.H. Leopard's Rushbrooke Rustic.

1958, Mr. H.C. Payne's Topscore of Tregwillym.

1959, Mr. T. Hubert Arthur's Brancourt Belinda.

1960, Mr. T. Hubert Arthur's Sh. Ch. Brancourt Belinda

1961, Mr. B.G. Thorpe's Ch. Kim of Cwm.

1962, Mr. H.C. Payne's Sh. Ch. Statesman of Tregwillym.

1963, Mr. Corbet and Miss Potter's Rambler of Da Miellette.

1964, Miss A. West's Sh. Ch. Deri Darrell of Linkhill.

1965, Miss A. West's Sh. Ch. Liza of Linkhill.

1966, Mr. H. Newman's Easter Parade.

1967, Mr. H.C. Payne's Golden Tint of Tregwillym

1968, Mr. J.K. Burgess' Sh. Ch. Plattburn Paramount

1969, Mr. G. Pattinson's Tidemarsh Rip

1970, Mr. & Mrs. J.K. Burgess' Plattburn Progressor

1971, Mr. & Mrs. J.K. Burgess' Sh. Ch. Plattburn Progressor

1972, Mr. & Mrs. J.K. Burgess' Sh. Ch. Plattburn Progressor

1973, Mr. H.C. Payne's Tregwillym Golden Gem

1974, Mr. H.C. Payne's Tregwillym Golden Gem

From 1933 to the beginning of World War II, the club in Britain continued with yearly championship shows, field trials, and the issuing of attractive Club Yearbooks, which are a rich source of information for any serious research about the breed. In the 1933 yearbook, two new names in Welsh Springer Spaniel history appeared that would have a lasting impact on the breed; Mrs. M. Mayall, the second consummate distaff fancier of Welsh Springers, and Mr. Harold Newman, a young owner-handler from Cardiff, Wales, recently into the breed after some work with Sealyham Terriers.

Mrs. M. Mayall, with many an outstanding specimen on both the working and the show side, first appeared in the upper ranks with Rockhill Rock, winning the Talbot-Fletcher Cup with the Best Puppy at the Club Field Trial in 1931. Following Mrs. S. Horsfield as the second woman to own and work Welsh Springers to winning positions in the field, Mrs. Mayall moved with even greater success with her own breeding in the show ring. In 1933 her Rockhill Rowdy took honors in both show and field, while her Rockhill Ranger earned Best Dog at the Ladies Kennel Association Show under Judge Mr. T. Williams. Some of the other Rockhill winners during the mid-thirtys were Rona, Roel, Ready, Rough, and Robina, while Champion Rockhill Rhiwderin, a very fine dog and winner of twelve Challenge Certificates, was the best known. Mrs. Mayall, a great supporter of the breed, was elected to the Committee of the Welsh Springer Spaniel Club in 1935 and served for close to twenty years in furthering club activities to advance the breed. One of her more lasting acts was the gift of the "Grove" Challenge Cup to the Club in 1935 to be given each year to the Best Dog or Bitch in Show at W.E.L.K.S. at Cheltenham. Always drawing a strong group of contenders, the winners of the "Grove" Cup listed above reads like a veritable "who's who" of Welsh Springer Spaniels since practically all the great dogs and bitches appear in the list of this longest-lived award for Welsh, still running after forty years.

While Mrs. Mayall has the honor of sponsoring the cup with the longest record of awards, Mr. H. Newman of Teorchy, Glamorgan has the distinction of being the dean of the all Welsh Springer Spaniel breeders, owners, and handlers. In 1929 he had his first Welsh Springer bitch that was the forerunner of all that has followed in the way of prized dogs from the Pencelli Kennel. Still working in the ring to further the breed, Mr. Newman has owned and bred ten Show Champions during his career. Included among them was Champion Dewi Sant, next to Champion Corrin, the most famous of all the Welsh Springers. Mr. Newman's first C.C.s were won with his bitch, Barmaid, under Judge Col. Downes-Powell in 1934 at the Abergavenny Champion Show. Mr. Newman recalled for a story in the 1967 Welsh

Springer Spaniel Club Yearbook the following scene:

> In those days this was one of the shows in the Principality that always attracted a wonderful entry of the breed and a win there was considered a bigger win than Crufts. For in those days the breed was strong in the working man's home and not everyone could afford the expense of going to show at Crufts. The breed would make a wonderful turnout and look a lovely sight in the beautiful surroundings of that part of the country. On one occasion I remember 19 exhibits in the Limit Class and 20 in the Open Dog Class and I took both classes with two different dogs. Those were the days! At the Abergavenny show in 1934 with its huge entry, Barmaid's son, Show Champion Dere Mhlaen took the Reserve C.C. in dogs. He was the result of the first mating between Barmaid and Ch. Marksman O'Matherne.

During the 1940-1945 period, breeding in Britain practically ceased just as it did during World War I, and if it were not for the vision and courage of Mr. Newman to carry on his kennel at a reduced scale, the place of the Welsh might well be quite different than what it is today. Mr. Newman acquired Dewi Sant at the height of the war from Miss M. C. Evans as the "pick of the litter" from the mating of his Dere Di with Tesco Thornycroft, and exhibited the dog at some of the war-time shows. After the war, Dewi Sant took his three Challenge Certificates in straight shows, one in 1946 and two in 1947 at Cardiff and Blackpool, and was the first dog in all breeds to finish in Wales. Show Champion Dewi Sant was considered by all Welsh fanciers as a "once in a life-time dog," full of breed characteristics, of ideal size, and true to type. In a recent letter to the author, Mr. Newman described Dewi Sant as:

> Quality from nose to tail and sound as a bell, with beautiful head, eye, and expression. He was a perfectly balanced dog who scored well in coat and color. He had personality plus. In fact, when someone asks me about him, I tell them that when he entered the ring, and if he could talk, he would look around as if to say, "Well who is going to be second to me today." A wonderful mover, he won many an Open against All Breeds on his movement.

This most attractive dog sired numerous winners and appears in practically all pedigrees of Welsh Springers as the foundation stock. Practically all breeding shortly after the War centered around Dewi Sant and it is reported that he earned over five-hundred pounds at stud when the fee was as low as five guineas. Because of his demand for stud service he was able to gain only four Challenge Certificates, but two sons, Show Champions Philosopher and Jester of Downland, also handled by Mr. Newman for their owner Miss D. H. Ellis, made up by winning over twenty C.Cs between them as dogs who were strikingly similar in all ways to their famous sire. Besides these two dogs, Champion Branksome Beauty and Show Champions Cofois Bon,

This bird-dog is considered by most authorities to be the forerunner of the Land Spaniel and Setter described by Johannes Caius in 1570. It is the central dog on the *Falconry* panel, one of the four 15' x 36' Devonshire Hunting Tapestries that hangs in the Victoria and Albert Museum. (Victoria and Albert Museum)

This scene of a hunting brace in action was painted by George Armfield in 1863 and is convincing evidence that the Welsh Springer Spaniel remains today true to type. (Ellis)

Painting by Thomas Gainsborough in 1775 of *Mrs. William Lowndes-Stone* with a spaniel-type dog. Note the dark eyes and the flesh-colored nose. (Calouste Gulbenkian Foundation Museum)

Stokecourt Jonathan, Denethorp Dido, Taliesin Ye Ail, and Welsh Lady, all owe him credit as their sire.

By 1947 the position of the Welsh Springer in Britain was greatly improved with fine specimens once again in the field and on the show bench and the club gaining in members under the leadership of Col. J. Downes-Powell as chairman and Mr. H.J.H. Leopard, honorary secretary. The list of winners during the 1947 season given below contains the names of a surprising number of the fanciers who would lead the breed for the next thirty years.

PRIZE WINNERS, 1947
KENNEL CLUB CHALLENGE CERTIFICATE WINNERS

Cardiff (March). Dog, Mr. H. Newman's Dewi Sant. Bitch, Mr. A.J. Dyke's Marglan Marchioness.

Blackpool. Dog, Mr H. Newman's Dewi Sant. Bitch, Mr. H. J.J. Leopard's Rushbrooke Rustle.

Cardiff (October). Dog, Miss D. H. Ellis' Philosopher of Downland. Bitch, Mr. T. H. Morgan's Dere Damsel.

Olympia (L.K.A.). Dog, Mr. H. Newman's Cofia Bon. Bitch, Mr. T. H. Morgan's Dere Damsel.

SHOWS

Cardiff (Ch.) (March). Judge, Mr. H.C. Hargreaves.
   Best Dog or Bitch not winning K.C. Certificate. Mr. H.J.H. Leopard's Rushbrooke Rustle.
   Best Dog or Bitch whose owner has not won a Club Special. Mr. J. Davis' Gunmaiden of Aeron.
Windsor (Ltd.). Judge, Mr. E.E. Turner.
   Best Novice. Mrs. D. Morriss' Stokecourt Beau.
   Best Dog or Bitch. Mr. H. Newman's Dewi Sant.
Cheltenham (Open). Judge, Mr. W. East.
   Best Novice. Mr. H. Newman's Cofia Bon.
   Best, owner not previously won a Club Special. Miss M.R. Campbell's Rushbrooke Ruadh.
Blackpool (Ch.). Judge, Mr. R.R. Kelland.
   Best Dog or Bitch. Mr. H.J.H. Leopard's Rushbrooke Rustle.
   Best, Exhibit or Exhibitor never having won a Club Special. Mr. T.H. Morgan's Dere Damsel.
Bedwelty (Open). Judge, Mr. J. Wright Ashworth.
   Best Novice. Mr. T.H. Morgan's Castle Court Countess.

Best, owner not previously won a Club Special. Mr. H.C. Payne's Gwenllian of Tregwillym.

Cardiff (Ch.) (October). Judge, Mr. J.H. Gibson.

The "Grove Cup." Mr. T.H. Morgan's Dere Damsel.

The "Lakefield Cup." Mr. H.J.H. Leopard's Rushbrooke Rustle.

Best Dog or Bitch not winning K.C. Certificate. Mr. H.J.H. Leopard's Rushbrooke Rustle.

Best Novice or Undergraduate. Mrs. D. Morriss' Stokecourt Beau.

Olympia, L.K.A. (Ch.). Judge, Mr. E.E. Turner.

The "Mathern Cup." Mr. H. Newman's Cofia Bon.

The "Tolworth Cup." Mr. T.H. Morgan's Dere Damsel.

Best Dog or Bitch not winning K.C. Certificate. Miss D.H. Ellis' Jester of Downland.

Best owned by an Exhibitor who has not previously won a Club Special. Mr. G. Cleeves' Elvet Lovely Lady.

FIELD TRIALS

W.S.S.C. Trials. Judges, G.C. Williams, Esq. and W.D. Edwards, Esq.

"O'Vara" Trophy. Mr. Selwyn Jones' F.T. Ch. Spark o'Vara.

Best Welsh Springer, Lt.-Col. J. Downes-Powell's Mona of Mathern.

Best Welsh Springer Puppy. Lt.-Col. J. Downes-Powell's Mona of Mathern.

Heading the list with a Challenge Certificate at Cardiff was Harold Newman's Dewi Sant. Other Show Champions developed by Mr. Newman after the war were Cofia Bon, Denethrope Dida, Welsh Lady, Easter Parade, and Maria, Roger, and Progress, all of Pencilli, the modern name of the Newman Kennel.

In recent years, Mr. Newman has again moved to the front ranks with his Show Champions Roger and Progress. Roger, as the Dog of the Year in the breed in 1972 has twelve C.C.s including Cruft's in 1972 and 1973 and twelve Reserve C.C.s with Best in Shows and many times Best Gundog at Open Shows, while his kennel mate, Progress, has gained fourteen C.Cs, three Best of Breeds, and three Reserve C.C.s. Show Champion Progress of Pencelli was Best in Show among a record entry at the 1973 Welsh Springer Spaniel Club Championship Show. Traveling to the United States, Mr. Newman had the honor of handling his American Champion Bachgen Dewr of Pencelli at the Westminister Kennel Club Show in Madison Square Garden in 1974. Mr. Newman's great enthusiasm for the breed remains unabated as he continues as President of the Welsh Springer Spaniel Club, is an approved judge to award Challenge Certificates, and remains the most senior breeder of Welsh Springers.

Also gaining a Challenge Certificate at the 1947 show at Blackpool, Mr. H.J.H. Leopard's Rushbrooke Rustle was the first of a line of Rushbrooke dogs and bitches that had to be reckoned with on the show bench or in the field. By 1950, Rushbrooke Runner was a dual champion after first showing her style by taking the reactived "Talbot-Fletcher" Cup in 1948 at the Welsh Springer Spaniel Club Field Trials. During the 1950s Mr. Leopard bred a large number of winners at field and show events, including Racer, Ruenelle, and Race-along, and Show Champions Rustle, Ruadh, and Rustic, all with the Rushbrooke prefix. Mr. Leopard was elected President of the Welsh Springer Spaniel Club in 1967 serving previously as first Hon. Secretary and Chairman of the Committee, rendering great service to the club for many years.

Another dog in the 1947 list of winners that would leave an important show and stud record both in Britain and America was Miss D.H. Ellis' Jester of Downland. Sired by Dewi Sant and handled to his Show Championship by Mr. H. Newman, Jester's dam was Merry Madcap of Downland, the first bitch in the Downland Kennel of Miss Ellis acquired in 1943 from Mr. J.S. Jones after a two-year search in the Welsh hills — so scarce were they in wartime England. An earlier Show Champion from Dowland was Philosopher, who, at the age of nine months, won the honored "Best of All Breeds in Show" awarded by the famous international judge, Mr. L. Wilson, at the Brighton Everyman Show in 1946 over six-hundred eager contestants. Philosopher won six Challenge Certificates during his show career, including the Cardiff (October) 1947. These two Dowland Champions, Jester and Philosopher, virtually dominated the 1949 season when they took seven Challenge Certificates at seven championship shows entered, of the ten authorized that year. Jester held eight Kennel Club Challenge Certificates and in 1952, went to America to join the kennel of Mrs. Eleanor Howes of East Bridgewater, Massachusetts. There he sired the first American Champion Welsh Springer, Holiday of Happy Hunting and later American Champion David of Happy Hunting. Earlier in 1950, Miss Ellis and some of her Downland dogs made a flight to the United States to appear at the Westminister, Hartford, and Boston shows and to leave behind her dogs to restart the breed in America after the war. Always enthusiastic about the breed, Miss Ellis was complimented by her long-time associate in the breed, Mr. H. Newman, as "having a wealth of knowledge about Welsh Springers and some very strong views." Judging by the records of achievement of the Downland dogs these views are sound, and their practice influenced greatly the postwar future of the breed in Britain and America.

Also on the 1947 list, Mrs. D. Morriss' Stokecourt Beau, bought for rough-shooting, was a grand worker and showdog, winning at Spaniel

Club Stakes on numerous occasions over a ten-year period. Shortly after election to the Welsh Springer Spaniel Club Committee in 1949, Mrs. Morriss purchased Stokecourt Jonathan from Mr. G.W. Hooper. Jonathan, sired by Dewi Sant, quickly gained his show championship, and in turn, sired a second Stokecourt Show Champion, Gillian. Always interested in preserving the working side of the Welsh Springer Spaniel, Mrs. Morriss, when writing to the author about her experiences with the breed, was most concerned "that the Welsh not develop into quite different types, the working and the show dogs, as is the case with so many of the gun-dog breeds." Mrs. Morriss followed her own advice perfectly having her show champions work regularly with the gun. She considered Jonathan, who won seven C.C.s, five of them Best of Breeds with two at Crufts in 1955 and 1957, as a "super retriever, both on land and in the water," while she thought her bitch Show Champion Stokecourt Gillian, eight C.Cs and a B.O.B. at Crufts in 1958, to be the "most beautiful Welsh Springer I have ever owned" yet "a useful rough-shooting dog." Elected Vice-President of the Welsh Springer Spaniel Club in 1970, Mrs. Morriss continues to be one of those who believe Welsh Springers to be the best-combined show and field dog, basically unchanged since earliest times, as evidenced by her record with the breed.

Mr. T.H. Morgans' Dere Damsel, with a Challenge Certificate at Cardiff in 1948 and wins for the "Grove" and "Tolworth" Cups in 1947, was the start of what is a long relationship with Welsh Springer Spaniels for the Morgan name. Winner of seven Challenge Certificates, six in one year, 1948, and four times Best of Breed at Championship Shows, Dere Damsel was sired by Dere Nol out of Cymro Girl. The first full Champion after the war, Champion Branksome Beauty, was bred and owned by Mrs. M.I. Morgan. This bitch sired by Show Champion Dewi Sant, won her first Best Bitch at Birmingham in 1949 under Judge David MacDonald and went on that year to take five Challenge Certificates and the "Tolworth" Cup at the Kensington Show. Within a few years Mr. and Mrs. T.H. Morgan gained championship status for Brancourt Bushranger. This latter dog was sired by Bang out of Champion Branksome Beauty and was rated to be one of the top dogs of the 1950s. Bushranger, bred by Mrs. M.I. Morgan, was joined in the Show Championship ranks five years later by a sister from a second breeding of Bang and Beauty, Brancourt Belinda. Both Bushranger and Belinda were picked from the litters by the Morgans and brought along to championship status, a feat of selection not yet matched by any other breeder of Welsh Springer Spaniels in Britain or America.

On the 1947 list of winners, the name H.C. Payne appears as the owner of Gwenllian of Tregwillym, having won first in the Club Special at the Bedwellty Open. The names Payne and Tregwillym are highly recurrent in postwar Welsh Springer breeding with three Champions and five Show Champions carrying the names. Aside from his substantial record as a champion maker, Mr. Payne is most remembered for the odd comment attributed to him in a book by C. Bede Maxwell, "Cut off a Welshie's head and all you've got left is just another Spaniel." Clearly there is more to a Welsh than what this statement implies, for most dogs would be the loser, yet easily distinguishable, with heads removed, horrible thought though it is. As for the head of dogs bred in the Tregwillym line, there is a tendency toward length and a difference in the "stop" not found in the older specimens and most other modern field and show champions. The distinguishing features of a Tregwillym head are seen best in Champion Statesman of Tregwillym who gained seven Challenge Certificates and was though by Mr. Payne to have been the best dog he ever owned. The highest C.C. winners from the Tregwillym Kennel were Show Champions Top Score, sixteen C.Cs, and Golden Tint, eighteen C.C.s, the latter bred by Mr. H. Pocock out of Show Champion Lady of Llangarna. Tregwillym stud dogs have also sired fourteen champions owned by Mr. Payne and others, while champion get from Tregwillym bitches number ten, a record in the breed that will not doubt stand for many years. One champion, Trigger of Tregwillym, is international, having gained his American Championship after being exported to Mr. D. Lawrence Carswell in 1958. Most recently, the Tregwillym name was honored by Golden Gem, who gained her championship in 1973.

In 1947 the activities of the club increased greatly with the lifting of the basic petrol ration, which permitted larger attendance at shows and the holding of field trials. Under the presidency of Capt. A. Talbot Fletcher and Chairman Lt-Col. J. Downes-Powell, two championship shows were held in Cardiff. One was in March and the other in October with additional Challenge Certificates granted for the breed at Blackpool and the L.K.A. Show at Olympia. At these shows Newman dogs took three of the C.C.s, while Miss D.H. Ellis gained the fourth. The bitch of T.H. Morgan won two C.C.s, while H.J.H. Leopard and A.J. Dykes each had a winner. A one-day field trial in November 1947 was held at Garth in Breconshire, which was the home of the event for the next three years. The best Field Welsh there were Rushbrooke Runner, Cyclo, Rushbrooke Racer, Spint O'Vara, and Shiela of Tregwillym.

Drawn to the Welsh Springers after interest in other sporting dogs, Dr. Esther Rickards, O.B.E., fielded Peridot of Tarbay in the early 1950s and gained two Challenge Certificates before she exported the bitch to France. Dr. Rickards with her Broomleaf and Tarbay dogs has set a steady pace in breeding, showing, and judging and as a leader of the Welsh Springer Spaniel Club, which she joined in 1953. Dr. Rickards is known widely for her fine work in guiding the Windsor Championship Show from its earliest beginnings and for her service as Secretary and Vice-President of the Society. She became a judge of Welsh Springers in 1958 and handled the breed for her first time out at Cruft's. Her efforts to advance the club started in earnest when she took on the job of chairman in 1966, following Mr. H.J.H. Leopard. This was jsut after the division of the club into branches with dominant interests for field work being handled by the Welsh and English Counties Spaniel Club. As indicated by the graph of Welsh Springer Spaniel Registrations, 1966 was a turning point in breed popularity in Britain with the number of litters raised increasing steadily ever since, tripling in 1974 to 462 registrations. Dr. Rickard's Chairmanship has paralleled this rise, which surely was caused in large part through her love and enthusiasm for dogs and Welsh in particular. Her first Show Champion was Mikado of Broomleaf, sired by Mrs. D. Morriss, Show

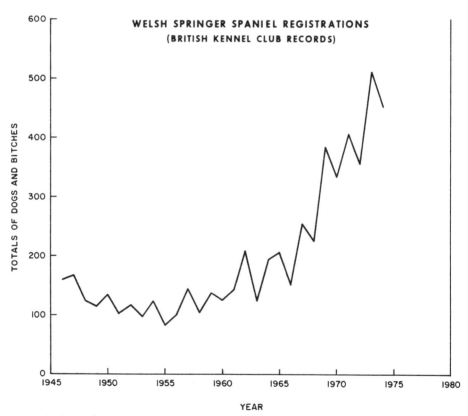

A chart of Welsh Springer Spaniel Registrations in Great Britain since 1945.

Champion Stokecourt Jonathan and breed by Mrs. K. Doxford. In all, Dr. Rickards has brought along four Welsh to championships—two dogs and two bitches—the last being Jenny of Tarbay, which she raised from her breeding of Show Champions Mikado of Broomleaf and Stokecourt Judith. These dogs and bitches dominated the show rings at champion and open shows during the 1950s and continued into the 1960s and 1970s as breed stock for fine Tarbay Kennel dogs.

In 1955 Miss A. West entered the top ranks of Welsh showwomen when her bitch Belinda of Linkton gained a championship. A year later this bitch was bred to Champion Brancourt Bang who sired the first West champion with the famous Linkhill suffix, Show Champion Arabella of Linkhill. Arabella, winner of six Challenge Certificates, was dam to two other Linkhill Show Champions, Deri Darrell and Liza, who between them gained thirty-one Challenge Certificates. Of these two, sired by Champion Statesman of Tregwillym from different litters, Deri Darrell is the more famous Welsh Springer Spaniel with twenty-one Best of Breeds and the holder of the supreme rating, winning Best In Show W.E.L.K.S. Champion Show in 1964, out of 5,900 dogs. Deri Darrell is known throughout the world of dogdom by his gracing the pages with a magnificent colored picture that appeared in one of the encyclopedia of dogs. He was truly a star in the Linkhill Kennel of Miss A. West and in the long history of the Welsh Springer Spaniel.

The third Welsh Springer Spaniel Champion crowned after World War II was Denethrop Danny, owned and bred by Mr. F.A.M. Hart. Additionally, the "Denethrop" Kennels have owned two champions, Dihewyd and Dido, who starred in the show ring. A memorable event involving Danny occurred in 1953 at the Three Counties Show when there were three full champions in the Open Dog lineup. The class was won by Champion Rockhill Rhiderin, bred by Mrs. M. Mayall, with Champion Snowdonian Lad, bred by Miss D.H. Ellis, second, and in third place, Champion Denethrop Danny. One hopes that such a championship grouping will reoccur soon to reaffirm that Welsh Springers for show or field are indistinguishable from one another. The more famous of the Denethrop dogs was Champion Dihewyd who won five Challenge Certificates and thirteen Reserve C.C.s and one Best Dog in the Spaniel Club Show.

Taking over the Morgan champions in the early 1960s, Mr. T.H. Arthur bred and owned three show champions under the "Of Hearts." suffix, two from Show Champion Brancourt Belinda, sired by Champion Statesman of Tregwillym from the same breeding. This pair, Fashion Plate and Diplomat, did well in the ring. Fashion Plate was awarded five Best of Breeds and seven Challenge Certificates and topped her show career with a final C.C. at Glasgow in 1965. Diplomat took four straight Challenge Certificates in 1965, two in 1966 and his last in 1967 at the Manchester Show. Between his duties as judge of groups at international shows, Mr. Arthur was able to finish Dewi of Hearts in 1970 at the Scottish Kennel Club Show under Judge J.H.J. Bradden to make a threesome for his effort in advancing the Welsh.

During this same period, Show Champion Mountararat of Broomleaf was winning Challenge Certificates and opens for Mr. C.J. Kitchener. Mountararat, with a superb temperament, always enjoyed being shown. He gained four C.C.s and twelve Best of Breeds, the last C.C. in 1966 at the Bath Show under Judge C. Brown. Sired by Show Champion Deri Darrell of Linkhill out of Iolanthe of Brooleaf, Mountararat was still roaming with vigor at the Devon countryside with two of his sons when last heard about in correspondence with Mr. Kitchener.

Now and then there occurs within the ranks of any breed, a dog or bitch that has a career somewhat different from the usual; so it was with Lady of Llangarna who entered the show ring at the mature age of four years after being trained in gun work. Lady, sired by Champion Statesman out of Tete-a-Tete of Tregwillym, was purchased by Mr. Howard Pocock as a puppy to build up his group of hunting Welsh that he owned and worked in support of his employment as gameskeeper on various estates in South Wales. The author learned from Mr. Pocock that one of his constant interests during a major portion of this century was the working quality of Welsh Springer Spaniels for the field. In 1924 he started in training with the Llanharran Strain of Welsh Springers with his father who obtained the dogs from Mr. Blandy Jenkins. Around 1930, he started his own kennel with stock from Random Shot of Llangarna and Megan owned by Mr. Sid Lewis, and Sky High Ruberta that Mr. Pocock purchased from Mr. Jenkins, also from the Llanharran Strain. His line of Welsh, though usually not registered, were expert hunters and always in demand on shooting days. Cumder Maid was followed by Lady of Llangarna as brood bitches for the Pocock Kennel but here lies the difference. Encouraged by friends and associates, Mr. Pocock entered the show ring in 1964 with the field trained Lady of Llangarna and in eighteen months against top competition took her to a championship — this after being a matron as well. Earlier, she was mated to Sportsman of Tregwillym and produced, as part of an exceptional litter, the all-time-high Challenge Certificate winning bitch, Show Champion Goldent Tint of Tregwillym. As Mr. Pocock said when asked to comment on his old bitch, "Lady," "I should have started to show her 3-½ years sooner than I did. She was difficult to fault!" Of course the lesson is that a top dog shows quality early or late and the Welsh, as a breed, is slow to fade. In fact, it is often observed that a Welsh is in its prime only after three years of age, both for show and gun work.

At the same time that Lady of Llangarna was winning in the show ring in 1966, a dog and bitch owned by Mr. D. Dobson, were also in contention for top honors. In fact, at Manchester they took the day, with the Dog Challenge Certificate going to Talysarn Colon Dewr and the Bitch Challenge Certificate won by Talysarn Golden Guinea, both Dobson trained. Colon Dewr went on to gain full championship to join the ranks of the select group of eighteen Welsh Springer Spaniels who have attained championship status in the show ring and at field trial. Golden Guinea also worked in the field but left her lasting mark in the show ring as she gained her first Challenge Certificate at her very first show at 9-½ months, and finished at twenty-two months, one of the youngest in the breed to achieve Show Championship status.

A new-to-Welsh Plattburn owner-team entered the show ring during this same period, and as noted in a pen protrait by Judge R.E. Hood, which appeared in the 1970 Welsh Springer Spaniel Club Yearbook, "the Plattburn rise can only be described as meteoric." A bitch named Penny, owned by Mr. and Mrs. J.K. Burgess, gained the first Plattburn Challenge Certificate in 1965 at W.E.L.K.S. From this start the record is exceptional by any standard—seven Show Champions in as many years. The burgess' started with Patmyn Pie Powder, purchased from Miss Collings of Hebden Bridge, and by breeding to Show Champion Denethrop Dihewyd and Champion Rockhill Rhiwderin, raised the first pair of Plattburn Show Champions, Paramount and Penny. A look at a Plattburn dog pedigree shows an exercise in studied breeding matched by only a few other kennels. As an example, Show Champion Plattburn Progressor, with fifteen C.C.s, has litter mates for grandparents and the same bitch appears as three of his great-grandparents. Out of this type of selective breeding came Plattburn Show Champions, Paramount, Penny, Progressor, Pweitt, Pegasus and the last, Pinetree in 1972. The Pen Portrait by Hood permits a telling glimpse of Burgess' thoughts about Welsh Springer Spaniels. Main faults in the breed are thought to be "long cast dogs and poor hind quarters . . ., and bad temperament." The Plattburn Kennel's goal for quality in the Welsh, as noted by Judge Hood, includes "good temperament, flat coat and short strong bodies with plenty of drive from behind." And how are they achieved? Why by "taking care in the selective breeding." The Plattburn people have obviously followed this advice and, in the process, created a line of Welsh Springer Spaniels of distinction.

The one dog in the late 1960s that stands out and demands special comment is Show Champion Bruce of Brent. Bred by Mrs. Hall out of her Bronwyn Trixie and sired by Benefactor of Brent owned by Mrs. D.M. Perkins, "Bruce" set a fine pace in the ring gaining nineteen Challenge Certificates and a Best Exhibit, All Breeds in November 1970 at the Ladies Kennel Association Show. Since then at stud he has sired two Show Champions, Roger of Pencelli and Dalati Helwr. Show Champion Bruce was Outstanding Young Welsh Springer of 1967 and Welsh Springer of the Year in 1968. The Brent Gun Dog Kennel of Mr. and Mrs. D.M. Perkins has produced but one Welsh Champion, but he is one to remember as a modern "great." In answering a letter from Joy Frelinger, an American admirer, Mr. Perkins rated "Bruce" as the only Welsh Springer Spaniel that he had seen in forty-five years of exhibiting dogs, which fit the "standard" to a "T." When asked about faults, he was firm in his belief that Bruce had none, where as in other dogs, he shunned "big, open feet . . . ski-slope from skull to nose . . . agressive or extremely shy dogs . . . and long bodied ones." Judging to these standards and others was demonstrated recently by Mr. Perkins as the feature in a recent program from the British Broadcasting Company (Wales) when he was filmed at Welsh Springer Spaniel judging at the Cardiff Show in 1973 — a performance that many rate as fine as a showing of "Bruce."

Entering the Welsh scene with a touch of humor that still holds after eight years with the breed, a record itself, the Mullins family has brought along two from their kennel to Show Championships — Athelwood Diaperoxide and Lily the Pink. Raising work and show Welsh, their best of the former group so far has been Athelwood Clifthesnif, the only Welsh Springer to win the F. Warner Hill Cup for best performance of day at the Show Spaniels Field Day (1969), and Lily the Pink who, although bred for working, has seven Challenge Certificates and Best Bitch awards (three times) at the Welsh Springer Spaniel Club Championship Shows.

The "Krackton" prefix of G.W.R. Couzens, Esq. JP, has been associated with terriers and gundogs since 1920. The latest to make Champion was Krackton Surprise Packet. Mr. Couzens, as Member of the Kennel Club serving on the Shows Regulation, Judges and Administrative Committees, and the General Committee, brings to Welsh Springer Spaniel activities, a wealth of experience in the handling, breeding, and judging, along with a style that is the model of many new to the breed. Some of Mr. Couzens views about raising dogs were aired recently in the W.S.S.C. 1971-72 Yearbook and deserve attention by all serious breeders. He stressed that dog temperament as seen in the show ring and in the community has its origins at the earliest of age. Mr. Couzens stated,

When puppies are sold at seven weeks to good private homes and are well reared in family surroundings they will have ideal temperaments . . . this is the best way to ensure a self confident, happy dog. It is a pity that more of our Breeders cannot bring their puppies up in a family atmosphere — the best thing for young puppies is the company of young children and going out and about from a very early age.

Advice such as this, along with the notion that dogs should be expected to fill the work role that was assigned to them through the long relationship with man, is timeless and "sound." For the Welsh Springer Spaniel puppy play with children should mimic the act expected of a gundog in the field. As in the old Welsh nursery rhyme, "catch, catch, fetch, fetch," should be first lessons. Mr. Couzens followed such advice, shown by his record with the Krackton working and show Welsh, Champion Surprise Packet and Ginger Bread, Gold Idol, Bright Future, and lastly, Rare Sequin, now a brood bitch in the United States at the Deckard Kennel.

Another Welsh Springer Spaniel fancier who holds to the working side with spectacular results is Mr. G.H. Pattinson with his Tidemarsh prefix. Taking his own advice about the choice of puppy, "choose stock from a working strain where at least the dam works," and adding the skill of an expert trainer, Mr. Pattinson has gained Championship status in 1969 and 1971 for his Tidemarsh Rip and Tidemarsh Tidemark. Some of the Pattinson methods of training field Welsh are dealt with in the last chapter, entitled "Your Pet for Show and Hunting." With many wins in field and show events, the top Tidemarsh honors were gained by Rip in 1971 as Best in Show at the W.S.S. Club Show and by Tidemark as Best in Show at the 1972 Club show, both winning also the Leacroft Trophy for "Best Qualified Worker in the Field."

Mr. Pattinson presented the following clear pictures of his dogs in a recent letter to the author:

Rip is a short coupled dog with good spring of rib and well boned. He has a very smooth, straight and silky coat, and intelligent head with a dark kind eye. A strong and active mover, he possesses great presence. Rip has a level temperament and it is often said of him that "he fills the eye." Of Tidemark he wrote, His is a classic head with nice eye and expression, a correct stop and a perfect mouth. He has a clean neck and very good front, a well bodied dog of a glorious deep color. He has a nice tail action and is a gay and sound mover.

One of the latest Welsh honored with champion status is Dalati Del, owned by Mr. and Mrs. N. Hunton Morgans, and sired by Show Champion Athelwood Diaperoxide. Other Dalati Show Champions are Anwylyd, Swynwyr and, most recently, Delwen, while Helwr, owned by L.L. Ross is of their breeding. Champion Dalati Del was the Top Challenge Certificate Winning Welsh Springer in 1972 and "Dog World" Welsh Springer of the Year in 1973. At the Spaniel Field Day in 1973 she qualified and was Best Novice Bitch in the Show. During her show career she gained fifteen Challenge Certificates. The Hunton Morgans have also led in exporting future champions to the continent where, in Holland, Dalati Dodi, Catrin, Pedi, and Illyricum Ganymede are champions and where, in Belgium, Dalti Pedrys gained the required wins.

The newest bitch to gain Show Champion status is Hillpark Pollyanna, owned by Mr. and Mrs. J.S. Walton, the latter also serving as Honorary Secretary of the Welsh Springer Spaniel Club. It was a pleasure to learn of Mrs. Walton's success with "Polly" as it proves that involvement in the show ring, breeding Welsh of quality, and handling the myriad of tasks that fall to an officer of a breed club are not incompatible and, in fact, can be expertly handled by talented and dedicated people. Anne Walton's help and patience in correspondence with many breed fanciers is truly appreciated and includes the gratitude of this author. The relatively new Hillpark Kennel of Mr. and Mrs. Walton, has, in addition to Show Champion Pollyanna, young stock destined for high honors. In fact one dog, Hillpark Mr. Polly, was Best of Breed at Cruft's in 1975 and was held in the last eight of the gun-dog groups. This youngster has gained additional Challenge Certificates and is now the second Hillpark Welsh show champion.

In recent years, a number of new breeders have entered the ranks of Welsh Springer enthusiasts and are showing and training successfully. Entering the Show Spaniel Field Day in November 1974 was Echo and Skylark of the Hackwood Kennels, owned by Mr. and Mrs. E. Falconer. Past their third generation in developing a dual-purpose, work and show Welsh Springer line, their bitch Echo won the Best Novice Performance of the day, beating twenty-seven dogs, while Skylark came through with a Qualifying Certificate. Colored prints of the Hackwood dogs in the act of field work were provided to the author by the Falconers and are striking proof of the working ability of a well-trained Welsh Springer Spaniel. The recent success in the field and show ring of the Hackwood Kennel name gives promise to a bright future. Others breeding for gun-dog temperament are Mrs. G. Burhouse with her Cholesbury prefix, Mr. and Mrs. B. Kidd, with their Lorcello Welshies, and B.O.B.s already attained by their Titus, Mr. and Mrs. J.M. Philips with Topmast Welsh trained for work and show, and Mrs. Shirley Skelton with the Bridgethorp Kennel.

Mr. A.R. Payne has gained show and field awards with his Leacroft dogs Prince, Duke, and Earl. The Pinymere name of Mrs. N. Peake is being carried forward most recently with Riplass, while at the Ricoris Kennel of Mr. A. Lewis, Red Satin is the working dog that has amassed the best field record. Mark Hamer's Sulicker Red Target has gained his first Challenge Certificate. The Trealvi Kennel of Mr. and Mrs. G.A. Buchanan is being advanced by Freddie Solo with two C.C.s and two Reserve C.C.s. Other dual purpose Welsh are trained by Mr. and Mrs. R. Jacobs of the Greyclouds Kennel as are the Amberheath Working Welsh of Mr. D. Baker.

For a look at what is ahead in the ranks of Champion Welsh Springer Spaniels, the results of the Class Winners at the Club Champion Show in 1974 and 1975 can be helpful. Here, as winners, are many of the future champions—dogs and bitches that gained their positions against the strongest competition offered in the breed. A total of one hundred dogs were shown filling two hundred and twelve entries in the 1973 show, while ninety-one dogs and two hundred and eleven entries filled the 1974 show. In the 1973 show, Progress of Pencelli gained his title and went on to take the trophy for Best in Show. He repeated Best Open Dog in 1974 to gain another of his fourteen Challenge Certificates and was awarded Best of Opposite Sex, finishing next to Payne's Sh. Ch. Tregwillym Golden Gem who took Open Bitch and Best in Show. Also in 1974, Ch. Tidemarsh Rip took Best Veteran, while Walton's Hillpark Sea Esther was awarded Best Puppy.

New to the breed is Mrs. B. Ordish with her Goldsprings prefix — dogs, Truffles and Gunflint, and bitches, Bright Amber and Guillemot. Although only a small kennel, the results of her breeding have attracted considerable attention as indicated by the number of Goldsprings winners at the 1975 Welsh Springer Spaniel Club Show at Stoneleigh, Warwickshire — Bright Spark, Truffles, Bright Embers, and Guillemot. In the final judging at the 1975 Show by F. Warner Hill, Goldsprings Guillemot gained Best Bitch in Show and her first Challenge Certificate, topping the Open Bitch Winner of Mr. and Mrs. N. Hunton Morgans, Show Champion Dalati Rhian. Also, against a very strong field of ninety-nine entries, she was awarded Best in Show over Mr. and Mrs. J.S. Walton's Hillpark Mr. Polly, who gained his third Challenge Certificate, and Show Champion status as Best Dog. Best Veteran Dog or Bitch went to Sh. Ch. Bruce of Brent, owned by Mrs. D. M. Perkins, while Best Puppy award was given to the Hunton Morgan's Dalati Math.

Class Winners At The Welsh Springer Spaniel Club Show In 1974

Judge:	Mr. J.K. Burgess
Sp. Puppy Dog:	Ordish's Goldsprings Truffles (Sh. Ch. Progress of Pencelli — Hillpark Trampoline)
Puppy Dog:	Purvis' Caronby Capability (Sh. Ch. Plattburn Perchance — Plattburn Prupride)
Junior Dog:	Hughes' Dalati Cador Dalati Dymn Fi — Sh. Ch. Dalati Anwylyd)
Maiden Dog:	Blinkhorn's Orielton Pendragon

	(Sh. Ch. Roger of Pencelli — Orielton Cateracker)
Novice Dog:	Hughe's Dalati Cador
	(Dalati Dymn Fi — Sh. Ch. Dalati Anwylyd)
Graduate Dog:	Allam's Goldsprings Firecracker of Empshott (N.A.F.)
	(Russet Ringtail of Pinemere — Goldsprings Dovet)
Post Graduate Dog:	Walton's Hillpark Mr. Polly
	(Plattburn Proclamation — Polly Garter of Doonebridge)
Limit Dog:	Walton's Hillpark Mr. Polly
	(Plattburn Proclamation — Polly Garter of Doonebridge)
Open Dog:	Newman's Sh. Ch. Progress of Pencelli
	(Sh. Ch. Plattburn Progressor — Sh. Ch. Marie of Pencelli)
Sp. Beginners Dog:	Williams' Cwmdows Cowboy
	(Progress of Pencelli — Pennar Mudlark)
Sp. Puppy Bitch:	Hughes' Dalati Ceiran
	(Dalati Dymn Fi — Sh. Ch. Dalati Anwylyd)
Puppy Bitch:	Walton's Hillpark Sea Esther
	(Sh. Ch. Plattburn Progressor — Sh. Ch. Hillpark Pollyanna)
Junior Bitch:	Hunton Morgans' Dalti Rhian
	(Dalati Dymn Fi — Sh. Ch. Dalati Anwylyd)
Maiden Bitch:	Peake's Pinymere Jasmin
	(Bracken of Pinymere — Pinymere Enchantress)
Novice Bitch:	Peake's Pinymere Jasmin
	(Bracken of Pinymere — Pinymere Enchantress)
Graduate Bitch:	Rickards' Tarbay Romola
	(Sh. Ch. Plattburn Perchance — Myfanwy of Tarbay)
Post-Graduate Bitch:	Decaux's Dalati Nanno
	(Sh. Ch. Bruce of Brent — Sh. Ch. Dalati Anwylyd)
Limit Bitch:	Hunton Morgan's Dalati Rhian
	(Dalati Dymn Fi — Sh. Ch. Dalati Anwylyd)
Open Bitch:	Payne's Sh. Ch. Tregwillym Golden Gem
	(Golden Shot of Tregwillym — Sh. Ch. Golden Tint of Tregwillym)

Class Winners at the Welsh Springer Spaniel Club Show — 1975

Judge:	F. Warner Hill
Minor Sp. Puppy Dog:	Hunton Morgan's Dalati Math (Dalati Syma Fi — Sh. Ch. Dalati Anwylyd)
Puppy Dog:	Hughes' Daiawn Siamsiwn (Dalati Cador — Orielton Yasmin)
Junior Dog:	Stratten's Goldsprings Bright Spark (Sh. Ch. Progress of Pencelli — Goldsprings Guillemot)
Maiden Dog:	Hughes' Daiawn Siamsiwn (Dalati Cador — Orielton Yasmin)
Novice Dog:	Young's Sandy of Wainfelin (Jason of Tregwillym — Roselle of Tregwillym)
Graduate Dog:	Payne's Duke of Leacroft (Prince of Leacroft — Rosaut Rhoda)
Post Graduate Dog:	Ordish's Goldsprings Truffles (Sh. Ch. Progress of Pencelli — Hillpark Trampoline)
Limit Dog:	Payne's Tregwillym Golden Gift (Golden Shot of Tregwillym — Cherryl of Tregwillym)
Open Dog:	Walton's Sh. Ch. Hillpark Mr. Polly (Plattburn Proclamation — Polly Garter of Doonebridge)
Minor Puppy Bitch:	Lewis/Morgan's Hillpark Sequin Taf (Sh. Ch. Progressor of Pencelli — Sh. Ch. Hillpark Pollyanna)
Puppy Bitch:	Payne's Contessa of Tregwillym (Dewi of Tregwillym — Maid of Tregwillym)
Junior Bitch:	Ormesher's Goldsprings Bright Embers (Sh. Ch. Progress of Pencelli — Goldsprings Guillemot)
Maiden Bitch:	Ormesher's Goldsprings Bright Embers (Sh. Ch. Progress of Pencelli — Goldsprings Guillemot)
Novice Bitch:	Payne's Contessa of Tregwillym (Dewi of Tregwillym — Maid of Henllys)
Graduate Bitch:	Mousley's Hackwood Skylark (Happy Lad of Hackwood — Hackwood Susan)

Post Graduate Bitch: Davies' Dalati Didra
                        (Rambler of Tregwillym — Dalati Sidan)
Limit Bitch: Ordish's Goldsprings Guillemot
                        (Sh. Ch. Roger of Pencelli — Hillpark
                        Trampoline)
Open Bitch: Hunton Morgan's Sh. Ch. Dalati Rhian
                        (Dalati Dymn Fi — Sh. Ch. Dalati Anwylyd)

With the growth of the breed in Britain during the last ten years, there
has occurred an increase in export of fine specimens to the continent
and the start of showing and breeding in a number of new centers of
enthusiasm for Welsh Springers. In Holland, at the June 1974
Champion Clubmatch, over thirty Welsh were entered with good dogs
such as Plattburn Proclaim owned by Mr. J. van Wijngaarden and the
dogs of Mrs. Cox Ohmstede-Evers. In France, nearly twenty Welsh
Springer Spaniels were registered in 1973 with the French Kennel Club,
while dogs such as Hillpark Polly Flinders and Plattburn Picasso were
winning prizes. The contingent of Welsh in Sweden is surprisingly large
with 150 registered in 1973, and twenty entered at the Stockholm
Show. Dogs that have gained recognition are Richard of Brent, Bryn of
Tarbay, Artmaster and Amanda of Tregwillym, Plattburn Pendews, and
Dalati Cai.

The future of the breed in Great Britain and neighboring countries
can be assured with progress in strong breeding, training, and showing
programs. With experienced leadership from Chairman Dr. Esther
Rickards, Vice-Chairman H.C. Payne, Esq., President H. Newman, and
Honorary Secretary and Treasurer Mrs. A. M. Walton, a recently formed
Working Subcommittee with Secretary G.G.H. Davies Esq. and many
other members who have a love for the breed, working to support the
interest of the club, the true British Spaniel — the Welsh Springer — will
continue, unabated, to give pleasure to its many owners as the flashy
showdog, tireless hunter, or devoted family pet, which it has been
throughout the years of recorded history.

Corrin, at ten years of age, belonged to Mr. A.T. Williams of Baglan Vale of Neath, Wales. Rated best spaniel at Cruft's in 1902, he sired the great Ch. Rover of Gerwn, from whom through Roverson can be traced many of the past English Springer Spaniel field trial winners. (W.S.S.C. 1936 Yearbook)

Longmynd Calon Fach, pre-World War One era champion, bred by Mrs. R.D. Greene and one of the best from her Grove Kennel. Also shown as the subject in the 1906 Maud Earl painting. (W.S.S.C. 1934 Yearbook)

Painting by Maud Earl in 1906 considered to be the best portrayal ever painted of Welsh Springer Spaniels. The two springers, Ch. Longmynd Calon Fach, 1823L, and Ch. Longmynd Megan, 1140K, belonged to Mrs. Greene. (Kennel Club)

Welsh Spaniels, Corrin of Gerwn and Mena of Gerwn, as painted by Maud Earl in 1902. These classic head studies are of two of the earliest champions and foundation dogs that were owned by the modern father of the breed, Mr. A.T. Williams. (Berlin Photographic)

At the 1935 Richmond Champion Show, second from right, Mr. Jack Philips with Show Champion Dere Mhlaen; fifth from right, Reverend D. Stewart, a well known breeder with the O'Silian suffix; sixth, Judge Major Harry Gunn. (Moore)

Two great foundation dogs of the breed, Champions Dewi Sant and Philosopher of Downland with "Wendy" during a moment of relaxation between shows. (Newman)

Miss D.H. Ellis, St. Mary's, Bramber, England, with the author. Miss Ellis is well known in the dog world for her flying trip to America with five young Welsh Springer Spaniels to restart interest in the breed after the War. (Pferd)

Champion Dewi Sant won his Challenge Certificates at the first three postwar championship shows and was the first dog in Wales of all breeds to achieve this distinction. After winning B.O.B.s at a few open shows, he was retired for stud service by his owner-handler, Mr. H. Newman. (Newman)

Doctor Esther Rickards, O.B.E., owner and breeder of many famous dogs, in Cockers, Irish Water and Welsh Springer Spaniels, has been Chairman of the Welsh Springer Spaniel Club since 1966. Shown here with her Tarbay Romolo Taf, Dr. Rickards has a love of gundogs and brilliant organizational talents that have been an inspiration to all who have known her. (Pferd)

Winners at the Three Counties Malvern Show in 1965, judged by Dr. E. Rickards. On the right is Best of Breed Medalist, Mr. H. Pocock's Lady of Llangarna, and on the left, Best Novice and Junior Medalist, Mr. H.C. Payne's Golden Tint of Tregwillym. (Pocock)

Under Judge M.C.W. Gilliat at Bath in 1964, the Best of Breed Medal was awarded to Miss A. West's Sh. Ch. Deri Darrell of Linkhill, and Best of Opposite Sex went to Mr. T. Hubert Arthur's Fashion Plate of Hearts. (Cooke)

Harold Newman of the Pencelli Kennel, dean of Welsh Springer Spaniel breeders and President of the British Club, shown along the Rhondda River, Mid Glamorgan, Wales, with Prospect and Show Champions Roger and Progress. (Pferd)

Setting up some of the best at the Windsor Show in 1974. Left to right: Open Dog Best of Breed Sh. Ch. Roger of Pencelli, handled by owner Mr. H. Newman; Sh. Ch. Progress of Pencelli, handled by Mr. G. Morgan; and Dalati Dynafi, handled by owner Mr. Hunton Morgans. (Newman)

Mr. F. Warner Hill, internationally known Judge, and Dr. Esther Rickards, the Welsh Springer Spaniel Club Chairman, during a moment of relaxation at the 1975 Club Show luncheon at Stoneleigh, England. (Pferd)

Mrs. Anne Walton, Hon. Secretary, Welsh Springer Spaniel Club of Great Britain, and her Sh. Ch. Hillpark Pollyanna. (Walton)

Goldsprings Guillemot, Challenge Certificate Winning Bitch and Best in Show at the 1975 Club Show handled by her owner, Mrs. B. Ordish. (Pferd)

6
BRITISH CHAMPIONS

Since Dewi Sant gained his third Challenge Certificate in 1947, seventy-nine other Welsh Springer Spaniels have gained top status in British dogdom—eighteen full Champions and sixty-one Show Champions. Of the total, thirty-eight are bitches, nine of these both Show and Field Champions—a fine showing of natural qualities in the field and show ring. In judging champions, more is needed than numbers or words as given in the Standard. As many an experienced breeder or judge has said, "To know a champion, you must handle, touch, and feel dogs—lots of dogs, preferably good dogs but in any case, dogs in great number!;" or, "When you can literally 'see' the body and skeleton of a dog when judging from a distance—why you can then make some reasonable judgments;" or, "Know the 'Standard' by heart, look at lots of dogs, handle good dogs and discuss the finer points with knowledgeable people—these are the steps to good judgments about your favorite breed."

Champions are dogs of quality in the breed that have an amalagamation of virtues of "type," "soundness," and "style." The first of these—"type"—relates to the Standards of the breed and the dog that most closely conforms in temperment and appearance. The most typical is not exaggerated, but rather is in perfect balance. Facts about type can be gained by study of pictures of breed champions while the second virtue, "soundness," can be judged only by observing the dog in motion. A "sound" dog has all physical parts in proper place functioning as nature intended with proper movement; included are the senses, reproductive capability, intelligence, and manner. In a phrase, the entire construction of the dog must be "sound". "Style" is a crucial virtue for top awards in the field or show ring. It is a condition born to the dog, as a manner of conduct or action. In the ring, a dog with "style" brings the "oohs" and "ahs" from the spectators.

Some dog fanciers believe that in great dogs "soundness" and "style" can show even in a picture. Can the virtues of "type," "soundness," and "style" be seen in the British Champions? Favorite photographs from the collections of many Welsh Springer Spaniel owners presented in the following register provides an opportunity to "judge the champions" at your own show.

Ch. Musketeer O'Matherne. (Kitchner)

CH. MUSKETEER O'MATHERNE

Dog   KC NO. 1878 PP   Whelped: 7/23/32

Owner: Lt. Col. J. Downes-Powell

Breeder: Capt. J. Gage-Williams

Ch. Barglam Bang

Ch. Merglam Bang

Shane Taff

Ch. Marksman O'Matherne

Cynon Taff

Goitre Lass

Rose

CH. MUSKETEER O'MATHERNE

Druid O'Garrett

Rockhill Rhon

Nell of Coopers

Merrymaid O'Matherne

Ch. Barglam Bang

Rockhill Rhoda

Adcombe Flush

Ch. Musketeer O'Matherne had seven wins in field trial competition during 1933 to 1935. He was judged by Colonel J.H.R. Downes-Powell, past present of the Welsh Springer Spaniel Club of Great Britain, to excell in type, movement, color and symmetry. Musketeer was the first winner of the "Grove" Challenge Cup in 1935 as the Best Dog at W.E.L.K.S.

Sh. Ch. Dere Mhlaen (Newman)

SH. CH. DERE MHLAEN

Dog   KC NO. 1342QQ   Whelped: 9/24/32

Owner: H. Newman, Treorchy, Mid Glamorgan

Breeder: H. Newman, Treorchy, Mid Glamorgan

                        Ch. Barglam Bang

               Ch. Merglam Bang

                        Shane Taff

        Ch. Marksman O'Matherne

                        Cynon Taff

               Goitre Lass

                        Rose (unreg'd)

SH. CH. DERE MHLAEN

                        Ch. Barglam Bang

               Jerry-y-Maer

                        Shane Taff

        Newman's Barmaid

                        Brynog Bang

               Chep Flo (unreg'd)

                        Seren Wyrnos

Sh. Ch. Dere Mhlaen was Mr. Harold Newman's first show champion, which he bred in 1932 from his bitch Barmaid. Mr. Newman is considered by many to be the dean of the breed and a leading exporter of Welsh. Dere Mhlaen and his dam were well-known winners during this period. Both were put up for C.C.s by Col. J.H.R. Downes Powell at Abergavenny in 1934.

Sh. Ch. Dewi Sant (Fall)

SH. CH. DEWI SANT
Dog   KC NO. 747AD   Whelped: 7/12/43
Owner: H. Newman, Treorchy, Mid Glamorgan
Breeder: Miss M.C. Evans

```
                              Ch. Marksman O'Matherne
               Sh. Ch. Dere Mhlaen
                              Newman's Barmiad
        Dere Di
                              Cere M'Laen
               Feltonette
                              Taffeta
SH. CH. DEWI SANT
                              Lord Bang
               Random Shot of Llangarna
                              Megan (unreg'd)
        Tesco Thornycroft
                              Sh. Ch. Dere Mhlaen
               Deuch Mhlaen
                              Shaun of Lynwood
```

Sh. Ch. Dewi Sant was undefeated in gaining his championship in three successive shows. Rated as one of the great Welsh, he was the leading stud dog after the war, siring six Champions, including Jester of Downland and Stokecourt Jonathan. A perfectly balanced dog, he scored in coat, color, and personality and has been a model to follow.

Sh. Ch. Jester of Downland (Fall)

SH. CH. JESTER of DOWNLAND

Dog   KC NO. 21AE   Whelped: 6/12/45

Owner: Miss D. Ellis, Bamber, Sussex

Breeder: Miss D. Ellis, Bamber, Sussex

                           Ch. Dere Mhlaen

               Dere Di

                           Feltonette

        Sh. Ch. Dewi Sant

                           Random Shot of Llangarna

               Tesco Thornycroft

                           Deuch M'hlain

SH. CH. JESTER of DOWNLAND

                           Cymro Gwyn

               Pencoed Lad

                           Clydach Mona

        Merry Madcap of Downland

                           High Game

               Tess of Tynywaun

                           Deuch Mhlaen

Sh. Ch. Jester of Downland, son of Dewi Sant, was one of the most consistent winners in the breed, gaining C.C.s in 1946 and 1947. He won Firsts at the Club Ch. Shows in Cardiff during this period and sired the first Welsh to gain a championship in the United States, Ch. Holiday of Happy Hunting.

Sh. Ch. Stokecourt Jonathan (Simms)

SH. CH. STOKECOURT JONATHAN

Dog   KC NO. 191AJ   Whelped: 2/17/48

Owner: Mrs. D. Morriss, High Wycombe, Bucks

Breeder: Mr. G. W. Hooper, Mortimer, Berks

```
                              Ch. Dere Mhlaen
                  Dere Di
                              Feltonette
         Sh. Ch. Dewi Sant
                              Random Shot of Llangarna
                  Tesco Thornycroft
                              Deuch Mhlaen
SH. CH. STOKECOURT JONATHAN
                              Cere M'Laen
                  Dere Nol
                              Barbara of Caegarw
         Camrose Lass
                              Pencoed Lad
                  Cymro Girl
                              Tess of Tynywaun
```

Sh. Ch. Stokecourt Jonathan, the first of the three champions owned or bred by Mrs. Morriss, was sired after the war by Sh. Ch. Dewi Sant. Trained for gun and show, Jonathan gained two B. of B.s at Crufts in 1955 and 1957 and had great movement as a super retriever on land or in water.

Sh. Ch. Stokecourt Gillian (Cooke)

SH. CH. STOKECOURT GILLIAN

Bitch   KC NO. 2303AN   Whelped: 4/20/53

Owner: Mrs. D. Morriss, High Wycombe, Bucks

Breeder: Col. C.R. Smith, West Wickham, Kent

Dere Di

Sh. Ch. Dewi Sant

Tesco Thornycroft

Sh. Ch. Stokecourt Jonathan

Dere Nol

Camrose Lass

Cymro Girl

SH. CH. STOKECOURT GILLIAN

Llywelyn of Llywn

Gwyn of Birchgrove

Llanilar Queen

Gwyneth Allt Bedw

Heddwch

Lady of Lluestnewydd

Pentre Queen

Sh. Ch. Stokecourt Gillian, won eight C.C.s and three B.O.B.s, one at Cruft's in 1958. Both a show and field performer, Gillian went Best Bitch in Show at the Winds Gun Dog Open in 1960 and was always ready for a rough shot through her sixteen years.

Sh. Ch. Mikado of Broomleaf (Simms)

SH. CH. MIKADO OF BROOMLEAF
Dog   KC NO. 118/AN   Whelped: 10/21/54
Owner: Dr. E. Rickards, Windsor, Berks
Breeder: Mrs. K. Doxford, N. Franham, Surrey

                              Dere Di
                    Sh. Ch. Dewi Sant
                              Tesco Thornycroft
          Sh. Ch. Stokecourt Jonathan
                              Dere Nol
                    Camrose Lass
                              Cymro Girl
SH. CH. MIKADO OF BROOMLEAF
                              Flick of Fossenay
                    Rockhill Raft
                              Rockhill Reine
          Broomleaf Dimple of Empshott
                              Sh. Ch. Dewi Sant
                    Treorchy Maid
                              Dewch Nol

Sh. Ch. Mikado of Broomleaf was the first champion owned by Dr.
Esther Richards, O.B.E. In all she has brought along four Show
Champions—two dogs and two bitches—the last being Jenny of Tarbay.
Mikado, the favorite in the Tarbay Kennel for many years, sired two
show champions, Jenny and Gamefeather of Siani.

Sh. Ch. Tarbay Florian of Broomleaf (Simms)

SH. CH. TARBAY FLORIAN OF BROOMLEAF
Dog   KC NO. 1427AS   Whelped: 3/17/58
Owner: Dr. E. Rickards, Windsor, Berks
Breeder: Mrs. K. Doxford, N. Farnham, Surrey

> Ch. Rockhill Rhiwderin
> Flush of Empshott
> Treorchy Maid
> Hilavion of Broomleaf
> Ch. Rockhill Rhiwderin
> Broomleaf Marigold of Empshott
> Broomleaf Dimple of Empshott
> SH. CH. TARBAY FLORIAN OF BROOMLEAF
> Ch. Rockhill Rhwiderin
> Broadwin Baccardi
> Rushbrooke Rum
> Broomleaf Little Buttercup
> Sh. Ch. Stokecourt Jonathan
> Pinafore of Broomleaf
> Broomleaf Dimple of Empshott

Sh. Ch. Tarbay Florian of Broomleaf, was the second of four Show Champions from the Tarbay Kennel of Dr. Esther Rickards. The Doctor, in her eighties, is famous in the dog world as breeder, exhibitor, judge, and organizer. She guided the Windsor Championship Show from its beginning and now serves as Chairman of the Welsh Springer Spaniel Club.

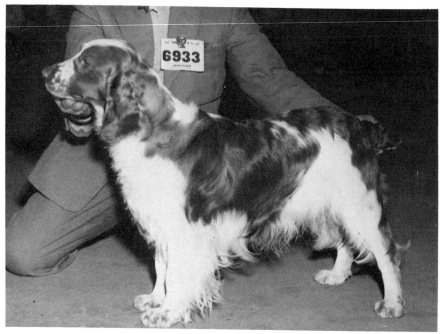

Ch. Statesman of Tregwillym (Cooke)

CH. STATESMAN of TREGWILLYM
Dog   KC NO. 1071AS   Whelped: 9/20/58
Owner: H.C. Payne, Cumbran, Gwent
Breeder: H.C. Payne, Cumbran, Gwent

                 Sh. Ch. Dewi Sant
        Sh. Ch. Taliesin Yr Ail
              Gillian of Tregwillym
    Sh. Ch. Token of Tregwillym
              Sh. Ch. Kim of Kenswick
        Titian of Tregwillym
              Gloria of Tregwillym
CH. STATESMAN of TREGWILLYM
              Ch. Brancourt Bang
        Tehran of Tregwillym
              Sh. Ch. Gwyneth
    Trinket of Tregwillym
              Sh. Ch. Taliesin Yr Ail
        Trudi of Tregwillym
              Titian of Tregwillym

Ch. Statesman of Tregwillym, one of the eight champions owned or bred by H.C. Payne, is the star of the Tregwillym Kennel with seven Challenge Certificates. In addition to his show record, he has sired six champions, qualified in the field and gained the "Grove" Challenge Cup for Best Dog, W.E.L.K.S., 1962.

Sh. Ch. Deri Darrell of Linkhill (Cooke)

SH. CH. DERI DARRELL of LINKHILL

Dog   KC NO. 2453AU   Whelped: 9/3/60

Owner: Miss A. West, Pulborough, Sussex

Breeder: Miss A. West, Pulborough, Sussex

Sh. Ch. Taliesin Yr Ail
Sh. Ch. Token of Tregwillym
Titian of Tregwillym
Sh. Ch. Statesman of Tregwillym
Tehran of Tregwillym
Trinket of Tregwillym
Trudi of Tregwillym
SH. CH. DERI DARRELL of LINKHILL
Lucky Laddie
Ch. Brancourt Bang
Ashfield Aristocrat
Sh. Ch. Arabella of Linkhill
Downland Diplomat
Ch. Belinda of Linkton
Elizabethan July

Sh. Ch. Deri Darrell of Linkhill, recognized as one of the great all time Welsh, was honored with his first C.C. in 1962, B.O.B.s in 1963 and 1964, and Reserve Best Gun dog, B.O.B. in 1965, 1966, and 1967, all at Crufts. His unmatched record also included twenty-four C.C.s, twenty-one times B.O.B. and Supreme B.I.S. W.E.L.K.S. Ch. Sh. 1964 out of 5,900 dogs.

Sh. Ch. Lady of Llangarna (Cooke)

SH. CH. LADY of LLANGARNA
Bitch   KC NO. 1749AY   Whelped: 12/7/61
Owner: H. Pocock, Pontypool, Gwent
Breeder: H.C. Payne, Cumbran, Gwent

```
                              Sh. Ch. Taliesin Yr Ail
                    Sh. Ch. Token of Tregwillym
                         Titian of Tregwillym
         Ch. Statesman of Tregwillym
                         Tehran of Tregwillym
                    Trinket of Tregwillym
                         Trudi of Tregwillym
SH. CH. LADY of LLANGARNA
                         Ch. Brancourt Bang
                    Tehran of Tregwillym
                         Sh. Ch. Gwyneth
         Tete-a-Tete of Tregwillym
                         Mynydd Marksman of Treg.
                    Rockhill Rosewell
                         Rockhill Rona
```

Sh. Ch. Lady of Llangarna was first trained by Mr. Pocock for gun work and entered in the show ring at the age of 4 years. After a strong start at the 3 Counties Show, 1965, where she was awarded the Bronze Medal under Judge Dr. E. Rickards, she gained her championship with firsts at the Cardiff shows of 1965 and 1966.

Ch. Talysarn Calon Dewr (Cooke)

CH. TALYSARN CALON DEWR

Dog   KC NO. 520AW   Whelped: 1/1/62
Owner: Mr. D. Dobson, Retford, Nottingham
Breeder: Miss Carol Potter, Hornsby, London

```
                    Lucky Laddie
               Ch. Brancourt Bang
                    Ashfield Aristocrat
          Tehran of Tregwillym
                    Begger-Me-Boy
               Sh. Ch. Gwyneth
                    Gwenllian Goch
CH. TALYSARN CALON DEWR
                    Sh. Ch. Taliesen Yr Ail
               Sh. Ch. Token of Tregwillym
                    Titian of Tregwillym
          Shot Silk of Tregwillym
                    Tehran of Tregwillym
               Trinket of Tregwillym
                    Trudi of Tregwillym
```

Ch. Talysarn Calon Dewr gained three C.C.s and nine Reserve C.C.s in the show ring and qualified for his Championship at the first All Show Spaniels Field Day in October 1966. "Taff" was a very placid, handsome dog who worked regularly in the field, a star in the Dobson Kennel.

Sh. Ch. Fashion Plate of Hearts (Cooke)

SH. CH. FASHION PLATE of HEARTS

Bitch   KC NO. 104AX   Whelped: 5/7/62

Owner: T.H. Arthur, Gower, West Glamorgan

Breeder: T.H. Arthur, Gower, West Glamorgan

Taliesin Yr Ail

Sh. Ch. Token of Tregwillym

Titian of Tregwillym

Ch. Statesman of Tregwillym

Tehran of Tregwillym

Trinket of Tregwillym

Trudi of Tregwillym

SH. CH. FASHION PLATE of HEARTS

Lucky Laddie

Ch. Brancourt Bang

Ashfield Aristocrat

Sh. Ch. Brancourt Belinda

Ch. Dewi Sant

Ch. Branksome Beauty

Castlecourt Countess

Sh. Ch. Fashion Plate of Hearts, litter mate to Sh. Ch. Diplomat of Hearts, was the last of seven champions which were owned, bred or handled by Judge T. Hubert Arthur. In 1964, Fashion Plate was awarded five B.O.B.s, and seven C.C.s and topped her show career with a final C.C. at Glasgow in 1965.

Sh. Ch. Mountararat of Broomleaf (Wiles)

SH. CH. MOUNTARARAT of BROOMLEAF

Dog   KC NO. 424AX   Whelped: 6/12/62

Owner: C.J. Kitchener, Barnstable, Devon

Breeder: Mrs. K. Doxford, N. Farnham, Surrey

                              Ch. Token of Tregwillym

                   Ch. Statesman of Tregwillym

                            Trinket of Tregwillym

       Sh. Ch. Deri Darrell of Linkhill

                             Ch. Brancourt Bang

                   Sh. Ch. Arabella of Linkhill

                            Ch. Belinda of Linkton

SH. CH. MOUNTARARAT of BROOMLEAF

                            Sh. Ch. Top Score of Tregwillym

                   Mog Madoc of Empshott

                            Blodwyn Gwanwyn

       Iolanthe of Broomleaf

                            Hilarion of Broomleaf

                   Oldhatch Fiery Farthing

                            Copper Coins of Reeth

Sh. Ch. Mountararat of Broomleaf gained his first C.C. at the L.K.A. Show in 1964 and finished at Three Counties in 1965 under Judge Dr. E. Richards. Mountie, during his show career, was awarded twelve Best of Breeds along with the "Newman Cup" in 1967 for Best Dog at the Cardiff Show, Wales.

Sh. Ch. Golden Tint of Tregwillym (Cooke)

SH. CH. GOLDEN TINT of TREGWILLYM

Bitch   KC NO. 2027AY   Whelped: 6/18/64
Owner: Mr. H.C. Payne, Cwmbran, Gwent
Breeder: Mr. H. Pocock, Pontypool, Gwent

                      Sh. Ch. Token of Tregwillym
                Ch. Statesman of Tregwillym
                      Trinket of Tregwillym
        Sportsman of Tregwillym
                      Tehran of Tregwillym
                Ch. Tulita of Tregwillym
                      Gilly of Beamends
SH. CH. GOLDEN TINT of TREGWILLYM
                      Sh. Ch. Token of Tregwillym
                Ch. Statesman of Tregwillym
                      Trinket of Tregwillym
        Sh. Ch. Lady of Llangarna
                      Tehran of Tregwillym
                Tete-A-Tete of Tregwillym
                      Rockhill Rosewell

Sh. Ch. Golden Tint, winner of thirty-three Challenge Certificates and numerous reserve C.C.s and B.O.B.s is rated as one of the top winning bitches in the world. She won the "Grove Challenge Cup" in 1967, the "Stokecourt" Cup in 1968 and 1969 and the Ch. Belinda of Linkton Cup in 1970 and 1971 for Best Bitch at Crufts.

Sh. Ch. Talysarn Golden Guinea (Cooke)

SH. CH. TALYSARN GOLDEN GUINEA

Bitch   KC NO. 1777AZ   Whelped: 5/26/65

Owner: Mr. D. Dobson, Retford, Nottingham

Breeder: Mr. D. Dobson, Retford, Nottingham

                         Hilarion of Broomleaf

              Wiston of Glensham

                         Gillian of Empshott

       Mynyddislwyn Lad

                         Alan Towzer

              Cymru Beauty

                         Twyn Judy

SH. CH. TALYSARN GOLDEN GUINEA

                         Ch. Brancourt Bang

              Tehran of Tregwillym

                         Sh. Ch. Gwyneth

       Talysarn Blodeuyn

                         Sh. Ch. Token of Tregwillym

              Shot Silk of Tregwillym

                         Trinket of Tregwillym

Sh. Ch. Talysarn Golden Guinea is one of the youngest Welsh to become a show champion gaining the award at twenty-two months. She won seven C.C.s during her show career along with a B.O.B. at the Cardiff Show in 1969 under Judge E.W. Painter.

Sh. Ch. Bruce of Brent (Perkins)

SH. CH. BRUCE of BRENT

Dog   KC NO. 2530BA   Whelped: 8/28/66

Owner: Mrs. D. N. Perkins, Rugby, Warwicks

Breeder: Mrs. N. Hall, Coventry, Warwicks

<pre>
                              Sh. Ch. Token of Tregwillym
               Ch. Statesman of Tregwillym
                              Trinket of Tregwillym
         Benefactor of Brent
                              Ch. Brancourt Bang
               Gwyneth Bach of Brent
                              Gwyn Coch Cora
SH. CH. BRUCE of BRENT
                              Ch. Rockhill Rhiwderin
               Denethorp Dorian
                              Denethorp Dannella
         Bronwyn Trixie
                              Ch. Tarbay Florian of Broomleaf
               Sally of Emscote
                              Tinkerborough Belle
</pre>

Sh. Ch. Bruce of Brent, winner of nineteen C.C.s had two group and two reserve group wins during his show career. At Cruft's Show in 1970, he was awarded Open Dog under Judge C.M. Francis and won Best Exhibit, All Breeds at the Ladies Kennel Association Show in November 1970.

Sh. Ch. Marie of Pencelli (Cooke)

SH. CH. MARIE of PENCELLI

Bitch   KC NO. 1713BC   Whelped: 3/14/67

Owner: H. Newman, Treorchy, Mid Glamorgan

Breeder: H. Newman, Treorchy, Mid Glamorgan

```
                              Sh. Ch. Top Score of Tregwillym
                 Sh. Ch. Easter Parade
                              Blodwyn Gwanwyn
          Priory Major
                              All Alone
                 Modern Maid
                              Lucy of Llanwenog
SH. CH. MARIE of PENCELLI
                              Sh. Ch. Top Score of Tregwillym
                 All Alone
                              Blodwyn Gwanwyn
          Bonny Legend
                              Sh. Ch. Token of Tregwillym
                 Lucy of Llanwenog
                              Bonnie Sally
```

Sh. Ch. Marie of Pencelli was handled by Mr. Harold Newman, owner-breeder, to seventeen Reserve C.C.s. She is dam to two champions, Bachgen Dewr in America and Rona of Pencelli in Canada. Maria is one of the nine Show Champions bred or owned by Mr. Newman since 1934.

Ch. Tidemarsh Rip (Cooke)

CH. TIDEMARSH RIP

Dog   KC NO. 2130BC   Whelped: 5/11/67

Owner: G.H. Pattinson, Maidstone, Kent

Breeder: G.H. Pattinson, Maidstone, Kent

```
                              Stokecourt Beau
                    Stokecourt Stephen
                              Stokecourt Fay
            Stokecourt Sam
                              Rushbrook Racer
                    Karushina
                              Anna Karina of Llagaron
CH. TIDEMARSH RIP
                              Stokecourt Simon
                    Shadow of Tarbay
                              Radiant Lass of Tarbay
            Lingholm Rhoda
                              Ch. Statesman of Tregwillym
                    Lingbelle Rose
                              Bell Heather Ruby
```

Ch. Tidemarsh Rip obtained six C.C.s, six Best of Breeds at Championship Shows and a Reserve to the Best in the Gundog Group at W.E.L.K.S. in 1969. He qualified in the field at seventeen months and was awarded Champion at the Welsh Springer Spaniel Club Show in 1971 under Judge Dr. Esther Rickards.

Ch. Krackton Surprise Packet (Pearce)

CH. KRACKTON SURPRISE PACKET

Bitch   KC NO. 1945BD   Whelped: 8/18/67
Owner: G.W.R. Couzens, Crickhowell, Powys
Breeder: S.G. Brabner,

                              Sportsman of Tregwillym
                     The Pride of Tregwillym
                              Sh. Ch. Lady of Llangarna
              Nobleman of Tregwillym
                              Sh. Ch. Top Score of Tregwillym
                     Lisa of Tregwillym
                              Tandi of Tregwillym
CH. KRACKTON SURPRISE PACKET
                              Ch. Statesman of Tregwillym
                     Sportsman of Tregwillym
                              Ch. Tulita of Tregwillym
              Pru of Gliffaes
                              Tehran of Tregwillym
                     Tag of Cwmcarvan
                              Theodora Hardy

Ch. Krackton Surprise Packet, pride of the Krackton Kennel, won six
C.C.s and two B.O.B.s, one under Judge H. Newman at the Royal Welsh
Open Show in July, 1971. An outstanding bitch, she is also an excellent
gun dog, having a second in advanced qualifying tests.

Sh. Ch. Athelwood Diaperoxide (Cooke)

SH. CH. ATHELWOOD DIAPEROXIDE

Dog   KC NO. 1490BC   Whelped: 3/26/68

Owner: Mr. and Mrs. B.J. Mullins, Little Birch, Herefordshire

Breeder: Mr. and Mrs. B.J. Mullins, Little Birch, Herefordshire

<pre>
                         Sportsman of Tregwillym
                 The Pride of Tregwillym
                         Sh. Ch. Lady of Llangarna
         Nobleman of Tregwillym
                         Sh. Ch. Topscore of Tregwillym
                 Lisa of Tregwillym
                         Tandi of Tregwillym
SH. CH. ATHELWOOD DIAPEROXIDE
                         Sh. Ch. Statesman of Tregwillym
                 Sportsman of Tregwillym
                         Sh. Ch. Tulita of Tregwillym
         Atalanta of Athelstone
                         Sh. Ch. Statesman of Tregwillym
                 Sherry of Tregwillym
                         Tete-a-tete of Tregwillym
</pre>

Sh. Ch. Athelwood Diaperoxide seems to deal in threes, with that number of C.C.s, reserve C.C.s, and B.O.B.s to his credit. His is a Mullins creation being bred, owned, and handled by Mrs. Mullins. To date he has also sired three show champions, including Ch. Dalati Del, a top C.C. winner.

Sh. Ch. Plattburn Progressor (Cooke)

SH. CH. PLATTBURN PROGRESSOR
Dog   KC NO. 2225BD   Whelped: 9/16/68
Owner: Mr. and Mrs. J.K. Burgess, Bishop Wilton, York.
Breeder: Mr. and Mrs. J.K. Burgess, Bishop Wilton, York.

```
                              Ch. Rockhill Rhiwderin
                  Plattburn Poacher
                              Patmyn Pie Powder
            Plattburn Proclamation
                              Sh. Ch. Denethorp Dihewyd
                  Plattburn Poppy
                              Patmyn Pie Powder
SH. CH. PLATTBURN PROGRESSOR
                              Sh. Ch. Denethorp Dihewyd
                  Sh. Ch. Plattburn Paramount
                              Patmyn Pie Powder
            Plattburn Penelope
                              Ch. Rockhill Rhiwderin
                  Sh. Ch. Plattburn Penny
                              Patmyn Pie Powder
```

Sh. Ch. Plattburn Progressor, one of the few systematically bred Welsh, gained seventeen C.C.s during his show career, the last under judge E.H. Perkins at Leeds in 1973. He has the distinction of winning the "Grove" Challenge Cup at W.E.L.K.S. in 1970, 1971, and 1972, more times than any other dog.

Ch. Tidemarsh Tidemark (Cooke)

CH. TIDEMARSH TIDEMARK

Dog   KC NO. 2128BE   Whelped: 9/24/69

Owner: G.H. Pattinson, Maidstone, Kent

Breeder: Mrs. Russen, London

```
                          Stokecourt Stephen
                  Stokecourt Sam
                          Karushina
          Ch. Tidemarsh Rip
                          Shadow of Tarbay
                  Lingholm Rhoda
                          Lingbelle Rose
CH. TIDEMARSH TIDEMARK
                          Ch. Statesman of Tregwillym
                  Wynnegate Lad
                          Nantgraw Girl
          Titian Beauty
                          Bartholomew
                  Brynwilach Queen
                          Pendoyland Princess
```

Ch. Tidemarsh Tidemark qualified in the Field in thirteen months, obtained his Junior Warrant at fourteen months and gained Championship status at twenty-five months. "Flash" was awarded six C.C.s, thirteen Reserve C.C.s, the Leacroft Trophy for Best Qualified Worker, and Best in Show at the 1972 Welsh Springer Spaniel Club Show under Judge D. Dobson.

Sh. Ch. Hillpark Pollyanna (Walton)

SH. CH. HILLPARK POLLYANNA

Bitch   KC NO. 3210BE   Whelped: 3/1/70

Owner: Mr. and Mrs. J.S. Walton, Sevenoaks, Kent

Breeder: Mr. and Mrs. J.S. Walton, Sevenoaks, Kent

Sh. Ch. Token of Tregwillym

Ch. Statesman of Tregwillym

Trinket of Tregwillym

Sportsman of Tregwillym

Tehran of Tregwillym

Ch. Tulita of Tregwillym

Gilly of Beamends

SH. CH. HILLPARK POLLYANNA

Ch. Rockhill Rhiwderin

Sh. Ch. Denethorp Dihewyd

Denethorp Dannella

Polly Garter of Doonebridge

Sh. Ch. Diplomat of Hearts

Doonebridge Diamond

Shepherdess of Broomleaf

Sh. Ch. Hillpark Pollyanna gained three C.C.s, the last under Judge Dr. E. Rickards at the East of England Show in 1974, and six reserve C.C.s, including Cruft's in 1974. Mrs. Anne Walton, owner and Secretary of the Welsh Springer Spaniel Club describes her champion bitch as thoroughly reliable and having a happy temperment.

Ch. Dalati Del (Hunton Morgans)

CH. DALATI DEL

Bitch   KC NO. 192-BG   Whelped: 12/8/70

Owner: Mr. and Mrs. N. Hunton Morgans, Llandovery, Dyfed
Breeder: Mr. and Mrs. N. Hunton Morgans, Llandovery, Dyfed

```
                            The Pride of Tregwillym
                    Nobleman of Tregwillym
                            Lisa of Tregwillym
            Sh. Ch. Athelwood Daiperoxide
                            Sportsman of Tregwillym
                    Atalanta of Athelstone
                            Sherry of Tregwillym
    CH. DALATI DEL
                            Benefactor of Brent
                    Sh. Ch. Bruce of Brent
                            Bronwyn Trixie
            Dalati Sidan
                            Gamefeather Brandy Snap
                    Freesia of Hearts
                            Sh. Ch. Fashion Plate of Hearts
```

Ch. Dalati Del, one of the four champions owned or bred by the Morgans, was the top C.C. winning Welsh Springer in 1972, gaining fifteen during her showing. She was Reserve Best in Show at the 1973 National Gun Dog Association Ch. Show.

Sh. Ch. Roger of Pencelli (Cooke)

SH. CH. ROGER of PENCILLI

Dog   KC NO. 3047BF   Whelped: 12/17/70

Owner: H. Newman, Treorchy, Mid Glamorgan
Breeder: H. Newman, Treorchy, Mid Glamorgan

```
                              Ch. Statesman of Tregwillym
                   Benefactor of Brent
                              Gwyneth Bach of Brent
          Sh. Ch. Bruce of Brent
                              Denethorp Dorian
                   Bronwyn Trixie
                              Sally of Emscote
SH. CH. ROGER OF PENCELLI
                              Sh. Ch. Easter Parade
                   Priory Major
                              Modern Maid
          Sh. Ch. Marie of Pencelli
                              All Alone
                   Bonny Legend
                              Lucy of Llanwenog
```

Sh. Ch. Roger of Pencelli was one of the youngest Champions of the breed and has since won thirteen C.C.s, including Cruft's in 1972 under Judge T.H. Arthur and in 1973 under Judge A.B. Nicholson. He was the Gun Dog of the Year, 1972 and Open Dog Winner in 1973 at the W.S.S. Club Ch. Show. He is rated by many as one of the best dogs in the breed.

Sh. Ch. Tregwillym Golden Gem (Payne)

SH. CH. TREGWILLYM GOLDEN GEM
Bitch   KC NO. 3772BG   Whelped: 1/1/72
Owner: Mr. H.C. Payne, Cumbran, Gwent
Breeder: Mr. H.C. Payne, Cumbran, Gwent

<pre>
                        Sportsman of Tregwillym
                Rambler of Tregwillym
                        Sherry of Tregwillym
        Golden Shot of Tregwillym
                        Ch. Diplomat of Hearts
                Honor May
                        Theresa of Hearts
    SH. CH. TREGWILLYM GOLDEN GEM
                        Ch. Statesman of Tregwillym
                Sportsman of Tregwillym
                        Ch. Tulita of Tregwillym
        Sh. Ch. Golden Tint of Tregwillym
                        Ch. Statesman of Tregwillym
                Sh. Ch. Lady of Tregwillym
                        Tete-a-Tete of Tregwillym
</pre>

Sh. Ch. Tregwillym Golden Gem, the tenth Champion from the Tregwillym Kennel of Mr. and Mrs. H. Clifford Payne, is a fourteen C.C. winner and many times Best Gundog and Reserve Best in Show.

Sh. Ch. Hillpark Mr. Polly (Walton)

SH. CH. HILLPARK MR. POLLY

Dog   KC NO. 1975BI   Whelped: 1/4/72

Owner: Mr. and Mrs. J.S. Walton, Sevenoaks, Kent

Breeder: Mr. and Mrs. J.S. Walton, Sevenoaks, Kent

                   Ch. Rockhill Rhiwderin

          Plattburn Poacher

                   Patmyn Pie Powder

     Plattburn Proclamation

                   Sh. Ch. Denethorp Dihewyd

          Plattburn Poppy

                   Patmyn Pie Powder

SH. CH. HILLPARK MR. POLLY

                   CH. Rockhill Rhiwderin

          Sh. Ch. Denethorp Dihewyd

                   Denethorp Dannella

     Polly Garter of Doonebridge

                   Sh. Ch. Diplomat of Hearts

          Doonebridge Diamond

                   Shepherdess of Broomleaf

Sh. Ch. Hillpark Mr. Polly, a natural worker with excellent temperment, gained his first Challenge Certificate at Cruft's, his third at the 1975 Welsh Springer Spaniel Club Show at Stoneleigh under Judge F. Warner Hill.

7
THE WELSHDOG IN AMERICA

Welsh Springer Spaniel fanciers the world over are familiar with the writings of the royal physician, Dr. Johannes Caius, who in 1583 described the "Spaniells" as "white, and if they be marked with any spottes, they are commonly red, and somewhat great therewithall, the heares not growing in such thicknesse but that the mixture of them maye safely bee preceaved." This description is part of his passable description of that fine hunting dog, the Welsh Spaniel. In America, it was in 1783 that the first book about dogs was written and here, also, one finds words that convey a picture of a Welsh Springer Spaniel type of hunting dog. A colonist's view of the spaniel is presented in the book, *Sportsman's Companion* wherein several different varieties of shooting dogs are described. Now this book was published in New York City just after the end of the War for American Independence and for reasons no doubt related to personal safety, the author (probably a Tory) chose to give his name as "A Gentleman, who has made shooting his Amusement upward of Twenty-Six Years, in Great-Britain, Ireland and North America." The book is interesting and authoritative. It was annotated and illustrated by Jan Thorton in 1948 in a limited edition of five-hundred copies, which are now, along with the originals, collectors items. This work includes a fine illustration of a typical "springer spaniel," by Philip Reinagle (1749-1833) which is almost exactly like a modern Welsh except for its fan tail.

Various phrases and comments cast the author of this early American work as a British officer who was familiar with the training of dogs for hunting in both common and aristocratic ways. Of interest to Welsh Springer fanciers is his description of his favorite type of spaniel.

> They are commonly red and white . . . have a resemblence to the Setters, but not so large, though much larger than the little spaniels (cocking) with a fan-tail and pretty large ears: This kind of Doge ranges well, and will make a sudden stand, or short pause or point, and, as you come up, bounce in upon, and spring the game.

Even at an earlier time the Welsh type spaniel was known in America. A painting by Justus Kuhn, dated 1712, of a little girl standing with her hand on the head of a red and white-coated spaniel now hangs in the Baltimore Hall of the Maryland Historical Society. Of interest here is the fact that these red and white spaniels described in paintings and prose are similar to those that appear in the paintings of Sir Joshua Reynolds, Thomas Gainsborough, George Stubbs, and George Romney of the same period in Britain. So, without a doubt, we can assign an equality of time to the presence of the Welsh Springer Spaniel in Britain and America at the beginning of the eighteenth century, and can see that the Welsh type "doggie" was imported from earliest times in settling "the new world."

Some sage once said, "imitation is the sincerest form of flattery." Surely such a view applies to the importing of dogs by individuals from one country to another. While the Welsh Springer Spaniel is identified at an early date in the United States, their numbers have always been small and, at times, they actually disappear from the record of recognizable breeds of sporting dogs. The extent of use of a particular type of dog for hunting and, in more recent times, in competitive showing, is clearly dependent on the advocation of the breed as evoked by a select group of people. It is the raising, training, and showing in the field or ring for the sheer love of it, as a hobby or for commercial reasons, which has caused one breed and then another to be raised to a position of great recognition. In the United States, the Welsh Springer Spaniel cannot be classed as a popular dog, or even one that is easily recognized. Only a few are born each year, bred just as in Wales and England by a small number of true advocates, people who have a genuine affection for the breed. There are one or two persons each year who, with their families, breed for the pleasure of the experience, and a small group who, with a professional thrust, show, breed, and sell Welsh Springer Spaniels. Most of the breeders in this latter group have imported from Wales and England their foundation dogs and bitches to imitate with their purchases the actions of their British associates who also fancy the Welsh Springer Spaniel as a hunter, family pet, or flashy showdog.

The record of registrations of Welsh Springer Spaniels with the American Kennel Club presents another view of the development of the breed in the United States since its formal recognition in 1906. The first Welsh Springer Spaniel to be registered was in 1914. Running records of breed registrations however have been kept by the AKC only since 1926 and the number of litters each year, since 1972. Of the litters, there were in the United States five in 1972, nine in 1973, and eleven in 1974. Preliminary information puts the 1975 litters at about fifteen. Individual dog registrations here and in Great Britain are listed for the years after 1946 in Appendix A. Until 1949 there were no registrations in the United States, which supports the claim that no Welsh Spaniels were alive here after World War II. Importing soon corrected the situation and in 1949 eleven dogs were registered. The plot of registrations in the graph below shows the zigzag nature of the breeding as it has progressed through 1974. In the figure, a more sustained effort appears to have started in 1963 and, except for the dip in the 1970-2 period, has caused a modestly upward growth pattern. Only time will tell whether it will continue or drop once again as in the past. A look at the graph of British registrations may give insights of the future here. It has a growth pattern starting in the same 1963-5 period

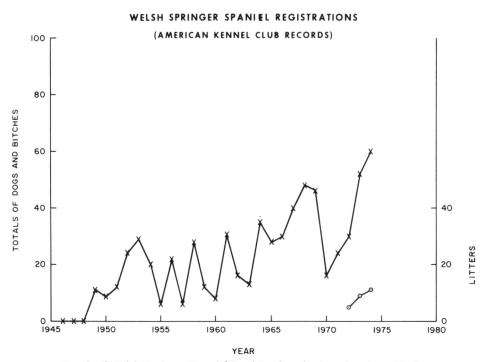

WELSH SPRINGER SPANIEL REGISTRATIONS
(AMERICAN KENNEL CLUB RECORDS)

TOTALS OF DOGS AND BITCHES

LITTERS

YEAR

Graph of Welsh Springer Spaniel Registrations in America since 1948.

as the beginning of a new interest in breeding, and the result has been a three-fold increase in registrations to 452 in 1974.

Of special note for the history of the Welshdog in America, is the first Welsh Springer registration with the American Kennel Club. Their records show that Mr. Harry B. Hawes of Kirkwood, Missouri registered a dog named Faircroft Bob in 1914 as owner-breeder. Faircroft Bob's pedigree was researched by George C. Reed of Reed Pedigrees at the request of the author with the following results. Mr. Reed learned that when Bob was registered with the AKC, the breed was called Welsh Springers. The word Spaniel was added sometime later and more recently has become the main title with the breed now known officially as Spaniel (Welsh Springer). Bob's father (sire), Faircroft Snip was two and one-half-year-older than Bob, and was also AKC registered. However, Bob's registration was handled first, a mere chance event, giving him the honor of being the first registered Welsh Springer in the United States. Bob's dam, Faircroft Sue, was never registered. Does this say something about the position of the female during this time? Not really, since Mr. Hawes subsequently registered two other bitches, Faircroft Lass and Vixen. In all, for the official start of the breed in America, Mr. Hawes registered six Welsh Springers. Of further note is the fact that running records of registrations by breeds was not started by the American Kennel Club until 1926, so it is not known how many other Welsh were registered. The record between 1926 and 1948 is available and shows a total blank for Welsh. If any were in the United States after the Hawes breeding activity as hunters or pets, they were not registered, rather they spent their days in official obscurity. The pedigree of the famous Bob shows an attempt at line breeding and at least one highly regarded British Champion Longmynd Calon Fach.

```
                                        Buller of Bout
                         Buller of Llyan
                                        Cora
              Faircroft Snip
                                        Topper
                         Nancy of Llyan
                                        Gipsy of Glyn
FAIRCROFT BOB
AKC NO. 185938
                                        Buller of Bout
                         Buller of Llyan
                                        Cora
              Faircroft Sue
                                        Longmynd Morgan
                         Longmynd May Gween
                                        Ch. Longmynd Calon Fach
```

Other Welsh imports during this period were by Mr. Hobart Ames (of Shovel Fame), Connecticut, who used dogs from Mr. A.T. Williams for shooting. The untimely death of Mr. Williams, some years before the First World War, brought this kennel to an end so, as the AKC records show, none were ever registered. Later, in the 1920s, Welsh from the Llanharan Kennels were exported to sportsman in the Midwest. It is reported that one of the last purebred Llanharan bitches, "Marged O'Matherne" was sold to America in 1927.

The year 1929 at the American Kennel Club was important for the Welsh Springer in a respect beyond the registering of the first dog. It was in December of that year the AKC published the standard for the breed that has remained unchanged to the present. An earlier standard appeared in 1921 in *The Complete Dog Book* by Dr. William R. Bruette, editor of the magazine, *Forest and Stream*. Almost all the phrases used to describe the Welsh Springer Spaniel in the Bruette description are to be found in the AKC standard for the breed; however, conspicuously absent are words about the jaw, "narrow when looked at downward;" the eyes, "intelligent;" the ears, "with feather not longer than the ear;" hindlegs, "not feathered below the hock on the leg;" weight, "between thirty and forty-two pounds;" and color, "red or orange and white (red preferable)." Some of these phrases have considerable merit and deserve attention during any effort to revise the standard. In most instances breed standards are the work of the parent club of the breed. The parent club is the sole source of changes and additions. The membership must approve the standard or revision; afterwards it can be submitted to the Board of Directors of the AKC for approval. No submission for change in the Welsh Springer Spaniel Standard has occurred in America but changes have been approved several times in Great Britain by the Kennel Club. The latest was the addition of a size limit for dogs of nineteen inches to the shoulder, and for bitches, eighteen inches, approximately. Since the standard is designed to protray an ideal dog of the breed the phrases must cover all aspects, defining type, structure, gait, and temperment. It is to represent a concept against which a dog owner or judge can measure for comparisons. Obviously, the standard is subject to interpretation by each user, yet it achieves surprisingly, considerable uniformity of view among dog fanciers. There will be greater accord when the American standard is revised to be the same as the British version, although the present differences between the two are slight. The British standard has sections on "Size" and "Faults" and there are differences in organization of the sections. The official standards from the British and American Kennel Clubs appear for comparison in the appendix of this book.

The most significant imports of Welsh occurred after the last war, which saw the decline in number of most dogs in Great Britain and the United States. It is probably safe to say that no Welsh Springer Spaniels survived in the United States and that it was only through the imaginative activities of people like Miss Dorothy H. Ellis of St. Mary's, Bramber, Sussex, that a resurgence in interest in the Welsh occurred as it did in America in the 1950s. It was the now-famous flight of Miss Ellis to New York and the Westminister Kennel Club Show with five young Welsh Springer Spaniels that is credited with starting the postwar interest of the breed. Ambassador of Downland and four relatives where flown in 1950 to compete in the New York, Hartford, and Boston shows. In the words of Miss Ellis, "They created a sensation. Ambassador finished in the gun-dog group at Westminister where he was loudly applauded by an enthusiastic American audience . . ." Another import from Miss Ellis, Jester of Downland, holder of eight K.C. Challenge Certificates, went to Mrs. Eleanor Howes of East Bridgewater, Massachusetts, in 1952. Jester, Ambassador, Souvenir, and the other young Welsh Springer Spaniels from the Downland Kennel were a new beginning for the breed in America. The restart of the Welshdog in America is told best by the woman who is responsible, Miss Dorothy Ellis, as she reported her experience for the British Club Yearbook in 1967.

MY FIRST AMERICAN SHOW — DOROTHY ELLIS

Of all the exciting shows I remember over more than 20 years, the one that will stay longest in my memory is the Westminster, at Madison Square Garden, New York, in 1950.

I made a sudden decision to exhibit there, as I discovered that the regulation that only dogs holding an American blue ribbon could be shown, was being waived in favour of pups under 1 year old. I had then two dogs and two bitch pups of eight months and thought I'd have a bash. 1950 was a "financial freeze" period and I had to ask the Bank of England to allow me to convert dollars for the purpose. They allowed me 100 worth (of my own money of course). No sooner had I received this permit than I was beseiged by reporters and photographic agencies—much to my surprise. I was still more surprised to be "seen off" by other papers. My plane, an early Stratocruiser—the only plane on which the dogs could travel with me—was twice returned from the end of the runway with engine trouble. It was some twenty four hours later that we got away. The journey took over twenty hours with a short stop at Shannon and at Monckton (Canada), and we arrived late on the evening before the show. I had been unable to secure kennelling for the five dogs (I had an adult bitch for two other shows I was attending) but to my amazement no objection whatever was raised to my keeping them in the bathroom of my hotel.

Just as soon as we were settled in, swarms of newspaper men came round, asking questions and flashing their cameras and it was not until I read their reports the following day that I understood why so much attention was being given. I was the first exhibitor from Britain since the war! It appears that the British Embassy was making sure that I sold my dogs and brought my dollars back to England, and a splendid job they did! A television interview (with dogs) followed, with that old movie veteran Edward Everitt Horton and since I did not know when I was on and when it was finished and my interviewer was a very entertaining person, it appears to have been very successful. Fortunately, after all this fuss, one of my young dogs was Best of Breed; (an honour which he went on to repeat at Hartford and Boston), and we had the exciting experience of the line-up for group judging. This indeed is an experience as it is so splendidly stage-managed. The whole floor is cleared as is Olympia, London, at such shows as the Royal Tournament, seats in tiers surround the exhibition area alongside which is stretched a long, wide carpet; each breed place is indicated by a large four-sided board bearing the name to be read from all sides and the whole area is vividly floodlit. The audience (every seat taken and some very expensively paid for) is quite silent except for applause for its particular favourites among the exhibits. The judges and instructions to exhibitors travel over loud-speaker to all parts of the hall. I felt very proud indeed to participate. Several of the top American handlers had offered free of charge to take the dog on the final run, but I had refused in view of the very trying two days he had passed through getting there and the two tiring days at the Show. Furthermore this was only the second show that this very inexperienced little pup had seen. I cannot pretend that he did very well against the magnificent best of breed winners with whom he competed, but he got a round of rousing applause from the generous American audience who had read of his arrival from England. It was indeed a day to remember.

Excerpted from the 1967 Year Book
of the Welsh Springer Spaniel Club

Also, in 1950, Mr. I.J. Smith of New Jersey imported a dog and bitch from the Rockhill Kennel of Mrs. M. Mayall of Great Britain, which served as the foundation for Mr. Smith's entry into Welsh Springer activities. Although an active breeder and showman, Mr. Smith is known best for his work in preparing the first paper devoted entirely to the history and characteristics of the breed. Entitled, "The Welsh Springer Spaniel" by I.J. Smith and reproduced by the Welsh Springer Spaniel Club of America, this six-page document was, until the publishing of this book, the only statement on Welsh Springers available in the United States to present to the newly interested or prospective owner. Mr. Smith also had the distinction of being the first American member of the British Welsh Springer Spaniel Club, setting a trend that has grown over the years so that today it is not uncommon for Americans who are active in the breed to hold British memberships as well as American in the Welsh Springer Spaniel Clubs. The dual memberships help solidify relationships and permit exchange through the yearbooks of breeding information and pictures of the more famous dogs.

By 1961 there were at least twenty families in Massachusetts, New York, New Jersey, and California who owned Welsh Springer Spaniels and who, as charter members, formed the Welsh Springer Spaniel Club of America. The organization of the club was led by Mr. James P. Parker, then Chief Steward of the Eastern Dog Club, Boston, Massachusetts. Mr. Parker accepted the position of secretary-treasurer and Mr. H.R. Randolph of Medford Station, New York, was elected president. Active in breeding and showing at this time were Mrs. Elenor Howes with her Downland imports and Mr. and Mrs. Randolph with their Randhaven line of Welsh Springers comprising Rockhill and Downland imports. It was Jester and Souvenir of Downland who became the parents of the first American show champion Welsh Springer Spaniel to be registered. He was Holiday of Happy Hunting, owned by Mrs. Howes, who remembers her "Rush" as being a "good dog and smart, one who always liked the woods." Rush sired three other American Champions, all from the Randhaven Kennel of Mr. and Mrs. Randolph from the same litter out of Randhaven's Geneth O'Rattle. Through the early 1960s, the Randhaven Kennel owned and bred eight show champions, setting the pace for development of the breed.

In 1962, Mr. D. Lawrence Carswell imported the British Show Champion, Trigger of Tregwillym, form Mr. H.C. Payne, Wales, to start a third strong and continuous breeding and handling program. Trigger quickly gained his American Championship at the Elm City K.C. show in February 1962, finishing under Judge Maxwell Riddle. To the present time, Trigger is the only dual British and American show champion, although some champions have done equally well in Canadian shows. Trigger placed in sporting group competition five times, more than any other Welsh Springer, gaining a second at the Delaware County K.C. show in June 1962. Since 1962, the DL'Car Kennel of Mr. and Mrs. Carswell has been responsible for the breeding and handling of twelve Welsh Springer Spaniel show champions.

During the sixties other fanciers imported dogs and bitches from such well-known British kennels as Broomleaf, Downland, Rushbrooke, and Stokecourt, and a steadily larger breeding program developed with American Kennel Club registrations during this period—averaging about thirty-five Welsh Springer Spaniels per year. In addition to David of Happy Hunting who had British Show Ch. Dewi Sant in the parentage of both his sire and dam, and Trigger of Tregwillym with British Ch. Brancourt Bang and British Show Ch. Taliesin-Ye-Ail as grandparents, American Ch. Filicia's Dylan has a place of distinction as one of the great dogs of this period. He was bred and owned by Mrs. Nettie Carswell and had five British and four American Champions in his parentage. He sired six American show champions and in twenty-eight shows was awarded twenty-three Best of Breeds. Filicia's Dylan gained his championship in five showings with a final B.O.B. at the Twin Brooks K.C. show under Judge Thompson in April 1965.

After its spirited beginning in 1961, the Welsh Springer Spaniel Club soon grew to include essentially all breeders and owners in the United States. Under the guidance of Jim Parker, who by 1962 had his own Champion, Cock Pluen of Randhaven, sired by Ch. David of Happy Hunting, out of Glannant Rattle, the usual club newsletters were issued and the Library Room of the Hotel Roosevelt in New York City became the meeting ground for the Club Annual Meeting, coincident with the American Spaniel Club Show, which soon listed Welsh Springer Spaniels as a group for judging. The Club Newsletter of March 1964 announced the first A.K.C. Sanctioned Match Show to be held on 24 May on the grounds of the Randhaven Kennel. This historic event for Welsh Springer Spaniels in America was attended by eleven members and nineteen guests, and was the largest gathering of Welsh Spaniels ever assembled, comprising fifteen dogs and bitches. Five puppies were shown and it is of interest that one of these went on to gain a championship, namely, Ch. Dilly, owned by Donna Kay Gatlin, Battletown, Kentucky. Dilly was a fast mover in the field as a hunter, and finished in the Midwest, appearing at Pontiac, Muncie, and the Detroit K.C. shows, while being handled by Mrs. Gatlin.

At the first show sponsored by the Welsh Springer Spaniel Club, of the dogs over one year, four were entered and two of these, DL'Car's Mister Lucky and Mikado's Tinker, had the distinction subseuqnetly of siring a future champion. Of the four bitches one year and older who entered this first Welsh Spaniel Match Show, two went on to gain their championships, Tair of Randhaven and Randhaven DL'Car Gini, a gratifying showing of the distaff side of the breed. The Best Older Dog and Best in Match went to Tair of Randhaven, one of the aforementioned bitches. At this match, eight owners handled their dogs. The judge was Mr. Edwin Cummings III, Stone Ridge, New York, long-time advocate of the breed and trainer of hunting Welsh. On the business side Jim Parker and H.R. Randolph were reelected to their previous positions and Mr. D. Lawrence Carswell was elected vice-president.

Another great dog, which arrived on the scene near the end of this period, was Champion Cicero Gus, owned by Mr. and Mrs. Charles Hatz of Cherry Hill, New Jersey. Cicero Gus was at home equally in the show and obedience ring as evidenced by his outstanding record of achievement. He was trained and handled by Mrs. Lori Hatz for his show championship and utility dog-tracking degree, having advanced further in obedience work than any other Welsh Springer Spaniel. As a showman, Gus finished in two months of showing, received a 1971 Dog

World Award as an undefeated dog, and gained the Canadian Award in 1972 as the top Welsh Springer Spaniel in breed competition in Canada. Cicero Gus set a blazing trail in the obedience ring, gaining at a steady pace his C.D., C.D.X., U.D., T.D. in America, and his C.D. and C.D.X. under Canadian judging.

During the 1960s, five other Welsh Spaniels were awarded C.D.s. Two of these were litter mates, Ch. Aduno of Randhaven and Coch Penion of Randhaven, owned, trained, and handled by Betty Jane Siegel of Babylon, New York. Of special interest to owners who train their dogs for field and obedience work is the experience of Mrs. Siegel. She was able to train her dogs to work as an obedience brace and, in one show, in brace competition, took one of the top honors.

By 1970, twelve Welsh Springer Spaniels had gained show championships and, in the previous ten years, a total of about forty litters and three hundred dogs were registered by their owners with the American Kennel Club. There were at least four professional breeders and the appearance of Welsh Springer Spaniels at champion shows was becoming a regular event. A small number of the dogs were purchased for field work and a reputation as spirited hunters was being established, so much so that there was a growing demand for Welsh Springer Spaniels as gundogs as well as for family pets. It was not uncommon during this period for people interested in acquiring a dog for hunting or pleasure to wait up to two years for their pup. Even today there is a general shortage of Welsh Springer Spaniels for purchase in the United States. The dog continues to have the distinction of being not only one of the oldest breeds but one of the rarest.

Since 1970, the ranks of Welsh Springer Spaniel breeders, owners, and handlers have swelled as awareness of the breed grew through the activities of the Welsh Springer Spaniel Club and the showing activities of the Randhaven, DL'Car, and Happy Hunting Kennels. The Club Newsletter took on a new tone as prepared first by Lori Hatz as Club Corresponding Secretary in 1974, by Mrs. D. Patterson Cannon and by Jane Pferd in 1975 as Newsletter Editor. On the show side, in the next five years through 1974, more dogs gained championships than in all previous years with twenty-five awards being made by the American Kennel Club. Also, an increasing interest was evident among sportsmen as calls for pups with good hunting ancestry were received by the club from all over the country, based on glowing reports about the field performance of Welsh Spaniels. Where dogs are available, filling such requests is particularly easy since, in all litters, there are many pups born with a good nose and searching ways. These are the natural hunters and, fortunately for the breed, have equal status to those that are selected for obedience and show training. In fact, no special characteristics or different appearance marks the show, pet, obedience, or field Welshdog, a condition that most serious breeders in America and Great Britain treat with great pride.

Since 1970, East and West Coast centers of interest for Welsh Springer Spaniels have developed, and a number of new breeders have entered their dogs in shows to gain championships. Of the new group the kennel names Sylabru, Bos'n, Pickwick, and Deckard in the East and owners Preston, Swonger, and Frelinger in the West are associated with the breeding and handling of champions. Of special note is the obedience work of Lawrence and Betty Siegel with the Bos'n dogs, Ch. Bos'n First Mate, and Bos'n Grand Finale. This brace had a number of group wins and placements as well as one all-breed and one specialty Best Brace in Show. These two fine Welsh went "Best Sporting Brace" in December 1970, at the Eastern Dog Show in Massachusetts with fine competition. A kennel mate, Ch. Bos'n Dick Deadeye took Best of Breed at the American Spaniel Club Speciality Shows in 1971 and 1972. This great showdog gained his championship in four straight Best of Breed wins—a record for the breed—and finished at the First Governors K.C. show in February 1971, under Judge Roling.

Another fancier to enter the ring in 1971 was Mrs. Sylvia Foreacre with her Sylabru's Copper Ibitz. Mrs. Foreacre came to Welsh after breeding other gundogs and in three years has caused a revitalization of interest that will be felt across the country for many years. Her first champion bitch, Copper Ibitz, sired by Ch. Filicia's Dylan, was bred by D.L. Carswell and ultimately gained a C.D., being trained and handled by Mrs. Foreacre. Caught up by the breed, Mr. and Mrs. Bruce Foreacre, Jr., traveled to Wales and England to obtain breeding stock for their fast-growing Sylabru Kennel. In four years, the Foreacres owned or bred nine Welsh Springer Spaniel champions. Their first import, Bachgen Dewr of Pencilli, bred by Mr. Harold Newman of Mid-Glamorgan, Wales, gained his American championship and serves as a leading stud dog. Another import to the Sylabru Kennel was Pencelli Rhyl bred by Mr. T. Hubert-Authur of Carmarthen, Wales, and sired by British Ch. Roger of Pencilli. Rhyl won her championship at the National Capital K.C. show in Washington, D.C., in March 1974. A third dog imported by the Foreacres to gain his championship was Gwilym of Brent, bred by Mrs. D. Perkins, Warwick, England. Of special note is the Foreacre Ch. Sylabru's Cimi Aberystwyth who has eight champions in his lineage of three generations. "Abbey" is full Foreacre creation, being bred, owned, and handled by Mrs. Sylvia Foreacre. He finished at Penn Treaty, Pennsylvania, K.C. show, and gained a Canadian championship and sixteen Best of Breeds during his show career.

In 1973, the new center in the Far West for Welsh Springer Spaniels was confirmed by the gaining of championships by Pickwick's Brychan, owned by Mr. Richard Preston, and Walter Gingham, owned by B. Swonger and G. Coffman. Ch. Pickwick's Brychan, a super dog among American Welsh has won over fifty Best of Breeds, was named the Top Welsh Springer Spaniel of 1973, and was awarded the Welsh Springer Spaniel Club of America Deckard's Cup as the 1974 Dog of the Year. Champion Walter Gingham has had the honor of placing four times in Sporting Group competition; with a second at the Dog Fancier's of Oregon Show in 1972.

Ch. Pickwick's Brychan was bred by Jane K. Seamans, of Dobbs Ferry, New York. Mrs. Seamans acquired her interest in the breed while living in England and on her return to the United States in 1971 brought a brace of Welsh Springer Spaniels of the Plattburn line to start her Pickwick Kennel. Brychan's dam, Plattburn Primrose, one of the imports, has since gained her championship along with Ch. Pickwick Dylan, who was brother to Brychan, although not litter mates. During this same period, championships were also gained by two more of the Carswell dogs, Ch. DL'Car's Prince of Wales and Ch. Peter Dewi Sant of DL'Car. The last dogs in 1974 to receive championships were Sylabru's Lollipop, bred by Constance J. Schuyler and owned by Edith DuBois, who is a new strong advocate and has entered the ranks of Welsh Springer breeders, and Wynfomeer's William the Welsh, bred by Louis Shoer and owned by handler Edwin J. Cummings III.

The latest burst of activity of the Welsh Springer Spaniel Club is due to the enthusiasm for the breed by Jane A. Pferd of Mendham, New Jersey. After experience with hounds, she became interested in spaniels in 1971 and purchased her first bitch from Mrs. Bryon E. Maine to start the Deckard Kennel. Subsequently she imported another bitch, Kraction Rare Sequin, from Mr. G.W.R. Couzens of Breconshire, Wales, and is now a leading breeder and guiding force in the East in advancing Welsh Springer Spaniels. Offering her home and hospitality for club meetings and taking the position of Membership Chairwoman, she caused a sharp growth in new members, and a revived interest in the club activities. She now serves as editor of the Club Newsletter.

In 1974, the organizing of a Club Show at the Saucon Rod and Gun Club at Coopersburg, Pennsylvania was planned by Mr. and Mrs. Ron Wade of Bear, Pennsylvania. There were seventeen Welsh Springer Spaniels, the most together up to that time in America, and the class judging was performed by Mrs. Margaret Migliorini, while Mrs. Edith DuBois covered the Junior Showmanship competition. The results of this show with winners and champions on exhibition are given the following table.

WELSH SPRINGER SPANIEL CLUB OF
AMERICA MATCH SHOW – 6 October 1974

Puppy Dogs

3-6 months	Sylabru's Streaker	Sylvia Foreacre
6-9 months	Deckard's Sir Barnye	Ken McCullough
	Dylan of Gwyln	Mary McGlynn

Best Puppy Dog — Deckard's Sir Barnye — Ken McCullough

Puppy Bitches

6-9 months	Deckard's Tamarama	Ruth Smith
	Penny	Nettie Carswell
9-12 months	Patches of Denbigh	Alex Nash

Best Puppy Bitch — Deckard's Tamarama — Ruth Smith

Best Puppy in Match — Deckard's Sir Barnye — Ken McCullough

Novice Dogs — Sylabru's Coupon Clipper — Paul & Joanne Alper

Open Dogs — Wynfomeer's William the Welsh — Edwin J. Cummings
Kyngsbree Aelwyn — Jane K. Seamans

Winners Dog — Wynfomeer's William the Welsh — Edwin J. Cummings

Novice Bitches — Sylabru's Serena — Sylvia Foreacre
Krackton Rare Sequin — Bill Pferd
Deckard's Tyn-Coed — Bobby Morris

Open Bitches — Deckard's Holyhead — Jane Pferd
Pencilli's Pandour — Ken McCullough

Winners Bitch — Sylabru's Serena — Sylvia Foreacre

Best in Match — Wynfomeer's William the Welsh — Edwin J. Cummings

EXHIBITION — Ch. Pencilli Rhyl — Cindy Foreacre
Ch. Peter Dewi Sant of DL'Car — Candy Carswell
Ch. Pickwick's Dylan — Jane K. Seamans

At the show the club was presented with the Deckard's Cup, donated by Mr. and Mrs. William Pferd III, to be awarded annually to the owner of the Welsh Springer Spaniel of the Year—that dog or bitch obtaining the most points in shows held under American Kennel Club rules during the previous two years. It is intended that this award will help stimulate and encourage owners of Welsh Springer Spaniels to show their dogs and to develop champions. Mr. Edwin J. Cummings is the present Award Chairman. The cup will be retired after ten years and will become the "symbol of office" of future presidents of the Welsh Springer Spaniel Club of America. In 1974, Champion Pickwick's Brychan, owned by Richard Preston and bred by Jane K. Seamans, won the award. In 1975, the Deckard's Cup winner was Champion Peter Dewi Sant of Dl'Car, owned by D. Lawrence Carswell and bred by Nettie Carswell.

In 1975, the Club Match Show was held at the Sylabru Kennel, Glen Mills, Pennsylvania, of Mr. and Mrs. Bruce Foreacre. There were eighteen Welsh Springer Spaniels judged by Mr. William Ring. With long experience in sporting dogs having started judging in 1928, Mr. Ring introduced a new feature in judging Welsh when he requested that the dogs be set up on a table for his examination. While a common event for the showing of small dogs, this arrangement was used to advantage by Mr. Ring in judging the Welsh and provided excellent viewing for spectators and eased the handler's task as well. The judge for junior handling was Miss Mary Samuels of Pennsville, New Jersey, an associate of Mrs. Edith DuBois of Pennhope Kennel who was Show Manager. In the following table are given the winners and Exhibition Champions with the names of their owners.

WELSH SPRINGER SPANIEL CLUB OF
AMERICA MATCH SHOW—19 October 1975

Puppy Dogs		
3-6 months	Sylabru's Scottney Castle	Sylvia Foreacre
6-9 months	Kenlyn's Duncan Dewr	David & Carol Merry
	Pennhope's The Conqueror	Edith DuBois
	Sylabru's Peter Lapin	Sylvia Foreacre
Puppy Bitches		
3-6 months	Sylabru's Welsh Taffey	Sylvia Foreacre
	Deckard's Lady Phyllis	C.P. Colwell III
	Sylabru's Llyr	Slyvia Foreacre
6-9 months	Becky	Barbara Wade
Best Puppy in Match	Sylabru's Scottney Castle	Sylvia Foreacre
Open Dogs	Sylvia's Clipper Coupon	Paul & Joanne Alper
	Sylabru's Streaker	Sylvia Foreacre
Best Dog	Sylabru's Streaker	Sylvia Foreacre
Novice Bitches	Krackton Rare Sequin	William Pferd III
	Robinsbrooks My Fanny	Nettie Carswell

Best Bitch	Krackton Rare Sequin	William Pferd III
Best in Match	Krackton Rare Sequin	William Pferd III
EXHIBITION	Ch. Deckard's Holyhead	Jane Pferd
	Ch. Peter Dewi Sant of DL'Car	Nettie Carswell
	Ch. Gwilym of Brent	Sylvia Foreacre
	Ch. Pencelli Rhyl	Cynthia Foreacre
	Ch. Sylabru's Lollipop	Edith DuBois
	Pennhope's Red Magic	Edith DuBois

For 1974 and 1975 directors and officers of the club are D. Lawrence Carswell, President and holder of this position for five years; William Pferd III, Vice-President, who also serves as Club Historian; Mrs. Barbara M. Wade, Secretary; Mrs. Lori Hatz, Treasurer and long-time member who has held positions of Secretary and Newsletter Editor; and Members-at-Large Mrs. Sylvia Foreacre and Mrs. Jane K. Seamans, both experienced breeders and handlers of Welsh Spaniels. Organized in April 1961, the Welsh Springer Spaniel Club of America has the following objectives:

1. To encourage and promote the breeding of purebred Welsh Springer Spaniels and to do all possible to bring their natural qualities to perfection.
2. To urge members and breeders to accept the standard of the breed as approved by The American Kennel Club as the only standard of excellence by which Welsh Springer Spaniels shall be judged.
3. To do all in its power to protect and advance the interests of the breed by encouraging sportsmanlike competition at dog shows, field trials, and obedience trials.
4. To conduct santioned matches and specialty shows and trials under the rules of The American Kennel Club.
5. As the national club for Welsh Springer Spaniels, to help organize other Welsh Springer Spaniel Clubs in localities where there are sufficient fanciers of the breed to meet requirements of the American Kennel Club.

The club does not operate for profit and all dues or donations to the club are used for club operations. Membership is open to all persons eighteen-years of age and older who subscribe to the purposes of the club. Inquiries about membership should be addressed to the Membership Chairperson, Joy Frelinger, the Secretary, Barbara M. Wade, or the American Kennel Club.

In the last few years a number of new breeders have entered the ranks of Welsh Springer enthusiasts and are showing and training successfully in the East and Midwest. Mr. Kenneth D. McCullough was the first in 1975 to gain a championship with his dog, Deckard's Sir Barnye, at the Suffolk County KC Show in September. Also a breeder, he imported a brood bitch Menna of Pencelli from Mr. Harold Newman of Treorchy, Wales and has an established program underway. In addition, he fills the role of Publicity Chairman of the Welsh Springer Spaniel Club of America and is responsible for the Welsh Springer Spaniel Brochure, which presents facts about the breed and is available from the club on request. Assisting Mr. McCullough with club publicity is Jane A. Pferd of Mendham, New Jersey who serves as Editor of the Club Newsletter. Mrs. D. Patterson "Pat" Cannon has also entered the breeders circle with a first litter from her Deckard bitch. Other breeders of Welsh Springers in the East are Louisa C. Gustafson, October Farm, and Sue Noble, Robinsbrook Kennel, both of Concord, Massachusetts, Edith DuBois of Pennsville, New Jersey, Edna Randolph of Medford Station, New York, and David R. Call of Virginia Beach, Virginia. In the Midwest Mrs. Gene Hodges of Fayetteville, North Carolina and Lt. Col. John W. Graff, AKC Delegate, have lines of Welsh bred for hunting and show while in the Far West, Joy Frelinger in Santa Monica, Richard and Emily Preston in Campbell, are breeders and showers in California. In Scottsdale, Arizonia, Donald and Sue Spahr are breeders with the Su Dawn prefix and Champion Ethorp Two. In California, the Prestons have made a strong showing to gain four champions in the last three years. Their dogs Pickwick's Brychan and Rickemshel Rainmaker, and bitches Olympian Rhonda Redhead and Olympian Brychan's Robyn have carried the field in the Far West for the Olympian Kennel and they appear to have fine young stock for the future. In 1976, Mr. Richard L. Preston will serve as a member-designate of the Welsh Springer Spaniel Club of America to represent the interests of club members in his part of the country. With breeding programs underway in at least ten states, the future of the Welsh Springer Spaniel in America is assured. A lively increase in litter and dog registrations should be experienced in the coming years with the position in the AKC standing of registrations rising along with the breed popularity.

Painting by Jutus E. Kuhn in 1712 of Eleanor Darnell at the age of six with her pet dog. The artist is the first portrait painter of record in the province of Maryland. Note the deep red tone to the patches on the white coat, long ears, stop, and catlike front feet—all typical features of this earliest American Welsh Spaniel type dog. (Maryland Historical Society)

Ch. Coch Pluen of Randhaven at the Ladies K.C. Show in 1962 with owners Mr. and Mrs. J.P. Parker. Jim Parker was cofounder and past Secretary-Treasurer of the Welsh Springer Spaniel Club of America. (Parker)

Ch. Cicero Gus at the Grayslake K.C. Show in 1969 with handler and treasurer of the W.S.S.C. of America, Mrs. Lori Hatz, and Judge Heckmann. (Ritter)

Ch. DL'Car's Gini Triggerboy at the Somerset Hills K.C. Show in 1972 with Judge Teeter and handler D. Lawrence Carswell. Mr. Carswell is President of the Welsh Springer Spaniel Club of America and a senior specialist in the breed. (Gilbert)

Ch. Bachgen Dewr of Pencelli when six-years-old at the Spaniel Club Show in 1973 with handler Mrs. Sylvia Foreacre. (Gilbert)

Ch. Pickwick's Brychan at the El Camino Fun Match in 1972 with Judge Michael Allen and owner-handler Robert L. Preston. (Lindstrom)

Welsh Springer Spaniel Club of America members at a planning session in 1973. From left to right: J. Christopher Cannon, Kenneth D. McCullough, Charles C. Hatz, Lori Hatz, D. Patterson Cannon, Barbara M. Wade, Edwin J. Cummings III, Sylvia Foreacre, Alfred E. Tucker, Mrs. Lester Morris, Mr. Lester Morris, Mrs. Alfred E. Tucker, Donald Traub, Ronald G. Wade, Jane A. Pferd, and Chris and Pat's Welsh Springer Spaniels. (Pferd)

Mr. William and Jane A. Pferd, sponsors of the Deckard's Cup awarded annually to the Welsh Springer Spaniel of the Year, convey the cup to Club President, D. Lawrence Carswell. (Pferd)

8

AMERICAN CHAMPIONS

There is no substitute for judging dogs in the flesh to arrive at a decision about the best in a group. This applies equally in the show or obedience rings and in the field. The search for the show dog of best "type," "soundness," "balance," "condition," or "style" requires close inspection of the group while posed and moving around the ring. Between shows however, and during moments of relaxation, pictures can give valuable information for making judgments about past and present champions. This register of Welsh Springer Spaniels contains pictures of all but a few of the forty-two who have been awarded championship status in the United States. Provided by Welsh fanciers from across the country, they represent the pick of the judges. Since the group can not be moved around the ring to observe such characteristics as style and balance, ring presence, soundness, reach and drive of stride, we must be satisfied with the dogs "setup" for inspection. As you will see, all but two are facing in the same direction toward your left hand just as in the ring. We can commence the examination with the dogs in silhouette. Check balance. Are the various parts in the desired proportion? Is the head slightly domed, with a clearly defined stop? Is the muzzle of medium length? How are the ears? Are they set moderately low, comparatively small, and covered with nice setterlike feathering? Let's move on to the neck. Is it long, clean in throat, and neatly set into long, sloping shoulders? Is the length of body proportionate to length of leg with loin slightly arched and well coupled up? The hindquarters require a close look. What about the second thighs? Are they fully developed and deep? Are the hocks well let down? Are the stifles moderately bent? And their feet, are they round, catlike, not too large or spreading? Are all the tails set on low and lightly feathered? Is feathering on the fore and hindquarters moderate? What about the coat, is it straight and flat rather than wavy? Much can be learned about "type" from these champions. Have you picked your Winners Dog and Winners Bitch and your Reserves? It would help to have them gait and move around the ring just once before making the final choice. But nevertheless, after giving time and attention equally to each champion, surely you can pick the top Welsh Springer Spaniel—the Best of Breed!

Ch. Holiday of Happy Hunting (Shafer)

CH. HOLIDAY of HAPPY HUNTING

Dog   AKC NO. S-588052   Whelped: 1/23/53

Owner: Happy Hunting Kennels, East Bridgewater, Mass.

Breeder: Mrs. Eleanor P. Howes, East Bridgewater, Mass.

Dere Di

Br. Sh. Ch. Dewi Sant

Tesco Thornycroft

Br. Sh. Ch. Jester of Downland

Pencoed Lad

Merry Madcap of Downland

Tess of Tynywaun

CH. HOLIDAY of HAPPY HUNTING

Br. Sh. Ch. Dewi Sant

Gay Rebel

Dewch Mewn

Souvenir of Downland

Br. Sh. Ch. Dewi Sant

Ballerina of Downland

Merry Madcap of Downland

Ch. Holiday of Happy Hunting was the first American Champion Welsh Springer Spaniel to be registered. His dam and sire were imported from the Downland Kennel of Mrs. D. H. Ellis, St. Mary's, Sussex, who brought them to the United States in 1950. Mrs. Howes remembers her "Rush" as being a "good dog and smart, and one who always liked the woods."

Ch. David of Happy Hunting (Shafer)

CH. DAVID of HAPPY HUNTING

Dog   AKC NO. S-826809   Whelped: 6/15/56
Owner: H. R. and E. B. Randolph, Medford Station, N.Y.
Breeder: Happy Hunting Kennels, Medford Station, N.Y.

Dere Di

Br. Sh. Ch. Dewi Sant

Tesco Thornycroft

Br. Sh. Ch. Jester of Downland

Pencoed Lad

Merry Madcap of Downland

Tess of Tynywaun

CH. DAVID of HAPPY HUNTING

Br. Sh. Ch. Dewi Sant

Br. Sh. Ch. Jester of Downland

Merry Madcap of Downland

Miss Timmy of Happy Hunting

Gay Rebel

Souvenir of Downland

Ballerina of Downland

Ch. David of Happy Hunting, sire of four champions and the first Welsh Springer Spaniel owned by H.R. and E.B. Randolph, was the top dog under the Randhaven banner for many years. He was from the first postwar American litter at the Happy Hunting Kennel that was then owned by Mrs. Eleanor P. Howes and Dr. Grace E. Philbrick.

Br. Sh. Ch. and Am. Ch. Trigger of Tregwillym (Shafer)

BR. SH. CH. AND AM. CH. TRIGGER of TREGWILLYM

Dog   AKC NO. SA-99450   Whelped: 8/13/56

Owner: D. Lawrence Carswell, Amityville, N.Y.

Breeder: H.C. Payne, Cumbran, Monmouth, G.B.

Lucky Laddie

Br. Ch. Brancourt Bang

Ashfield Aristocrat

Tehran of Tregwillym

Beggar-Me Boy

Br. Sh. Ch. Gwyneth

CH. TRIGGER of TREGWILLYM

Br. Sh. Ch. Dewi Sant

Br. Sh. Ch. Taliesin Yr Ail

Gillian of Tregwillym

Teresa of Tregwillym

Br. Ch. Kim of Kenswick

Titian of Tregwillym

Gloria of Tregwillym

After gaining his British show championship under Mr. H.C. Payne of Wales, Ch. Trigger of Tregwillym was imported by Mr. D. Lawrence Carswell from Britain and gained his American championship at the Elm City KC show on 18 February 1962, finishing under Judge M. Riddle. He placed in sporting group competition five times, more than any other Welsh Springer Spaniel, gaining a 2nd at the Delaware County KC show in June of 1962.

Ch. Dien Glynis of Randhaven (Shafer)

CH. DIEN GLYNIS of RANDHAVEN

Bitch AKC NO. S-900546 Whelped: 12/24/57
Owner: H.R. and E.B. Randolph, Medford Station, N.Y.
Breeder: H.R. and E.B. Randolph, Medford Station, N.Y.

Br. Sh. Ch. Dewi Sant
Br. Sh. Ch. Jester of Downland
Ch. David of Happy Hunting
Br. Sh. Ch. Jester of Downland
Miss Timmy of Happy Hunting
Souvenir of Downland
CH. DIEN GLYNIS of RANDHAVEN
Lancelot of Llwyn
Glannant Ariel
Glannant Symphony
Randhaven's Geneth O'Rattle
Rushbrooke Rufus
Rockhill Rattle
Rockhill Regina

Ch. Dien Glynis of Randhaven was the first of four champions sired by Ch. David of Happy Hunting. She finished at the Staten Island KC show on 21 June 1959, preceding her litter mate as the first bitch Welsh Springer Spaniel champion in the United States.

Ch. Dere Nol of Randhaven (Shafer)

CH. DERE NOL of RANDHAVEN
Bitch   AKC NO. S-900545   Whelped: 12/24/57
Owner: Robert Gelfand, Yonkers, N.Y.
Breeder: H.R. and E.B. Randolph, Medford Station, N.Y.

Br. Sh. Ch. Dewi Sant
Br. Sh. Ch. Jester of Downland
Merry Madcap of Downland
Ch. David of Happy Hunting
Br. Sh. Ch. Jester of Downland
Miss Timmy of Happy Hunting
Souvenir of Downland
CH. DERE NOL of RANDHAVEN
Lancelot of Llwyn
Glannant Ariel
Glannant Symphony
Randhaven's Geneth O'Rattle
Rushbrooke Rufus
Rockhill Rattle
Rockhill Regina

Ch. Dere Nol of Randhaven was finished in October 1960 after her litter sister Ch. Dien Glynis of Randhaven and her litter brother Ch. Gwaint of Randhaven. She was handled by Mr. H.R. Randolph to a first on 4 January 1959 at the American Spaniel Club Show in New York City.

Ch. Gwaint of Randhaven (Shafer)

CH. GWAINT of RANDHAVEN

Dog   AKC NO. S-935878   Whelped: 12/24/57

Owner: J.B. Worthington, Stony Brook, N.Y.

Breeder: H.R. and E.B. Randolph, Medford Station, N.Y.

Br. Sh. Ch. Dewi Sant

Br. Sh. Ch. Jester of Downland

Merry Madcap of Downland

Ch. David of Happy Hunting

Br. Sh. Ch. Jester of Downland

Miss Timmy of Happy Hunting

Souvenir of Downland

CH. GWAINT of RANDHAVEN

Lancelot of Llwyn

Glannant Ariel

Glannant Symphony

Randhaven's Geneth O'Rattle

Rushbrooke Rufus

Rockhill Rattle

Rockhill Regina

Ch. Gwaint of Randhaven gained his championship on 7 June 1959 and was the first Welsh Springer Spaniel to place in the Sporting Group in the United States.

Ch. Coch Pluen of Randhaven (Parker)

CH. COCH PLUEN of RANDHAVEN

Dog   AKC NO. SA-34836   Whelped: 4/30/60

Owner: J.P. Parker, Ft. Glover, Marblehead, Mass.

Breeder: H.R. and E.B. Randolph, Medford Station, N.Y.

                    Br. Sh. Ch. Dewi Sant

           Br. Sh. Ch. Jester of Downland

                 Merry Madcap of Downland

       Ch. David of Happy Hunting

                 Br. Sh. Ch. Jester of Downland

           Miss Timmy of Happy Hunting

                 Souvenir of Downland

CH. COCH PLUEN of RANDHAVEN

                 Lancelot of Llwyn

           Glannant Ariel

                 Glannant Symphony

       Glannant Rattle

                 Rockhill Ransom

           Glannant Symphony

                 Rockhill Rattle

Ch. Coch Pluen of Randhaven was the first Welsh Springer Spaniel to gain a championship in New England, appearing at the Eastern Dog Club, North Shore, and Worchester K.C. shows. Owned by Jim Parker, long time Secretary of the W.S.S. Club of America, Coch Pluen finished at the Worchester show, put up by Judge Hall.

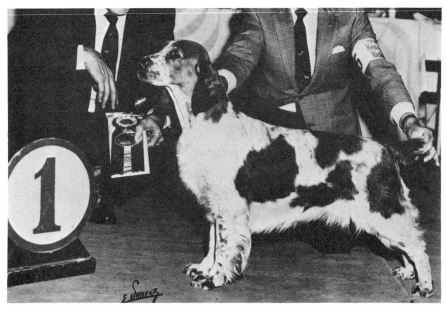

Ch. Randhaven's D'LCar Gini. (Shafer)

CH. RANDHAVEN'S D'LCAR GINI
Bitch   AKC NO. SA-111091   Whelped: 9/17/61
Owner: Nettie Carswell, Amityville, N.Y.
Breeder: Nettie Carswell, Amityville, N.Y.

Br. Ch. Brancourt Bang
Tehran of Tregwillym
Br. Sh. Ch. Gwyneth
Br. Sh. Ch. and Am. Ch. Trigger of Tregwillym
Br. Sh. Ch. Taliesian Yr Ail
Teresa of Tregwillym
Titian of Tregwillym
CH. RANDHAVEN'S D'LCAR GINI
Br. Sh. Ch. Jester of Downland
Ch. David of Happy Hunting
Miss Timmy of Happy Hunting
Ch. Dien Glynis of Randhaven
Glannant Ariel
Randhaven's Geneth O'Rattle
Rockhill Rattle

Ch. Randhaven's D'LCAR Gini has the distinction of being the first of the three American champions to have champions for parents. She was the second champion to be bred and owned by Nettie Carswell. "Gini" finished at the American Spaniel Club Show in January 1968, where she was handled by D. Lawrence Carswell and given a first by Judge Roling.

Ch. Tair of Randhaven (Shafer)

CH. TAIR of RANDHAVEN

Bitch   AKC NO. SA-131752   Whelped: 1/31/62

Owner: H.R. and E.B. Randolph, Medford Station, N.Y.

Breeder: H.R. and E.B. Randolph, Medford Station, N.Y.

                       Br. Sh. Ch. Jester of Downland

             Ch. David of Happy Hunting

                       Miss Timmy of Happy Hunting

        Rhudd O'Randhaven

                       Glannant Ariel

            Glannant Rattle

                       Glannant Symphony

CH. TAIR of RANDHAVEN

                       Br. Sh. Ch. Token of Tregwillym

             Br. Ch. Statesman of Tregwillym

                       Trinket of Tregwillym

        Showgirl of Tregwillym

                       Tehran of Tregwillym

             Br. Ch. Tulita of Tregwillym

                       Gilly of Beamends

Ch. Tair of Randhaven was the daughter of Showgirl of Tregwillym, an import from the Payne Kennels in Wales. She was owned and handled by Mr. and Mrs. Randolph and finished over five dogs at the Twin Brooks KC show in April 1965 under Judge Thompson.

Ch. Filicia's Dylan (Gilbert)

CH. FILICIA'S DYLAN

Dog   AKC NO. SA-229796   Whelped: 8/28/63

Owner: Nettie Carswell, Amityville, N.Y.

Breeder: Nettie Carswell, Amityville, N.Y.

<pre>
                              Br. Ch. Statesman of Tregwillym
                  Br. Sh. Ch. Deri Darrell of Linkhill
                              Br. Sh. Ch. Arabella of Linkhill
            Gamelad of the Downs
                              Br. Sh. Ch. Mikado of Broomleaf
                  Downland Redhead
                              Downland Red Gem
CH. FILICIA'S DYLAN
                              Tehran of Tregwillym
                  Br. Sh. Ch. and Am. Ch. Trigger of Tregwillym
                              Teresa of Tregwillym
            Ch. Randhaven's D'LCAR Gini
                              Ch. David of Happy Hunting
                  Ch. Dien Glynis of Randhaven
                              Randhaven's Geneth O'Rattle
</pre>

Ch. Filicia's Dylan, sire of six Welsh Springer Spaniel champions, was a strong showman, obtaining twenty-three Best of Breeds after finishing at the Twin Brooks KC show on April 1965. "Dylan" was bred and owned by Nettie Carswell. The Carswell name is well known in Welsh Springer Spaniel circles since the family have bred or owned eleven champions.

Ch. Dilly (Ritter)

CH. DILLY

Bitch   AKC NO. SA-268705   Whelped: 8/28/63

Owner: Nettie Carswell and Donna K. Gatlin, Battletown, Ky.

Breeder: Nettie Carswell, Amityville, N.Y.

<pre>
                              Br. Ch. Statesman of Tregwillym
                  Br. Sh. Ch. Deri Darrell of Linkhill
                              Br. Sh. Ch. Arabella of Linkhill
          Gamelad of the Downs
                              Br. Sh. Ch. Mikado of Broomleaf
                  Downland Redhead
                              Downland Red Gem
CH. DILLY
                              Tehran of Tregwillym
                  Br. Sh. Ch. and Am. Ch. Trigger of Tregwillym
                              Teresa of Tregwillym
          Ch. Randhaven's D'LCAR Gini
                              Ch. David of Happy Hunting
                  Ch. Dien Glynis of Randhaven
                              Randhaven's Geneth O'Rattle
</pre>

Ch. Dilly was the first Welsh Springer Spaniel to gain a championship in the midwest, appearing at Pontiac, Muncie, and the Detroit KC shows. She finished at the later show while being handled by Mrs. Gatlin and judged by Mr. R. Beale. "Dilly" was both a champion showgirl and good hunter.

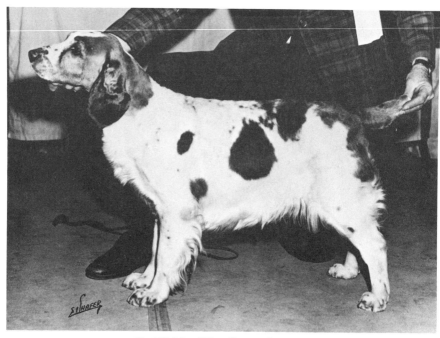

Ch. Llitith of Randhaven (Shafer)

CH. LLITITH of RANDHAVEN

Bitch   AKC NO. SA-266414   Whelped: 12/5/63
Owner: Nettie Carswell, Amityville, N.Y.
Breeder: E.B. Randolph, Medford Station, N.Y.

                       Br. Ch. Brancourt Bang
              Tehran of Tregwillym
                       Br. Sh. Ch. Gwyneth
     Br. Sh. Ch. and Am. Ch. Trigger of Tregwillym
                       Br. Sh. Ch. Taliesin Yr Ail
              Teresa of Tregwillym
                       Titian of Tregwillym
CH. LLITITH of RANDHAVEN
                       Br. Ch. Statesman of Tregwillym
              Br. Sh. Ch. Deri Darrell of Linkhill
                       Br. Sh. Ch. Arabella of Linkhill
              Redhead Debutante
                       Br. Sh. Ch. Mikado of Broomleaf
              Downland Redhead
                       Downland Red Gem

Ch. Llitith of Randhaven, on the show circuit for five years, was granted her championship at the Gloucester KC show in October 1970. She was handled by Nettie and D. Lawrence Carswell and finished under Judge Cowie and was the second champion out of Redhead Debutante.

Ch. Aduno of Randhaven, C.D. (Siegel)

CH. ADUNO OF RANDHAVEN, C.D.
AKC NO. SA-377588

Dog   Whelped: 1/26/66

Owner: Betty June Siegel, Babylon, N.Y.

Breeder: E.B. Randolph, Medford Station, N.Y.

```
                              Br. Sh. Ch. Stokecourt Jonathan
                Br. Sh. Ch. Mikado of Broomleaf
                              Broomleaf Dimple of Empshott
        Mikado's Tinker
                              Br. Sh. Ch. Stokecourt Simon
                Br. Sh. Ch. Stokecourt Judith
                              Br. Sh. Ch. Stokecourt Gillian
CH. ADUNO of RANDHAVEN, C.D.
                              Br. Ch. Statesman of Tregwillym
                Br. Sh. Ch. Deri Darrell of Linkhill
                              Br. Sh. Ch. Arabella of Linkhill
        Redhead Debutante
                              Br. Sh. Ch. Mikado of Broomleaf
                Downland Redhead
                              Downland Red Gem
```

Ch. Aduno of Randhaven was a great champion in both the show and obedience ring, being the first champion Welsh Springer Spaniel to gain a Companion dog degree. He was trained and handled by Betty Siegel and performed as an obedience brace with litter mate Coch Penion of Randhaven—C.D.

Ch. Bachgen Dewr of Pencelli (Gilbert)

CH. BACHGEN DEWR of PENCELLI

Dog   AKC NO. SB-183550   Whelped: 3/14/67

Owner: Sylvia and Bruce Foreacre, Jr., Glen Mills, Pa.

Breeder: Harold Newman, Treorchy, Wales, G.B.

```
                                    Br. Sh. Ch. Top Score of Tregwillym
                     Sh. Ch. Easter Parade
                                    Blodwyn Gwanwyn
            Priory Major
                                    All Alone
                     Modern Maid
                                    Lucy of Llanwenog
CH. BACHGEN DEWR of PENCELLI
                                    Br. Sh. Ch. Top Score of Tregwillym
                     All Alone
                                    Blodwyn Gwanwyn
            Bonny Legend
                                    Br. Sh. Ch. Token of Tregwillym
                     Lucy of Llanwenog
                                    Bonnie Sally
```

Ch. Bachgen Dewr of Pencelli, after gaining C.C.s in Britain, was imported by the Foreacres as a stud for their Sylabru Kennel. He was a steady winner in America, going BOB at the American Spaniel Club Show in January 1973, and gaining his American championship at Penn Treaty K.C. show in April.

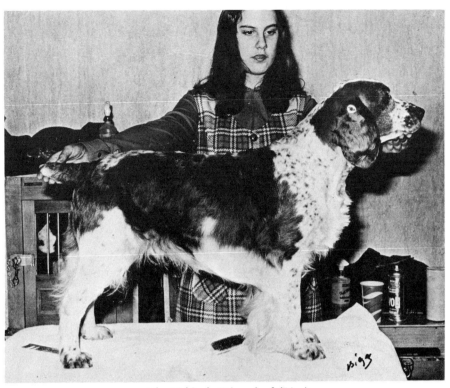

Ch. DL'Car's Triggerleaf (Bigg)

CH. DL'CAR'S TRIGGERLEAF

Dog   AKC NO. SA-667998   Whelped: 6/1/67

Owner: D. Lawrence Carswell, Amityville, N.Y.

Breeder: D. Lawrence Carswell, Amityville, N.Y.

<pre>
                        Tehran of Tregwillym
          Br. Sh. Ch. and Am. Ch. Trigger of Tregwillym
                        Teresa of Tregwillym
          DLCAR'S Mister Lucky
                        Ch. David of Happy Hunting
                 Gwen Coch of Randhaven
                        Randhaven's Geneth O'Rattle
CH. DL'CAR'S TRIGGERLEAF
                        Br. Sh. Ch. Top Score of Tregwillym
                 Mog Madoc of Empshott
                        Blodyn Gwanwyn
          Iolanthe of Broomleaf
                        Hilarion of Broomleaf
                 Oldhatch Fiery Farthing
                        Copper Coins of Reeth
</pre>

Ch. DL'Car's Triggerleaf, handled by owner/breeder D. Lawrence Carswell, gained his championship at the Bronx County KC show in March 1972, under Judge Lawreck. He was the third champion out of the dam Iolanthe of Broomleaf who was also owned by Mr. Carswell.

Ch. Cicero Gus, U.D. (Mattern)

CH. CICERO GUS, U.D.
Dog   AKC NO. SA-611116   Whelped: 5/10/68
Owner: Mr. and Mrs. Charles Hatz, Cherry Hill, N.J.
Breeder: Stanley Spirala

```
                                Br. Sh. Ch. Mikado of Broomleaf
                    Mikado's Tinker
                                Br. Sh. Ch. Stokecourt Judith
            Shadow of Storyland
                                Casowasco's Schroeder
                    Coeth Coch of Randhaven
                                Ch. Dien Glynis of Randhaven
CH. CICERO GUS, U.D.
                                Br. Sh. Ch. Deri Darrell of Linkhill
                    Gamelad of the Downs
                                Downland Redhead
            Jewel of Mayfield
                                Br. Sh. Ch. and Am. Ch. Trigger of Treg.
                    Ch. Randhaven's D'LCAR Gini
                                Ch. Dien Glynis of Randhaven
```

Ch. Cicero Gus was equally at home in both the show and obedience ring as evidenced by his outstanding record of achievement. He was handled by Mrs. Hatz to his championship and utility and tracking dog degrees, having advanced further in obedience training than any other Welsh Springer Spaniel. He was finished in two months, and received a 1971 Dog World Award, as an undefeated dog.

Ch. Walter Gingham (Bennett)

CH. WALTER GINGHAM
Dog   AKC NO. SA-620071   Whelped: 5/10/68
Owner: B. Swonger and G. Coffman, Sacramento, Calif.
Breeder: S.C. Spirala

```
                        Br. Sh. Ch. Mikado of Broomleaf
              Mikado's Tinker
                        Br. Sh. Ch. Stokecourt Judith
        Shadow of Storyland
                        Casowasco's Schroeder
        Coeth Coch of Randhaven
                        Ch. Dien Glynis of Randhaven
CH. WALTER GINGHAM
                        Br. Sh. Ch. Deri Darrell of Linkhill
              Gamelad of the Downs
                        Downland Redhead
        Jewel of Mayfield
                        Br. Sh. Ch. and Am. Ch. Trigger of Treg.
        Ch. Randhaven's D'LCAR Gini
                        Ch. Dien Glynis of Randhaven
```

Ch. Walter Gingham has the honor of placing four times in Sporting Group competition, with a second at the Dog Fanciers of Oregon Show under Judge Tuttle in August 1972. He finished for his championship at the Golden Gate KC in July 1973.

Ch. Peter Dewi Sant of DL'Car (Bushman)

CH. PETER DEWI SANT of DL'CAR

Dog   AKC NO. SA-618775   Whelped: 6/5/68

Owner: Nettie Carswell, Amityville, N.Y.

Breeder: D. Lawrence Carswell, Amityville, N.Y.

Tehran of Tregwillym

Br. Sh. Ch. and Am. Ch. Trigger of Tregwillym

Teresa of Tregwillym

Gary's Jethro of Randhaven

Br. Sh. Ch. Deri Darrell of Linkhill

Redhead Debutante

Downland Redhead

CH. PETER DEWI SANT of DL'CAR

Br. Sh. Ch. Top Score of Tregwillym

Mog Madoc of Empshott

Blodyn Gwanwyn

Iolanthe of Broomleaf

Hilarion of Broomleaf

Oldhatch Fiery Farthing

Copper Coins of Reeth

Ch. Peter Dewi Sant of DL'Car is another star of the DL'Car Kennel going thirty-three times Best of Breed after gaining his championship at the Long Island K.C. show in May 1974. He was placed fourth in the Sporting Group by Judge Brady at the Twin Brooks K.C. show in July 1974.

Ch. DL'Car's Gottowin (Gilbert)

CH. DL'CAR'S GOTTOWIN

Dog   AKC NO. SA-667456   Whelped: 6/25/68

Owner: Mrs. D.L.Carswell, Amityville, N.Y.

Breeder: D. Lawrence Carswell, Amityville, N.Y.

Tehran of Tregwillym

Br. Sh. Ch. and Am. Ch. Trigger of Tregwillym

Teresa of Tregwillym

Gary's Jethro of Randhaven

Br. Sh. Ch. Deri Darrell of Linkhill

Redhead Debutante

Downland Redhead

CH. DL'CAR'S GOTTOWIN

Br. Sh. Ch. Top Score of Tregwillym

Mog Madoc of Empshott

Blodyn Gwanwyn

Iolanthe of Broomleaf

Hilarion of Broomleaf

Oldhatch Fiery Farthing

Copper Coins of Reeth

Ch. DL'Car's Gottowin opened his show career with a first over eight dogs at the Boardwalk, New Jersey KC show in November 1970. He was finished in four more shows with a final win when handled by Nettie Carswell at the Bronx County KC show in March 1971, under Judge Tuddenhan.

Ch. DL'Car's Gini Triggerboy

CH. DL'CAR'S GINI TRIGGERBOY
Dog   AKC NO. SA-756822   Whelped: 8/20/68
Owner: Nettie Carswill, Amityville, N.Y.
Breeder: N. Carswell and D.K. Gatlin, Amityville, N.Y.

Tehran of Tregwillym
Br. Sh. Ch. and Am. Ch. Trigger of Tregwillym
Teresa of Tregwillym
Gary's Jethro of Randhaven
Br. Sh. Ch. Deri Darrell of Linkhill
Redhead Debutante
Downland Redhead
CH. DL'CAR'S GINI TRIGGERBOY
Tehran of Tregwillym
Br. Sh. Ch. and Am. Ch. Trigger of Tregwillym
Teresa of Tregwillym
Ch. Randhaven's D'LCAR Gini
Ch. David of Happy Hunting
Ch. Dien Glynis of Randhaven
Randhaven's Geneth O'Rattle

Ch. DL'CAR's Gini Triggerboy is one of the stars of the DL'Car dogs and of Welsh Spaniels in America, going BOB over fifty times. He was the top dog in 1972 and gained his big wins for championship at the Boardwalk and Philadelphia KC shows in December of 1971. One of the few sporting group placers, he finished fourth in November 1972 at the Ramapo K.C. show.

Ch. Plattburn Primrose (Seamans)

CH. PLATTBURN PRIMROSE

Bitch AKC NO. SA-818004 Whelped: 7/2/69

Owner: Jane K. Seamans, Dobbs Ferry, N.Y.

Breeder: J. Kenneth Burgess, York, England

```
                              Br. Ch. Rockhill Rhiwderin
                    Plattburn Poacher
                              Patmyn Pie Powder
            Plattburn Proclamation
                              Br. Sh. Ch. Denethorp Dihewyd
                    Plattburn Poppy
                              Patmyn Pie Powder
CH. PLATTBURN PRIMROSE
                              Br. Sh. Ch. Denethorp Dihewyd
                    Br. Sh. Ch. Plattburn Paramount
                              Patmyn Pie Powder
            Plattburn Pretty Pepps
                              Br. Ch. Rockhill Rhiwderin
                    Br. Sh. Ch. Plattburn Penny
                              Patmyn Pie Powder
```

Ch. Plattburn Primrose, dam of Champions Pickwick's Dylan and Pickwick's Brychan, was imported from the Plattburn Kennel in England. She gained her championship at the Bucks County K.C. show, Erwinna, Pennsylvania, in May 1974, under British Judge T. Hubert Arthur.

Ch. Sylabru's Copper Ibitz, C.D. (Klein)

CH. SYLABRU'S COPPER IBITZ, C.D.
Bitch   AKC NO. SA-787337   Whelped: 11/12/69
Owner: Sylvia Foreacre, Glen Mills, Pa.
Breeder: D. Lawrence Carswell, Amityville, N.Y.

                        Br. Sh. Ch. Deri Darrell of Linkhill
                  Gamelad of the Downs
                        Downland Redhead
            Ch. Filicia's Dylan
                        Br. Sh. Ch. and Am. Ch. Trigger of Treg.
                  Ch. Randhaven's D'LCAR Gini
                        Ch. Dien Glynis of Randhaven
      CH. SYLABRU'S COPPER IBITZ, C.D.
                        Br. Sh. Ch. Top Score of Tregwillym
                  Mog Madoc of Empshott
                        Blodyn Gwanwyn
            Iolanthe of Broomleaf
                        Hilarion of Broomleaf
                  Oldhatch Fiery Farthing
                        Copper Coins of Reeth

Ch. Sylabru's Copper Ibitz was the first Welsh Springer Spaniel owned
by the Foreacre family and the first of seven champions which have
been owned or bred under their banner. She was finished with a five
point win at the New Brunswick KC show in September 1971 under
Judge Given.

Ch. Bosn's First Mate (Gilbert)

CH. BOSN'S FIRST MATE

Dog   AKC NO. SA-767379   Whelped: 2/8/70

Owner: L. and B.J. Siegel, Babylon, N.Y.

Breeder: L. Siegel, Babylon, N.Y.

```
                              Br. Sh. Ch. Mikado of Broomleaf
                    Mikado's Tinker
                              Br. Sh. Ch. Stokecourt Judith
          Coch Penion of Randhaven, C.D.
                              Br. Sh. Ch. Deri Darrell of Linkhill
                    Redhead Debutante
                              Downland Redhead
CH. BOSN'S FIRST MATE
                              Ch. David of Happy Hunting
                    Ch. Coch Pluen of Randhaven
                              Glannant Rattle
          Bo Forte's Ballerina, C.D.
                              Br. Sh. Ch. Mikado of Broomleaf
                    Bo Forte's Befana
                              Br. Sh. Ch. Stokecourt Judith
```

Ch. Bosn's First Mate went five straight wins to gain his championship, finishing at Westminister in February 1971, under Judge Irmio. Together with his brother, Bosn's Grand Finale, in Brace competition there were a number of group wins as well as one all-breed Best Brace in Show, all handled by Betty Siegel.

Ch. Bosn's Dick Deadeye (Siegel)

CH. BOSN'S DICK DEADEYE

Dog   AKC NO. SA-767383   Whelped: 2/8/70

Owner: L. and B.J. Siegel, Babylon, N.Y.

Breeder: L. Siegel, Babylon, N.Y.

                          Br. Sh. Ch. Mikado of Broomleaf

              Mikado's Tinker

                          Br. Sh. Ch. Stokecourt Judith

      Coch Penion of Randhaven, C.D.

                          Br. Sh. Ch. Deri Darrell of Linkhill

              Redhead Debutante

                          Downland Redhead

CH. BOSN'S DICK DEADEYE

                          Ch. David of Happy Hunting

              Ch. Coch Pluen of Randhaven

                          Glannant Rattle

      Bo Forte's Ballerina, C.D.

                          Br. Sh. Ch. Mikado of Broomleaf

              Bo Forte's Befana

                          Br. Sh. Ch. Stokecourt Judith

Ch. Bosn's Dick Deadeye was Best of Breed at the New York Spaniel Specialty Show for two years. He gained his championship in four straight Best of Breed wins, finishing at the 1st Governors KC show in February 1971, under Judge Roling.

Am. and Can. Ch. Sylabru's Cimri Aberystwyth (Gilbert)

AM. AND CAN. CH. SYLABRU'S CIMRI ABERSYTWYTH
Dog   AKC NO. SA-924093   Whelped: 1/11/71
Owner: Cynthia and Sylvia Foreacre, Glen Mills, Pa.
Breeder: Sylvia Foreacre, Glen Mills, Pa.

                              Br. Sh. Ch. Deri Darrell of Linkhill
                    Gamelad of the Downs
                              Downland Redhead
          Ch. Filicia's Dylan
                              Br. Sh. Ch. and Am. Ch. Trigger of Treg.
                    Ch. Randhaven's D'LCAR Gini
                              Ch. Dien Glynis of Randhaven
CH. SYLABRU'S CIMRI ABERYSTWYTH
                              Gamelad of the Downs
                    Ch. Filicia's Dylan
                              Ch. Randhaven.s D'LCAR Gini
          Ch. Sylabru's Copper Ibitz, CD
                              Mog Madoc of Empshott
                    Iolanthe of Broomleaf
                              Oldhatch Fiery Farthing

Ch. Sylabru's Cimri Aberstywyth has the distinction of having eight
champions in his lineage back to his great-grandparents, including
champion parents. "Abbey" is a full Foreacre creation; being bred,
owned, and handled by Mrs. Sylvia Foreacre. He finished at Penn
Treaty KC show under Judge Freman, gained a Canadian championship,
and went BOB at the 1975 American Spaniel Club Show.

Ch. DL'Car's Prince of Wales (Bushman)

CH. DL'CAR'S PRINCE OF WALES
Dog   AKC NO. SB-51976   Whelped: 3/18/71
Owner: Nettie Carswell, Amityville, N.Y.
Breeder: Bryon E. Maine, Allamuchy, N.J.

                         Br. Sh. Ch. Deri Darrell of Linkhill
                  Gamelad of the Downs
                         Downland Redhead
          Ch. Filicia's Dylan
                         Br. Sh. Ch. and Am. Ch. Trigger of Treg.
                  Ch. Randhaven's D'LCAR Gini
                         Ch. Dien Glynis of Randhaven
CH. DL'CAR'S PRINCE OF WALES
                         Br. Sh. Ch. and Am. Ch. Trigger of Treg.
                  Gary's Jethro of Randhaven
                         Redhead Debutante
          Tara Fina of Bo Forte
                         Ch. Coch Pluen of Randhaven
                  Bo Forte's Ballerina
                         Bo Forte's Befana

Ch. DL'Car's Prince of Wales carries forward the winning conformation
of Trigger of Tregwillym and Filicia's Dylan. In gaining his championship, Prince of Wales had one of his majors at the Boardwalk K.C. show
in December 1973, where he placed first over nine dogs, one of the
largest groups of Welsh to compete. He is shown by Candy Carswell, a
well-known Junior Handler.

Ch. Randhaven Return of D'LCar (Shafer)

CH. RANDHAVEN RETURN OF D'LCAR

Dog   AKC NO. SB 48827   Whelped: 3/18/71

Owner: Edna Randolph and Merle Bauer, Medford Station, N.Y.

Breeder: Bryon E. Maine, Allamuchy, N.J.

                       Br. Sh. Ch. Deri Darrell of Linkhill

           Gamelad of the Downs

                       Downland Redhead

      Ch. Filicia's Dylan

                       Br. Sh. Ch. and Am. Ch. Trigger of Treg.

           Ch. Randhaven's D'LCAR Gini

                       Ch. Dien Glynis of Randhaven

CH. RANDHAVEN RETURN OF D'LCAR

                       Br. Sh. Ch. and Am. Ch. Trigger of Treg.

           Gary's Jethro of Randhaven

                       Redhead Debutante

      Tara Fina of Bo Forte

                       Ch. Coch Pluen of Randhaven

           Bo Forte's Ballerina

                       Bo Forte's Befana

Ch. Randhaven Return of D'LCar, in nine shows, went Best-of-Breed six times. He finished with a five-point major over two Specials at the Maryland K.C. Show under Judge E.I. Eldridge. With his symbolic name, Randhaven Return has again put the Randolph name into the Welsh Springer Spaniel winners circle.

A well-trained Welsh presenting game to the handler, while another, at attention, watches the action. (Falconer)

Ch. Deckard's Holyhead (Ashbey)

CH. DECKARD'S HOLYHEAD

Bitch   AKC NO. SA-942727   Whelped: 3/18/71

Owner: Jane A Pferd, Mendham, N.J.

Breeder: Bryon E. Maine, Allamuchy, N.J.

<pre>
                          Br. Sh. Ch. Deri Darrell of Linkhill
                  Gamelad of the downs
                          Downland Redhead
          Ch. Filicia's Dylan
                          Br. Sh. Ch. and Am. Ch. Trigger of Treg.
                  Ch. Randhaven's D'LCAR Gini
                          Ch. Dien Glynis of Randhaven
CH. DECKARD'S HOLYHEAD
                          Br. Sh. Ch. and Am. Ch. Trigger of Treg.
                  Gary's Jethro of Randhaven
                          Redhead Debutante
          Tara Fina of Bo Forte
                          Ch. Coch Pluen of Randhaven
                  Bo Forte's Ballerina
                          Bo Forte's Befana
</pre>

Ch. Deckard's Holyhead was first trained for obedience work and serves as a brood bitch (twenty-eight pups) in the Deckard Kennel of Jane A. Pferd. Entering the show ring at four years, she gained her final points at the Twin Brooks KC Show in July 1975 under Judge H.D. Roling, being handled by D.L. Carswell.

Ch. Sylabru Pocketfull of Pennies (Gilbert)

CH. SYLABRU POCKETFUL of PENNIES
Bitch   AKC NO. SB-39076   Whelped: 3/18/71
Owner: Sylvia Foreacre, Glen Mills, Pa.
Breeder: B.E. Maine, Allamuchy, N.J.

                            Br. Sh. Ch. Deri Darrell of Linkhill
                Gamelad of the Downs
                            Downland Redhead
        Ch. Filicia's Dylan
                            Br. Sh. Ch. and Am. Ch. Trigger of Treg.
                Ch. Randhaven's D'LCAR Gini
                            Ch. Dien Glynis of Randhaven
CH. SYLABRU POCKETFUL of PENNIES
                            Br. Sh. Ch. and Am. Ch. Trigger of Treg.
                Gary's Jethro of Randhaven
                            Redhead Debutante
        Tara Fina of Bo Forte
                            Ch. Coch Pluen of Randhaven
                Bo Forte's Ballerina
                            Bo Forte's Befana

Ch. Sylabru's Pocketful of Pennies, one of the four champions sired by
Ch. Filicia's Dylan, has herself had three champions as offspring. Owned
and handled by Sylvia Foreacre, she was finished at the Westminister
K.C. show in February 1973.

Ch. Pickwick's Brychan (Lindstrom)

CH. PICKWICK'S BRYCHAN

Dog   AKC NO. SA-923666   Whelped: 4/15/71

Owner: R.L. Preston, Champbell, Calif.

Breeder: J.K. Seamans, Tarrytown, N.Y.

```
                              Br. Sh. Ch. Plattburn Paramount
                    Plattburn Penrip
                              Br. Sh. Ch. Plattburn Penny
          Plattburn Pickwick
                              Br. Ch. Statesman of Tregwillym
                    Plattburn Playfull
                              Patmyn Pie Powder
CH. PICKWICK's BRYCHAN
                              Plattburn Poacher
                    Plattburn Proclamation
                              Plattburn Poppy
          Ch. Plattburn Primrose
                              Br. Sh. Ch. Plattburn Paramount
                    Plattburn Pretty Peeps
                              Br. Sh. Ch. Plattburn Penny
```

Ch. Pickwick's Brychan was the first Welsh Springer Spaniel to win a championship in the far west, finishing at the Lizard Butte KC show in May 1973. He went on to win over fifty BOBs, was named the Top Welsh Spaniel of 1973 and was awarded the Welsh Springer Spaniel Club of America Deckard's Cup as the 1974 Dog of the Year.

Ch. Gwilym of Brent (Stonham)

CH. GWILYM of BRENT

Dog   AKC NO. SB-212651   Whelped: 6/5/71

Owner: Sylvia Foreacre, Glen Mills, Pa.

Breeder: Mrs. D. Perkins, N. Rugby, Warks, G.B.

Plattburn Poacher
Plattburn Proclamation
Plattburn Poppy
Br. Sh. Ch. Plattburn Progressor
Br. Sh. Ch. Plattburn Paramount
Plattburn Penelope
Br. Sh. Ch. Plattburn Penny
CH. GWILYM of BRENT
Benefactor of Brent
Br. Sh. Ch. Bruce of Brent
Bronwyn Trixie
Rhiannon of Brent
Br. Ch. Brancourt Bang
Gwyneth Bach of Brent
Gwyn Coch Cora

Ch. Gwilym of Brent, an English import from the Brent Kennel, was the fifth champion to be owned and handled by Mrs. Sylvia Foreacre. He gained his championship at the Carroll County KC show in July 1973, under Judge Stevenson.

Ch. Pickwick's Dylan (Shafer)

CH. PICKWICK'S DYLAN

Dog   AKC NO. SB-97241   Whelped: 4/8/72

Owner: Jane K. Seamans, Dobbs Ferry, N.Y.

Breeder: Jane K. Seamans, Dobbs Ferry, N.Y.

```
                            Br. Sh. Ch. Plattburn Paramount
                   Plattburn Pickwick
                            Br. Sh. Ch. Plattburn Penny
          Plattburn Pickwick
                            Br. Ch. Statesman of Tregwillym
                   Plattburn Playfull
                            Patmyn Pie Powder
CH. PICKWICK'S DYLAN
                            Plattburn Poacher
                   Plattburn Proclamation
                            Plattburn Poppy
          Ch. Plattburn Primrose
                            Br. Sh. Ch. Plattburn Paramount
                   Plattburn Pretty Peeps
                            Br. Sh. Ch. Plattburn Penny
```

Ch. Pickwick's Dylan was the first of the Seamans champions and of the same breeding as Ch. Pickwick's Brychan, who was awarded the Deckard's Cup for 1974. Dylan gained his last major at the Penn Treaty K.C. show in April 1974, under Judge Laytham.

Ch. Pencelli Rhyl (Gilbert)

CH. PENCELLI RHYL

Bitch   AKC NO. SB-192100   Whelped: 4/13/72

Owner: Cynthia Foreacre, Glen Mills, Pa.

Breeder: T. Hubert-Authur, Carmarthen, Wales

```
                          Benefactor of Brent
                  Br. Sh. Ch. Bruce of Brent
                          Bronwyn Trixie
          Br. Sh. Ch. Roger of Pencelli
                          Priory Major
                  Br. Sh. Ch. Marie of Pencelli
                          Bonny Legend
  CH. PENCELLI RHYL
                          Br. Ch. Statesman of Tregwillym
                  Gamefeather Brandy Snap
                          Br. Sh. Ch. Gamefeather Siani
          Br. Sh. Ch. Freesia of Hearts
                          Br. Ch. Statesman of Tregwillym
                  Br. Sh. Ch. Fashionplate of Hearts
                          Br. Ch. Brancourt Belinda
```

Ch. Pencelli Rhyl was handled to her championship by "Cindy" Foreacre who has the honor of being the youngest owner-handler of a champion Welsh. They gained their final major at the National Capitol K.C. show in March 1974.

Ch. Sylabru's Penny Candy (Bennett)

CH. SYLABRU'S PENNY CANDY

Bitch AKC NO. SB-114607 Whelped: 5/27/72

Owner: R.L. Preston, Campbell, Calif.

Breeder: S. Foreacre, Glen Mills, Pa.

```
                        Gamelad of the Downs
              Ch. Filicia's Dylan
                        Ch. Randhaven's D'LCAR Gini
       Am. and Can. Ch. Sylabru's Cimri Aberystwyth
              Ch. Filicia's Dylan
       Ch. Sylabru's Copper Ibitz, C.D.
                        Iolanthe of Broomleaf
CH. SYLABRU'S PENNY CANDY
                        Gamelad of the Downs
              Ch. Filicia's Dylan
                        Ch. Randhaven's D'LCAR Gini
       Ch. Sylabru Pocketful of Pennies
                        Gary's Jethro of Randhaven
              Tara Fina of Bo Forte
                        Bo Forte's Ballerina
```

Ch. Sylabru's Penny Candy, of champion parents both sired by Champion Filicia's Dylan, was an easy winner on the California circuit in 1973. She was the first Welsh Spaniel bitch to gain a championship in the far west, being finished at the San Joaquin KC show in November 1973, under Judge Gilliland.

Ch. Pencelli Pandour

CH. PENCELLI PANDOUR

Bitch   AKC NO. SB 59501   Whelped: 7/29/73
Owner: Kenneth D. McCullough, Westfield, N.J.
Breeder: Harold Newman, Treorchy, Mid Glamorgan, Wales.

```
                             Benefactor of Brent
                   Br. Sh. Ch. Bruce of Brent
                             Bronwyn Trixie
           Br. Sh. Ch. Roger of Pencelli
                             Priory Major
                   Br. Sh. Ch. Marie of Pencelli
                             Bonny Legend
CH. PENCELLI PANDOUR
                             Plattburn Proclamation
                   Br. Sh. Ch. Plattburn Progressor
                             Plattburn Penelope
           Paula Girl of Pencelli
                             Priory Major
                   Br. Sh. Ch. Marie of Pencelli
                             Bonny Legend
```

Ch. Pencelli Pandour, an import from the kennel of Harold Newman, gained her final points with a five point major at the Kennel Club of Philadelphia Dog Show on December 6, 1975 under the International Judge George W.R. Couzens. "Mena" was trained and shown to her championship by Junior Handler Linda McCullough.

Ch. Deckard's Sir Barnye (Ashbey)

CH. DECKARD'S SIR BARNYE

Dog   AKC NO. SB 485490   Whelped: 2/6/74
Owner: Kenneth D. McCullough, Westfield, N.J.
Breeder: Jane A. Pferd, Mendham, N.J.

Priory Major
Ch. Bachgen Dewr of Pencelli
Bonny Legend
Sir Henry Cardiff
Ch. Filicia's Dylan
Deckard's Holyhead
Tara Fina of Bo Forte
CH. DECKARD'S SIR BARNYE
Monarch of Granville
Daniel of Tregwillym
Red Rocket
Krackton Rare Sequin
Sportsman of Tregwillym
Trealvi Jessica
Br. Sh. Ch. Lady of Llangarna

Ch. Deckard's Sir Barnye was the first Welsh Springer Spaniel in the McCullough family and was handled to his championship by his owner. Sir Barnye started his show career with the Best Puppy in Match at the W.S.S. Club of America 1974 show and finished at the Suffolk County KC Show in September 1975 with a fourth major.

9
YOUR PET FOR SHOW
AND HUNTING

Most books about a breed of dog contain pages and pages and words and words about the subject contained in this chapter. It has been my experience that most are never read and, worst of all, when finally, in desperation, one wants to find the answer to a question, why of course, one never can. All those words seem to get in the way and the instructions are lost in extra verbiage. No doubt these thoughts have offended some of the readers of this book but, those of you so inclined, please press on, for I hope that you too will be satisfied. I believe that some things should and must be read, history and commentary for example, other things should be looked at, like pictures of Welsh Springer Spaniels and even their handlers, owners, and judges, but the identification and use of what is principally instructional material is best presented in ways that are "easy to use." This has been the goal in preparing this chapter and the variety of subjects that are included. Tracing the types of associations between you and your pet gives a format for subjects that will be of interest during your days and years together. Some of the more important follow and for those who wish to read further and enjoy the full pciture with their Welsh, please consult the recommended texts in the "Guide to Further Study."

DOG REGISTRATION PROCEDURES

At the Time of Purchase of Your Puppy or Dog, OBTAIN:
1 – A blue American Kennel Club Application form so you can register your puppy, or
2 – An endorsed individual American Kennel Club registration certificate transferring ownership to you, or
3 – A signed bill of sale if papers are not available at the moment you obtain your pup or dog, plus
4 – A written contract if restrictions are placed on future breeding or stud use (See American Kennel Club Registration Rules Section 6).

Before Accepting the Papers Examine Them For:
1 – Completeness and Accuracy.
2 – Separate certification by each person who owned the dog previously.
3 – Changes or erasures. Each must be initialed by the person required to complete the changed portion.

Before Accepting a Bill of Sale, Examine it for Statements of:
1 – Dog Breed – Welsh Springer Spaniel or Spaniel (Welsh Springer)
2 – Sex
3 – Coat Color
4 – Date of Birth
5 – Names of Sire and Dam
6 – Name and Address of Breeder
7 – Litter Registration Number, if registered.
8 – Full refund provision if proper papers are not forthcoming within a specified period.

At Home the Next Day:
1 – Mail application to the American Kennel Club to register your dog or to record transfer of ownership.

Sometime Later:
1 – Obtain at least a three generation pedigree from the breeder or the Kennel Club.
2 – Make a few copies of your dog's official registration certificate.
3 – Obtain Litter Registration Forms before breeding.

HOUSEBREAKING YOUR PUPPY

Things To Remember:

1 — Use the million-year-old instinct of your den-dwelling pup to keep his box clean and to be trained.
2 — Have his new box ready when he arrives.
3 — Never forget to carry your pup out-of-doors immediately when he leaves his box, no matter what the weather.
4 — Expect success after one week.
5 — Make his box his permanent home, no matter where he visits.

His Den:

1 — Construct a box with a wire lid or purchase a wire or plastic transport cage for the puppy's den.
2 — For a Welsh, have the den fifteen inches wide, thirty inches long, and twenty inches high.
3 — Partition off the back half until the puppy is trained.
4 — Make the den just big enough for the puppy to turn about in or lie at full length, but no longer.
5 — Have a secure lid or door so that he can not get out.
6 — Use a piece of rug as bedding.

The Training Process:

1 — From the first, day naps and nightime sleep should be taken in the box.
2 — Keep the puppy in his box at all times except to go out-of-doors, to eat, to drink, and to play.
3 — Place his box in the kitchen.
4 — Select a spot where he will always relieve himself in or out-of-doors.
5 — ALWAYS take him to his spot—before and after meals.
    —when he awakes from a nap.
    —first thing in the morning.
    —after all meals.
    —last thing at night.
6 — Compliment him when he goes on his spot.
7 — After mistakes, scold him and take him to his spot.
8 — Clean up with ammonia solution on linoleum. On rugs, use club soda to neutralize urine and to stop staining.

9 — Use his den as his permanent home, he'll love it.

10 — Puppies can stay up to eight hours in their den if properly relieved before hand.

11 — For apartment dwellers, the spot can be a piece of newspaper in the bathroom as well as a place out-of-doors.

LIVING WITH YOUR PUPPY

Plan In Advance—

To keep your dog in a house, either yours of his.

To take your dog on escorted walks, regularly.

To have him checked for worms.

To have protective shots at ten to twelve weeks of age.

To know about registration papers.

Preparing His Outdoor Pen—

Have it ready when he arrives.

For a Welsh, make it four feet wide and eight feet long.

Make it six foot high, and cover if he is a jumper.

Fencing should be of steel and have a gate.

Surface the pen with concrete, bricks or round gravel.

Have a water outlet near for cleaning and drinking.

Preparing His Outdoor House—

Have it ready when he arrives.

For a Welsh, make it eighteen inches wide and thirty inches long.

Shield the entrance with a baffle to stop drafts.

Hinge the top for easy cleaning.

Have the floor at least two inches off the ground.

Provide an overhang at the door to stop the rain.

Provide a sloping roof.

Insulate the walls in cold climates.

If He Lives In Your House—

He will be happier and learn faster, even if a hunter.

Provide an overhead wire with slip ring as a run.

Provide a box or cage for his den.

Schedule play periods and outdoor walks.

Feed your dog a modest diet.

IN SICKNESS AND IN HEALTH

Welsh Spring Spaniels are a surprisingly hardy breed and it is rare that one hears of illness or a lack of vitality. Of course, the particular temperament of the dog will vary from extreme activity in youth to a more sedate manner that could be the character of some dogs throughout their life. The recommendations that follow are for conditions that most owners will experience during a portion of the dog's life and are considered to be routine. All other illnesses or discomforts experienced by the dog should be treated by your veterinarian.

Dog won't eat — Try a change in feed, at least twice. Welsh can get along on a light diet of one meal a day and should be on the thin side and never more than fifty pounds in weight.

Fleas — Nothing helps like a flea collar.

Ticks — A collar helps, but first spray the yard and bushes with *Sevan.* Also jerk ticks off dog with fingers. Dispose of tick in toilet.

Worming — Can be done routinely for puppies with purchased medication. If suspected in dogs, have the vet check a stool. Have a yearly blood test for heart worm prevention.

Foreign Bodies In Mouth — If dog is pawing at mouth, pull out dog's tongue and look in. Use fingers to feel for object and pull it out.

Minor Cuts — Remove surrounding hair, cleanse with mild soap and water, swab with a diluted tincture of merthiolate. Your dog will take over from there.

Shedding — Kennel-housed dogs will shed once a year starting in May. House dogs shed all the time — due to their exposure to home lighting.

Anal Gland Accumulation — Seat dragging by dog indicates discomfort. With the thumb and second finger behind and slightly below the anal glands, force out smelly yellow liquid. Do it out-of-doors!

Ear Scratching — Clean with cotton swab soaked in alcohol to dissolve wax and dirt. Apply a drop of mineral oil into the ear channel or swab with calomine lotion.

Feet chewing — Due to long nails, a thorn, excess hair between pads, or most likely ticks or fleas that can be removed by dust or spray.

Bad Breath — Use dry food for two months — if it persists, see vet.

Hairless Spots — Due to sleeping on hard surface such as concrete or linoleum. Apply psoriasis medication on bare spot and provide a deep pile rug or mat as a sleeping surface for your dog.

Dry Coat — Add one tablespoon of linoleic acid food supplement to daily meal.

Gray Hair — For that youthful appearance, stain graying hair with strong tea.

GROOMING YOUR WELSH SPRINGER SPANIEL

Compared to many breeds, the Welsh Springer is easy to maintain. One advantage is that his coat is self-cleaning. He can become completely covered with mud but when he dries, the dirt falls away without any trace of odor, and a simple combing restores his coat to its natural flat and glossy appearance. Since his coat is thick but not long, grooming consists of only an occasional brushing and trimming of excess hair from his feet and ears to a natural shape. Trimming excess hair from his tail and clipping his whiskers and toe nails takes care of the end-points. The grooming of a Welsh Springer Spaniel is not a time-consuming task and results in a healthy bloom, which is very attractive and sure to gain compliments from your friends and even from strangers as you pass them in your trips to town. Preparing your dog for the show ring will mean a somewhat more careful effort, which should start well before showtime. For guidance in this task and for some everyday grooming tips follow the steps given here:

1. Avoid a barbered look by starting several weeks before show time to groom a bit at a time in stages.
2. Let the dog run about once or twice during the grooming period to observe your progress.
3. Use a grooming table with chock leash to save your back and to control the dog.
4. Fine-comb carefully all the short body coat to remove dead and loose hair.
5. Fine-comb the top of the skull and back of the neck to thin and smooth the coat.
6. Use a larger mesh comb sparingly for thinning the feathering on the ears, legs, and under the body so as to leave as much fringe as possible.
7. Thin the outside of the legs, removing extra and discolored hair to produce a neat appearance.
8. Thin the abundant frill of hair on the front and sides of the neck and down the chest with the finger and thumb or with the aid of a stripping knife.
9. Remove with a thinning scissors the unwanted hair from the underside of the ears and side of the head to allow the ears to fall closer to the skull.
10. Remove wild or stray hairs on the ears and shoulders with a stripping knife or your fingers.
11. Use a stripping knife or thinning scissors to remove excess hair from around the anus and from between the hind legs.

12. Remove excess hair with a curved blunt scissors from the tail and round the end.
13. With a curved scissors cut out the hair between the pads and the matted hair between the toes to give a cat's paw appearance.
14. Cut toe nails as short as possible without cutting down into the quick with a guillotine-type cutter.
15. Groom with a hound glove or brush to smooth the coat and raise stray hairs that should be removed.
16. Wash the dog, if needed, at least three days before showtime to permit the coat to regain its sleek glossy appearance.
17. Remove whiskers the day of the show with a curved blunt scissors.

SOCIAL TRAINING OR "GOOD DOG!"

Your Welsh Springer Spaniel has natural, inherited characteristics that will gain him praise and get him into trouble, unless you help. From eight weeks he learns rapidly, either what he picks up on his own, or things you wish him to know. He can be spoiled or he can be trained! Do not wait until he is bigger — start now. A "socialized" Welsh Springer should enjoy a life that contains the following restrictions:

1. No lunging at people.
2. No jumping on people.
3. No uncontrolled barking.
4. No biting.
5. No dashing off wildly unless he follows the command "Come."

For simple social training you will need a few aides for all beginning lessons and for refresher sessions later.

- Choke collar (Puppy — fourteen inches, Dog — twenty-four inches)
- Long thin leather lead (six feet)
- Tidbits
- Praise

Dogs that are allowed always to run freely can hardly be trained. Walk your dog regularly while restrained with the choke collar and lead. Position the dog on your left, keep him on a shortened lead, and give it a "jerk" to move him close to your side. Of course give him full lead when he wishes to relieve himself. Walk near or through groups of people, giving him a sharp "jerk" if he lunges toward any child or adult. Many people will instinctively try to pet or talk to the dog. Typically, the dog will rush toward or jump on the person. Now this is your

Hackwood Echo, trained by Mrs. Eileen Falconer of Ascot, Berkshire, making a perfect up-and-over retrieve of a bird during a cold game test. (Falconer)

Freckles II at two years—an experienced Welsh Springer Spaniel from the Deckard Kennel who was trained by her owner, Mr. Jack L. Dumbleton of Geneva, New York. (Dumbleton)

American Champion Deckard's Holyhead, right, and British Show C.C. winner Krackton Rare Sequin, left, brood bitches at the Deckard Kennel. (Pferd)

Painting by Maud Earl in 1906 considered to be the best portrayel ever painted of Welsh Springer Spaniels. The two springers, Ch. Longmynd Calon Fach, 1823L, and Ch. Longmynd Megan, 1140K, belonged to Mrs. Greene. (Kennel Club)

chance. A sharply sounding "No" and a "jerk" is given immediately followed by a "Good Dog" command and a pat as the dog settles down. Treat barking in the same manner, a sharp "No" with a "jerk." Do these things whenever or wherever your dog lunges, jumps, or barks at people when on a lead. The "No" should be loud and terse. The "jerk" should be sharp and produce mild discomfort. The words "Good Dog" should convey pleasure and friendship. These simple instructions will produce a dog that knows his first three "Nos"—No lunging, no jumping, and no barking.

The desire to bite and chew must be controlled, yet they are natural acts that your new puppy will also do instinctively. For these to cease, your dog must sense discomfort at the source, which is his mouth. Dogs dislike a whack under the chin or on the nose since it jars the teeth, can pinch the tongue, and forces the head back against the neck. He will soon associate biting or chewing with the receiving of mild rebuke near his mouth if you tap the palm of your hand against his nose sharply when he is chewing or nipping and if you chuck him sharply under the chin with your hand when he bites. Start when he is a puppy and he will be a gentleman dog. Bumping the nose of a puppy also cures jumping up on a person when off the lead. Don't forget to say "No" when you bump his nose or wack his chin. There is no need to say "Good Dog" here. Since chewing or biting is still fun for your dog, even when trained, buy him a toy that he can work over to his heart's content.

The last "No" cure for a socially adjusted dog really makes the two of you a civilized team. A dog who dashes wildly, ignores his owner, and chases people or cars is an embarrassment and a menace. A good free run in the park is fine, but is even better when followed by strict adherence to the command, "Come." To gain this type of relationship with your dog requires bribery and praise on your part, which is applied best at the height of your walk with your dog under control on his choke collar and lead. Go out before he has eaten and is hungry to a large open area. Drop the lead to the ground but do not unclip it from his collar. He will move off a lead length, about six feet. Call "Hynaf!. . . Come!" Pause briefly between his name and the command to get your dog's attention. Show him the tidbit. If necessary pull him toward you with the lead and give him the reward with lots of loud praising, "Good Dog!" Do this only two or three times at the beginning of training, gradually building up to longer distances and more tests, but always before dinner and end on a successful "Come" with lavish praise and the tasty reward.

It may take a full year of your attention to his brief lessons before you are completely confident that your dog has learned his "social

Nos." It will be fun, a success, and an achievement for you and your "Good Dog," which will amaze your friends.

SO YOU WANT TO "SHOW" YOUR DOG

You may have bought your dog with an eye toward showing or you may be so proud of the beauty of your Welsh Springer that you decide that you want to show your dog. In either case, study of the many pictures in this book that show Welsh Springer Spaniels in the ring or just after receiving their championship awards should be helpful in your decision-making. If you think that your dog satisfies the standards set forth for the breed at the back of this book and looks very much like one or another of the past champions, then you have good reason to learn about grooming and training your dog for the show ring. By the age of nine months, your dog will have filled out to permit judgments to be made about his conformation, and by one year his growth will be essentially completed for show purposes. Only his weight will increase with age. For a dog who meets these tests, the award of champion could be gained within another year.

Champion status in the United States and Britain are obtained by different rules. The American Kennel Club requires that your Welsh win fifteen points to become a Champion of Record; six or more points must be won at two shows with three or more points each and under two different judges; the remaining points must be won under other judges. Points are recorded equivalent to the number of eligible dogs competing in the classes of each sex. In Great Britain, the title of Show Champion is attached by the Kennel Club to any gundog awarded three Challenge Certificates under three different judges, provided at least one of the Challenge Certificates was awarded when the dog was more than twelve months of age. The C.C. is awarded to the Best of Sex exhibit provided the judge is clearly of the opinion that the dog is worthy of the title of Champion.

The Welsh Springer Spaniel, as a member of the Gundog or Sporting Dog Group, can qualify for even higher honors by also competing in field trials and gaining awards that permit the title of a dual-purpose champion. In Britain, after obtaining a Qualifying Certificate under Kennel Club Field Trial Regulations or Awards of Merit at authorized Field Trials, a Show Champion is henceforth recorded as a Champion, while in the United States, after winning an Open All-Age Stake at a field trial licensed by the American Kennel Club, the dog will be recorded as a Field Champion and may be designated as "Dual Champion." This title has not yet been gained by a Welsh Springer

Spaniel in the United States, but eighteen have been awarded their Champion title in Great Britain since 1945.

The showing of dogs for most people is a sporting event and a form of entertainment. For the serious owner or professional, it is an opportunity to promote the breed and gain an independent judgement on the quality of the entry. The cost is to pay for the judge's opinion. Since fees and expenses will be about twenty-five dollars per exhibit plus at least an equal amount for the services of a professional handler—it is sport to enter with forethought. Much can be achieved by entering first those matches and shows that offer prizes and ribbons but lack the awarding of points or C.Cs necessary for championship status. The costs are nominal and the experience invaluable, both for you and your dog. Training sessions sponsored by local dog clubs or schools, usually held on weekday evenings, can provide the basic skills of handling. For you and your dog, showing must be fun and a challenge. A top showdog loves to go into the ring and move with spirit and style. Visit a championship show or two and see how it is done. Training toward this end should start during puppyhood, but can be learned at any time as shown by the record of some champions who gained the title after first entering the ring at three years. Set up your puppy and walk him a short distance on a show lead once a day. This should be a fun time so never, never "jerk" the dog when on the show lead. After some weeks take him for a short walk on his show lead among crowds and noises of all kinds since he must be confident in the circuslike atmosphere of the dog show. With an early start, a course with an experienced handler and a few turns at a local match show, you and your dog will be ready for the big time!

IN THE OBEDIENCE RING

While your dog's conformation is all important in the show ring and his instincts are the controlling factor in field work, a third characteristic—intelligence—dominates his working and obedience manner. A smart dog is helpful for show and hunting roles, but to gain high honors in working trials or the obedience ring, it is an essential condition. In many respects, similarities exist in the tasks performed by the field and working Welsh Springer Spaniel, but the pace, setting, and the duration of the events are radically different. Both are classed as sports for the dog and handler but with quite different objectives. Yet obedience or working is considered by many to lay a foundation for the training of a field dog and also to reinforce field work during off season for the experienced hunting spaniel. Clearly, obedience training is a sport open to all who live in city surroundings and lack either the place or inclination to hunt or to train their dogs. The number of participants has grown hugely since its inception during the early 1930s, testimony to the pleasure and satisfaction that dog training and testing affords dogs owners. A dog from an obedience school is a better dog by far, even if he barely graduates. He is no doubt socially acceptable, reasonably mindful, responsive to commands from his owner, and accustomed to working around other handlers and their dogs. If he graduated with "honors," he is sure to win a Companion Dog (C.D.) Award under Obedience Show conditions and may even be able to go on to gain higher awards if his owner is motivated to enter the obedience ring.

But what accomplishments are necessary to gain these obedience degrees? Just as there are differences in requirements for gaining champion awards in Great Britain and the United States, so also are there differences in this field. Briefly, the degrees are earned by mastering the following:

Great Britain
(Kennel Club Rules)

Companion Dog (C.D.)

1. Heel on Leash
2. Heel Free
3. Sit (two Minutes)
4. Recall to Handler
5. Sending Dog Away
6. Down ten Minutes
7. Agility Jumps
8. Retrieving Dumbbell
9. Elementary Search

Utility Dog (U.D.)

1. Heel free
2. Drop on Order (twenty yrds.)
3. Retrieving Dumbbell
4. Long Down (ten Minutes)
5. Steadiness to Gunshot
6. Scale Wall (six ft.)
7. Clear Jump (three ft.)
8. Long Jump (nine ft.)
9. Search (twenty-five yrds.)
10. Leash Track (½ mile)

United States
(American Kennel Club Rules)

Companion Dog (C.D.) — Open

1. Heel Free
2. Drop on Recall
3. Retrieve on Flat
4. Retrieve over High Jump
5. Broad Jump
6. Long Sit (one minute)
7. Long Down (three minutes)

Utility Dog (U.D.)

1 Signal Exercise
2. Scent Discrimination (No. 1)
3. Scent Discrimination (No. 2)
4. Directed Retrieve
5. Directed Jump
6. Stand Alone Examination

A candid assessment leads to the view that the British standards are more demanding and more closely related to hunting activity. Such tasks as "recall," "sending away," "steadiness to gun," and "searching" are not found in the American tests yet, surely, must be accomplishments of a trained field dog and a hunting spaniel in particular. Beyond these degrees in both countries there are programs for the more devoted fancier. Working, Tracking and Police Dog Titles are awarded for more specialized accomplishments that require your dog to demonstrate exceptional skill in obedience to command and patterns of behavior. Whether you go on to such heights of achievement with your dog or just squeek through to gain his C.D., it will be fun, and you and your dog will meet a fine group of new friends and companions.

THE HUNTING SPRINGER SPANIEL

A perfectly trained Welsh Springer Spaniel:
- hunts eagerly, silently and with drive,
- works close-in and never tires,
- is not gun-shy when off the lead,
- willingly faces cover of brush, woods, and briar,
- is equally at home in water and in the field,
- is always under control and responds to signals,

- never barks, chases, or catches unwanted game,
- stops to game and shot automatically,
- shows a game marking ability,
- retrieves on command all small game quickly and tenderly,
- delivers the game well up to the hand of the trainer.

But of course there are few if any perfect dogs, or owners for that matter, so we usually settle for less, and in the case of the working spaniel it is for the sportsman to have a dog that quite simply and consistently can:

1. seek and flush game
2. drop to shot
3. retrieve on command
4. perform in a merry and active manner.

It is entirely possible to train your Welsh Springer to do these things as shown by the record of the British Champions and the pictures of Welsh in various acts of hunting within this book. Just as your spaniel can be trained for show and obedience work, so can he be trained to work in the field on a hunt. Of the three sports, field training is the most demanding for the dog and owner since it requires the dog to display intelligence and keenly developed instincts. Most spaniels possess these in abundance, but the better working dog will also exhibit at an early age a willingness to pay attention and reasonable emotions. These last are seen in the expression of your dog and a desire to almost talk or read your mind. While instincts may be present, often they are dormant and must be aroused by the trainer. The entire process of training is one of gradualism. Starting as a pup, it will take eighteen months to reach a level of performance that could lead to qualifying or Field Champion Status — in all cases, to a level that will permit great satisfaction as a hunting companion.

All strains of Welsh Springer Spaniels seem to take naturally to gun work, but it is prudent to choose your pup from among those with working parents. While the finely tuned dog and field champion is a joy to the owner, it also takes an amount of time not usually available for most sportsmen. As Mr. Jack Dumbleton, an experienced Welsh Springer man, said in a recent letter to the author, "I'm not a fancy hunter. I do it for leisurely enjoyment and I train my own dogs. I think the Welshman is a very easy dog to train if you set up a routine and spend a little time at it each day." As little as ten to fifteen minutes a day with your puppy will produce ample progress. By six months, more serious training in the field can begin. While opinions differ on this point, there are many Welsh house pets trained to be good steady hunters and not relegated to a closed kennel to sharpen their interest.

Early training should start with a training dummy and bird scent in or near the house with activity in the field as the dog gains in experience and ability. Training to "come" and "sit" should be followed by learning to "stay," exercises exactly like those to be learned by any Welsh with good social manners or one destined for the obedience ring. If you wish, training with hand signals or a silent whistle can then commence based on following the "sit" command prior to giving new direction signals. At five to six months, a blank starting pistol can be used at a distance to introduce your dog to shot, which should go well if you have toughened your pup to noises by hand clapping and food dish banging during earlier weeks. By one year he should be able to hunt well between five and twenty yards away from you in semicircular patterns. He will most likely pick scents from the air, working cover carefully with few misses of game. Tail action will be a guide to the closeness of game, going faster when game is found. He will not balk at dense cover or ditches and most will enter water fearlessly. The Welsh is classed as a general purpose gundog, good with pheasant, rabbit, grouse and duck, and also used to advantage for across water retrieves. He has ancient instincts and temperament designed for the hunt and a coat color easy to see in the field. All that is lacking is the response to commands that patience and skill on the part of the owner can instill in the dog to make the "perfectly trained Welsh Springer Spaniel."

MARRIAGE IS A SERIOUS BUSINESS

This essay will help those owners of bitches who for fun or profit decide to mate their Welsh Springer and, hopefully, have a litter of fine pups. The number of registerd bitches who enter the marriage circle is surprisingly small, both in total and as a percentage of bitches born each year. Since the number is limited, it is particularly important that some care be given to the choosing of the mate, as well as the decision to breed a particular bitch. Typically, the bitch has a delightful personality since it would be a rare owner or professional breeder who would be motivated to mate a bitch that exhibits offensive behavior patterns. Additionally, she might demonstrate fine field work and fill the role of aide to hunting members of the family. If she had a successful show career or has conformation that fits the standard as well, then all of the reasons for mating this bitch prevail—temperament, instincts, and beauty. The choice of the mate is the next serious issue the breeder must face.

Many people have spent great efforts in trying to find the right male and female combination to raise the perfect litter. All too often they are disappointed. More logically the goal should be a fine healthy litter, uniform in appearance and perky in disposition. But even here there will be disappointments as differences from pup to pup appear through the workings of heredity. There are two basic laws that control the results of breeding: the Law of Similarity and the Law of Dominance. The first means simply that the offspring will possess a combination of the sire's and dam's characteristics in varying degrees. The second explains why two champions do not necessarily get a third. Each dog possesses unseen weak characteristics, and if mated to a champion with one or more of the same dormant characteristics, a certain percentage of these weaknesses will be transferred. Since male and female each contribute one-half the chromosomes, and the genes in the chromosomes combine in pairs, the sum of the offspring's characteristics is indeed a changy business, with different results to be expected each time. Fortunately, greater control occurs when the dog and bitch come from stock that possess the same desirable qualities. This is especially true where certain characteristics such as good scenting ability, intelligence, or good conformation have been evident over a period of three or four generations. It can be assumed that these qualities are fixed in the line and the controlling genes will be dominant when bred. Clearly, the choice of male is crucial.

When ready to choose a mate, first identify the desirable and undesirable characteristics of the bitch and select a stud with qualities that will offset the dam's weak points. If both sire and dam are deficient in the same way, the breeding should not take place, but the search should continue for a more complimentary stud. With two or more studs available, questions about outcrossing, line-breeding, or inbreeding will arise. These terms cover the range of matings from unrelated lineage to close relatives. In-breeding involves close mating, such as father and daughter, or son to mother, and should never be undertaken unless the stock is absolutely sound in all ways. More typically, line-breeding is followed, which consists of the mating of relatives with common ancestors appearing in the second, third or fourth generation, or outcrossing, the mating of totally unrelated dogs. Whichever system is used, it is necessary to have knowledge of the ancestry through pictures or personal encounter of the lineage through two generations. Additionally, judgments regarding subtle physical features of the stud are important. While Welsh Springer Spaniels have breed classification and are of ancient origin, there is typing within the breed as the result of conscientious effort by owners to breed to the standard. Being a prose statement, the standard is subject to some personal interpretation that manifests itself in the breeding of dogs that have distinguishing appearnace factors. These subtle line-breeding features should be understood in planning the mating.

In summary, the business of marriage starts with a good young bitch and a search for an acceptable stud. Family relationships should be studied along with pictures and visits to see the relatives are in order. When all else fails and mating time is fast approaching, the best decision may be just that — mate the best to the best and then sit back and hope for the best. Good luck in your quest for future champions!

WHELPING CARE — BEFORE AND AFTER

Whelping Box — At least two by three feet with torn newspapers as bedding.

Grooming — Remove long hair around breasts, stomach, and around the vulva.

Whelping — At the onset, the bitch becomes uneasy, shows restlessness, pants, and has a rather anxious expression. She goes to her bed, begins to scratch and tear at the bedding and attempts to make a nest. This can last for twelve to twenty-four hours.

— True labor is characterized by purposeful straining. Normally, the sac containing the puppy soon protrudes, followed by a few forceful, expulsive efforts that usually produces the pup along with the placental membrane. The mother removes the placenta from around the puppy, chews the umbilical cord, and usually eats the membranes. She then licks the puppy dry, which stimulates breathing.

— Young or tired mothers may need help. If the sac is not broken within fifteen seconds, tear it with your fingernail, otherwise the puppy will smother in the air-tight sac.

— To revive the pup, snip off with a blunt scissors the naval cord about ¼ inch from the body and rub the pup vigorously in a towel until it begins to struggle.

— The bitch will rest for ten to sixty minutes between deliveries. When labor is finished and all the pups (four to eleven) are delivered, the bitch will lie quietly and let the puppies nurse.

— To ensure survival of the pups during whelping, keep all but one pup in an electric blanket-lined basket while the mother is still delivering.

— Call Veterinarian
   If no pup is delivered after one hour of straining;
   If a greenish-black discharge appears before any pups are whelped;
   If you're worried.

Diet — Offer milk and dog food after the birth of a few puppies at intervals during whelping, since the labor can carry over many hours (three to six).

Following Whelping — The mother should be exercised outside long enough to relieve herself. Manually carry out the bitch if she refuses to leave the puppies.

The Next Day — Take mother to your veterinarian to determine if all pups and afterbirths are out of the uterus and to have medication.

The Third or Fourth Day — Dock tails at the second joint after the taper begins, about ½ the tail, by cutting with a sharp scissors and swabbing the end with powdered permanganate of potash. Remove all dew claws in a similar manner, as close as possible to the leg.

WELPING CALENDER

Most puppies will be born 62 days after the bitch is mated. This whelping calendar makes it easier to determine the date to expect the birth of a litter. Simply read the "due date" below the date of mating.

Mated / Due	Day numbers (mated = top row, due = bottom row)	Due
January	1 2 3 4 5 6 7 8 9 10 11 12 13 14 15 16 17 18 19 20 21 22 23 24 25 26 27 28 29 30 31	
March	5 6 7 8 9 10 11 12 13 14 15 16 17 18 19 20 21 22 23 24 25 26 27 28 29 30 31 1 2 3 4	April
February	1 2 3 4 5 6 7 8 9 10 11 12 13 14 15 16 17 18 19 20 21 22 23 24 25 26 27 28	
April	5 6 7 8 9 10 11 12 13 14 15 16 17 18 19 20 21 22 23 24 25 26 27 28 29 30 1 2	May
March	1 2 3 4 5 6 7 8 9 10 11 12 13 14 15 16 17 18 19 20 21 22 23 24 25 26 27 28 29 30 31	
May	3 4 5 6 7 8 9 10 11 12 13 14 15 16 17 18 19 20 21 22 23 24 25 26 27 28 29 30 31 1 2	June
April	1 2 3 4 5 6 7 8 9 10 11 12 13 14 15 16 17 18 19 20 21 22 23 24 25 26 27 28 29 30	
June	3 4 5 6 7 8 9 10 11 12 13 14 15 16 17 18 19 20 21 22 23 24 25 26 27 28 29 30 1 2	July
May	1 2 3 4 5 6 7 8 9 10 11 12 13 14 15 16 17 18 19 20 21 22 23 24 25 26 27 28 29 30 31	
July	3 4 5 6 7 8 9 10 11 12 13 14 15 16 17 18 19 20 21 22 23 24 25 26 27 28 29 30 31 1 2	August
June	1 2 3 4 5 6 7 8 9 10 11 12 13 14 15 16 17 18 19 20 21 22 23 24 25 26 27 28 29 30	
August	3 4 5 6 7 8 9 10 11 12 13 14 15 16 17 18 19 20 21 22 23 24 25 26 27 28 29 30 31 1	September
July	1 2 3 4 5 6 7 8 9 10 11 12 13 14 15 16 17 18 19 20 21 22 23 24 25 26 27 28 29 30 31	
September	2 3 4 5 6 7 8 9 10 11 12 13 14 15 16 17 18 19 20 21 22 23 24 25 26 27 28 29 30 1 2	October
August	1 2 3 4 5 6 7 8 9 10 11 12 13 14 15 16 17 18 19 20 21 22 23 24 25 26 27 28 29 30 31	
October	3 4 5 6 7 8 9 10 11 12 13 14 15 16 17 18 19 20 21 22 23 24 25 26 27 28 29 30 31 1 2	November
September	1 2 3 4 5 6 7 8 9 10 11 12 13 14 15 16 17 18 19 20 21 22 23 24 25 26 27 28 29 30	
November	3 4 5 6 7 8 9 10 11 12 13 14 15 16 17 18 19 20 21 22 23 24 25 26 27 28 29 30 1 2	December
October	1 2 3 4 5 6 7 8 9 10 11 12 13 14 15 16 17 18 19 20 21 22 23 24 25 26 27 28 29 30 31	
December	3 4 5 6 7 8 9 10 11 12 13 14 15 16 17 18 19 20 21 22 23 24 25 26 27 28 29 30 31 1 2	January
November	1 2 3 4 5 6 7 8 9 10 11 12 13 14 15 16 17 18 19 20 21 22 23 24 25 26 27 28 29 30	
January	3 4 5 6 7 8 9 10 11 12 13 14 15 16 17 18 19 20 21 22 23 24 25 26 27 28 29 30 31 1	February
December	1 2 3 4 5 6 7 8 9 10 11 12 13 14 15 16 17 18 19 20 21 22 23 24 25 26 27 28 29 30 31	
February	2 3 4 5 6 7 8 9 10 11 12 13 14 15 16 17 18 19 20 21 22 23 24 25 26 27 28 1 2 3 4	March

WELSH DOG NAMING VOCABULARY

A

Able - gallu
after - wedi
again - eto
apple - afal
aunt- modryb

B

baby - baban
bad - bag
banner - baner
bard - bardd
beautiful - prydferth
bell - cloch
best - gorau
big - mawr
born - geni
boy - bachgen
breeze - pont
brother - brawd

C

cake - teisen
castle - castell
catch - dal
cheerful - llawan
chief - prif
child - plentyn
clear - clir
crown - coron

D

daughter - merch
dawn - gwaur
dear - annwyl
dog - ci
drink - yfed

E

easy - hawdd
eat - bwyta
evening - noson
ever - byth

F

fair - teg
faith - ffydd
farm - fferm
fast - cytlym
father - tad
fire - tan
first - cyntaf
flower - blodeuyn
fond - hoff
friend - cyfaill

G

gift - aurheg
girl - geneth
go - mynd
gold - aur
good - da

H

hair - gwallt
hat - poeth
happy - hapus
head - pen
headmaster - prifathro
heart - calon
help - help
her - ei
high - bryn
his - ei

I

ice cream - hirfen ia
ideal - delfryd
idol - eilun
idyll - canig
illustrious - enwog
imp - dieflyn
important - pwysig
infant - maban
ivory - ifori

J

jaunty - hoenus
jest - cellwair
jit - muchudd
jolly - braf
jovial - llawen
joy - llawenydd
jubilee - jiwbili

K

keepsake - cofrodd
kennel - cwb ci
kid - myn
kind - rhyw
king - brenin
kiss - cusanu

L

lad - hogyn
lady - arglwyddes
lamb - oen
lass - llances
laughter - chwertin
lawyer - cyfreithiwr
lazy - diog
leash - cynllyfan
leather - lledr
liberty - rhyddid
life - bywyd
light - golau
love - cariad

M

magic - cyfareddol
maid - merch
majesty - mawrhydi
male - gwryw
manhood - dyndod
marshal - cadlywydd
mate - cymar
miracle - gwyrth
mistletoe - uchelwydd
model - cynllun
moon - dyn
moonshine - ffiloreg
mother - mam
muddle - dryswch

N

neat - eidion
neighbor - cymydog
neophyte - newyddian
night - noswaith
nobleman - pendefig
nuzzle - trwyno

O

obedient - ufudd
obliging - caredig
offspring - hiliogaeth
original - gwreiddol
outlaw - herwr
overture - cynnig

P

paradise - paradwys
paradox - gwrthddywediad
paramount - pennaf
party - mintai
passion - gwyn
pastor - bugail
patch - clwt
peace - heddwch
peasant - gwladwr
pebble - gioyn
peer - gogyfurdd
penny - ceiniog
perfect - perffaith
periwinkle - gwichiad
petticoat - pais
pheasant - ceilog coed
playful - chwareus
pleasant - byfryd
preacher - pregethur
precious - gwerthfawr
premier - blaenaf
prize - gwobr
prophet - proffwyd
prospect - rhagoliwg
prowd - balch
prudent - pwyllog
puppy - ci bach

Q

quality - ansawdd
queen - brenhines
quick - byw
quiet - llonydd
quixotic - rhamaullyd

R

rabbit - cwningen
race - hil
racy - blasus

razor - ellyn
regular - rheolaidd
reluctant - aufodlon
remarkable - nodedig
renaissance - dadeni
rider - marchogwr
rifle - dryll
rigamarole - ffregod
rocket - roced
royal - brenhiniaeth

S

sailor - morwr
saint - sant
salute - cyfarch
saucy - digywilydd
school - ysgol
scientist - gwyddonydd
scion - impyn
scout - sgowt
senior - hynaf
shaggy - cedenog
shepherd - bugail
signal - arwyddol
silk - sidan
siren - mor-forwyn
smart - gwyn
soldier - milwr
souvenir - cofrodd
spaniel - adargi
specialist - arbenigwr
spokesman - liefarwr
statue - delw
strawberry - mefysen
strong - cryf
student - myfyriwr
sunbeam - pelydryn
sunshine - heulwen
supreme - goruchaf
sweet - melys

T

tail - cynffon
teacher - athro
tender - cynnig
thief - lleidr
thunder - taran
tomboy - hoeden
treasure - trysor
trigger - cliced
trumpet - utgorn
twilight - cyfnos
tyro - newyddian

U

uncle - ewythr
upland - ucheldir

V

valley - dyffryn
victor - gorchfygwr
visitor - ymwelwr

vixen - cadnawes

W

wayfarer - fforddol
Welsh - Cymreig
Welshman - Cymro
Welshwoman - Cymraes
whelp - cenau
wind - gwynt
wizard - swynwr
worthy - teiliwng

Y

youngster - plentyn
youth - mebyd
youthful - ieuanc

Z

Zealous - selog
zephyr - awel dyner

SIMPLIFIED WELSH PRONOUNCING GUIDE

Alphabet

A   — as in Halleluja
B   — as in bat
C   — as in cat
CH   — as in Bach
D   — as in dog
DD   — as "th" in this
E   — as in ball or pen
F   — as English V
FF   — as in phone
G   — as in get
NG   — as in hang
H   — as in help
I   — as in Mil (meal)

J   — as in Jam
L   — as in lot
LL   — a consonant whose pronouncing is fun. Put the tip of the tongue against the roof of the mouth and hiss. Try these: Llan (church), Lleth (lodging), Llyfr (book).
M   — as in make
N   — as in not
O   — as in more
P   — as in pot
PH   — as in pheasant
R   — trilled as in robin
RH   — as English r
S   — as in sat
SI   — as English sh
T   — as English t
TH   — as in think
U   —as in een
W   — as in fool
Y   — as in dean

Chief Vowel Sounds

ae, ai, au — are pronounced as an English "aye, aye, sir".
aw   — aa-oo as in fowl
ew   — The e sound is an open one as in pell-mell, not dew
iw, yw   — pronounced somewhat like (y)ew in English.
wy   — as in oo-ee
oe, oi, ou — as in oil

Ch. Deckard's Holyhead with her week-old litter of nine sired by Ch. Bachgen Dewr of Pencelli. (Pferd)

A Merry Madcap of Downland litter at two months sired by Ch. Dewi Sant in 1945. (Ellis)

Three happy, youthful girls—Sarah D. Pferd, Krackton's Rare Sequin, and Deckard's Holyhead—looking for sport. (Pferd)

A sporting group at the Welsh Springer Spaniel Club of Great Britain Cold Game Test, February 1975. (Falconer)

Happy Hackwood Welsh, Happy Lark, left; Susan, center; and Happy Lad, right. (Falconer)

APPENDIX A

YEARLY REGISTRATIONS OF WELSH SPRINGER SPANIELS
(AKC and KC Data)

Year	G.B.	U.S.	Year	G.B.	U.S.
1946	160	0	1961	153	31
1947	168	0	1962	210	16
1948	126	0	1963	124	13
1949	116	11	1964	195	35
1950	136	9	1965	208	28
1951	102	12	1966	157	30
1952	109	24	1967	253	40
1953	99	29	1968	229	48
1954	122	20	1969	385	46
1955	82	6	1970	335	16
1956	101	22	1971	409	24
1957	143	6	1972	357	30
1958	105	28	1973	511	52
1959	139	12	1974	452	60
1960	128	8			
	1836	189		3978	656

APPENDIX B

GREAT BRITAIN – WELSH SPRINGER SPANIEL CHAMPIONS

GREAT BRITAIN — WELSH SPRINGER SPANIEL CHAMPIONS

Name	Sex	Sire	Dam	Owner	Breeder	Born
1949 Ch. Branksome Beauty	B	Dewi Sant	Castlewood Counctss	Mrs. M. I. Morgan	Mrs. M. I. Morgan	17.5.48
1950 Ch. Rushbrooke Runner	B	Rushbrooke Rufus	Rushbrooke Ruff	Mr. H.J.H. Leopard	Mr. H.J.H. Leopard	16.4.47
1952 Ch. Denethorp Danny	D	Rushbrooke Rufus	Jenny of Denethorp	Mr. F.A.M. Hart	Mr. F.A.M. Hart	5.549
Ch. Snowdonian Lad	D	Gay Rebel	Freckled Fanny	Mr. L. Hughes	Miss D.H. Ellis	7.1.148
1953 Ch. Rockhill Rhiwderin	D	Myrydd Marksman of Tregwillym	Rockhill Rona	Mr. Hart, previously Mrs. Mayall	Mrs. M. Mayall	26.9.51
1954 Ch. Broadweir Bracken	B	Rushbrooke Rust	Rushbrooke R Rum	Mrs. J.A. Foster	Mrs. J.A. Foster	13.4.51
Ch. Lassie of Menai	B	Ch. Snowdenian Lad	Ceri Menai	Mr. L. Hughes	Mr. D.F. Hughes	1.3.52
1955 Ch. Belinda of Linkton	B	Downland Diplomat	Elizabeth Judy	Miss A. West	Mr. D. Lawrie	12.7.53
1956 Ch. Brancourt Bang	D	Lucky Laddie	Ashfield Aristocrat	Mr. and Mrs. T.H. Morgan	Mrs. D. Thomas	30.11.51
1959 Ch. Tulita of Tregwillym	B	Tehran of Tregwillym	Gilly of Beameads	Mr. H.C. Payne	Mr. L. Bourne	11.9.56

Year / Name	Sex	Sire	Dam	Breeder	Owner	Date
1960 Ch. Kim of Cwm	D	Sh. Ch. Top-Score of Tregwillym	Tudor Lass of Tregwillym	Mr. B.G. Thorpe	Mr. H.C. Payne	21.9.57
1962 Ch. Mandy of Tregwillym	B	Sh. Ch. Trigger of Tregwillym	Lady Blanche of Broomleaf	Mr. H.C. Payne	Lt. Col. J.C. Lewis	26.8.59
1962 Ch. Statesman of Tregwillym	D	Sh. Ch. Token of Tregwillym	Trinket of Tregwillym	Mr. H.C. Payne	Mr. H. C. Payne	20.9.58
1965 Ch. Talysarn Calon Dewr	D	Tehran of Tregwillym	Shot Silk of Tregwillym	Mr. D. Dobson	Miss C. Potter	1.1.62
1969 Ch. Tidemarsh Rip	D	Stokecourt Sam	Lingholm Rhoda	Mr. G.H. Pattinson	Mr. G.H. Pattinson	11.5.67
1971 Ch. Krackton's Surprise Packet	B	Nobleman of Tregwillyn	Pru of Gliffaes	G.W.R. Cousens	S.G. Brabner	18.8.67
1972 Ch. Tidemarsh Tidemark	D	Ch. Tidemarsh Rip	Titian Beauty	G.H. Pattinson	Mrs. Russen	24.9.69
1973 Ch. Dalati Del	B	Sh. Ch. Athelwood Diaperoxide	Dalati Sidan	Mr. and Mrs. N. Hunton Morgans	Mr. and Mrs. N. Hunton Morgans	12.8.70

APPENDIX C

GREAT BRITAIN – WELSH SPRINGER SPANIEL SHOW CHAMPIONS

GREAT BRITAIN – WELSH SPRINGER SPANIEL SHOW CHAMPIONS

Name	Sex	Sire	Dam	Owner	Breeder	Born
Sh. Ch. Dewi Sant	D	Deri Di	Tresco Thornycroft	Mr. H. Newman	Mrs. M.C. Evans	10.6.43
Sh. Ch. Rushbrooke Rustle	B	Goblin Goch	Rushbrooke Rose	Mr. H.J.H. Leopard	Mr. H. J. H. Leopard	30.3.46
Sh. Ch. Jester of Downland	D	Dewi Sant	Merry Madcap of Downland	Miss D. Ellis	Miss D. Ellis	12.6.45
Sh. Ch. Cofois Bon	B	Dewi Sant	Doweli Meweh Nol	Mr. H. Newman	Mr. H. Newman	6.9.45
Sh. Ch. Rushbrooke Ruadh	D	Dere Nol	Rushbrooke Ruff	Mr. H.J.H. Leopard	Mr. H.J.H. Leopard	7.2.46
Sh. Ch. Stokecourt Jonathan	D	Dewi Sant	Camrose Lass	Mrs. D. Morriss	Mr. G. Hooper	17.2.46
Sh. Ch. Denethorp Dido	B	Dewi Sant	Treorchy Megan	Mr. H. Newman	Mr. F.A.M. Hart	26.7.49
Sh. Ch. Taliesin Ye Ail	D	Dewi Sant	Gillian of Tregwillym	Mr. G. Taylor	Mr. J. Kemp	10.5.47
Sh. Ch. Moelwyn Melody	B	Melwyan Marksman	Tebay	Mr. E.W. Painter	Mr. T. Jones	27.0.40
Sh. Ch. Kestrel of Kenswick	B	Glenross of Tregwillym	Fidget of Fosseway	Mrs. M.G. King	Mrs. M.G. King	4.5.50
Sh. Ch. Rushbrooke Rustic	B	Rushbrooke Rust	Rushbrooke Rum	Mr. H.J.H. Leopard	Mrs. J.A. Foster	13.4.57

Name	Sex	Sire	Dam	Owner	Breeder	Born
Sh. Ch. Kim of Kenswick	D	Glenross of Tregwillym	Fidget of Fosseway	Mrs. M.G. King	Mrs. M.G. King	4.5.50
Sh. Ch. Welsh Lady	B	Dewi Sant	Merch Dewi	Mr. H. Newman	Mr. H. Newman	28.9.49
Sh. Ch. Brancourt Bushranger	D	Ch. Brancourt Bang	Ch. Branksome Beauty	Mr. and Mrs. T.H. Morgan	Mrs. M.I. Morgan	23.12.53
Sh. Ch. Token of Tregwillym	D	Taliesin Ye Ail	Titian of Tregwillym	Mr. H.C. Payne	Mr. H.C. Payne	22.6.54
Sh. Ch. Gwyneth	B	Beggar Me Boy	Gwenlilian Goch	Mr. G.E. Bounds	Mr. G.E. Bounds	19.6.52
Sh. Ch. Mikado of Broomleaf	D	Sh. Ch. Stokecourt Jonathan	Broomleaf Dimple of Empshott	Dr. E. Rickards	Mrs. K. Doxford	2.10.54
Sh. Ch. Stokecourt Gillian	B	Sh. Ch. Stokecourt Jonathan	Gwyneth Alit Bedw	Mrs. D. Morriss	Col C.R. Smith	30.4.53
Sh. Ch. Top Score of Tregwillym	D	Tehran of Tregwillym	Rockhill Rosewell	Mr. H.C. Payne	Mr. H.C. Payne	11.1.57
Sh. Ch. Brancourt Belinda	B	Ch. Brancourt Bang	Ch. Branksome Beauty	Mr. and Mrs. T.H. Morgan	Mrs. M.I. Morgan	22.5.57
Sh. Ch. Coombelane Fidelia	B	Ch. Brancourt Bang	Sh. Ch. Gwyneth	Miss D.M. Norman	Mr. G.E. Bounds	4.5.55
Sh. Ch. Trigger of Tregwillym	D	Tehran of Tregwillym	Terlesa of Tregwillym	Mr. H.C. Payne	Mr. H.C. Payne	13.8.56

Name	Sex	Sire	Dam	Breeder	Owner	Date
Sh. Ch. Arabella of Linkhill	B	Ch. Brancourt Bang	Ch. Belinda of Linkton	Miss A. West	Miss A. West	4.10.56
Sh. Ch. Tarbay Florian of Broomleaf	D	Hilarion of Broomleaf	Broomleaf Little Buttercup	Dr. E. Rickards	Mrs. K. Doxford	17.3.58
Sh. Ch. Statesman of Tregwillym	D	Sh. Ch. Token of Tregwillym	Trinket of Tregwillym	Mr. H.C. Payne	Mr. H.C. Payne	20.9.58
Sh. Ch. Stokecourt Judith	B	Stokecourt Simon	Sh. Ch. Stokecourt Gillian	Dr. E. Rickards	Mrs. D. Morriss	27.5.55
Sh. Ch. Jenny of Tarbay	B	Sh. Ch. Mikado of Broomleaf	Sh. Ch. Stokecourt Judith	Dr. E. Rickards	Dr. E. Rickards	25.8.58
Sh. Ch. Deri Darrell of Linkhill	D	Sh. Ch. Statesman of Tregwillym	Sh. Ch. Arabella of Linkhill	Miss A. West	Miss A. West	3.9.60
Sh. Ch. Denethorp Dihewyd	D	Ch. Rockhill Rhiwderin	Denethorp Danella	Mr. F.A.M. Hart	Mr. F.A.M. Hart	2.8.58
Sh. Ch. Rambler of Miellette	D	Hackpen Redwyn Lad	Thora of Empshott	Mr. A.H. Corbett and Miss C. Potter	Mrs. E.A. Rowe	24.7.57
Sh. Ch. Amber Rose of Tregwillym	B	Ch. Statesman of Tregwillym	Tete-a-Tete of Tregwillym	Mr. H.C. Payne	Mr. H.C. Payne	1.11.59
Sh. Ch. Liza of Linkhill	B	Ch. Statesman of Tregwillym	Sh. Ch. Arabella of Linkhill	Miss A. West	Miss A. West	26.10.61
Sh. Ch. Gamefeather of Siani	B	Sh. Ch. Mikado of Broomleaf	Blodyn Gwanwyn	Major and Mrs. K. Stevens	Mr. H. Newman	14.7.60

Name	Sex	Sire	Dam	Owner	Breeder	Born
Sh. Ch. Fashion Plate of Hearts	B	Ch. Statesman of Tregwillym	Sh. Ch. Brancourt Belinda	Mr. T.H. Arthur	Mr. T.H. Arthur	7.8.62
Sh. Ch. Mountararat of Broomleaf	D	Sh. Ch. Deri Darrell of Linkhill	Iolanthe of Broomleaf	Mr. C.J. Kitchener	Mrs. K. Doxford	12.6.62
Sh. Ch. Diplomat of Hearts	D	Ch. Statesman of Tregwillym	Sh. Ch. Brancourt Belinda	Mr. T.H. Arthur	Mr. T.H. Arthur	7.8.62
Sh. Ch. Easter Parade	D	Sh. Ch. Topscore of Tregwillym	Blodyn Gwanwyn	Mr. H. Newman	Mr. H. Newman	1.4.61
Sh. Ch. Lady of Llangarna	B	Ch. Statesman of Tregwillym	Tete-a-Tete of Tregwillym	Mr. H. Pocock	Mr. H. C. Payne	7.12.61
Sh. Ch. Golden Tint of Tregwillym	B	Sportsman of Tregwillym	Sh. Ch. Lady of Llangarna	Mr. H.C. Payne	Mr. H. Pocock	18.6.64
Sh. Ch. Plattburn Paramount	D	Sh. Ch. Denethorp Dihewyd	Patmyn Pie Powder	Mr. and Mrs. J.K. Burgess	Mr. and Mrs. J.K. Burgess	7.2.65
Sh. Ch. Talysarn Golden Guinea	B	Mynyddislwyn Lad	Talysarn Blodeuyn	Mr. D. Dobson	Mr. D. Dobson	26.5.65
Sh. Ch. Plattburn Penny	B	Ch. Rockhill Rhiwderin	Patmyn Pie Powder	Mr. and Mrs. J.K. Burgess	Mr. and Mrs. J.K. Burgess	27.11.63
Sh. Ch. Bruce of Brent	D	Benefactor of Brent	Bronwyn Trixie	Mrs. D. M. Perkins	Mrs. N. Hall	28.8.66
Sh. Ch. Dewi of Hearts	D	Ch. Talysarn Calon Dewr	Fashion Model of Hearts	Mr. T.H. Arthur	Mr. and Mrs. N.P. Campbell	30.3.66

Name	Sex	Sire	Dam	Breeder	Owner	Date
Sh. Ch. Plattburn Progressor	D	Plattburn Proclamation	Plattburn Penelope	Mr. and Mrs. J.K. Burgess	Mr. and Mrs. J.K. Burgess	16.9.68
Sh. Ch. Maria of Pencelli	B	Priory Major	Bony Legend	Mr. H. Newman	Mr. H. Newman	14.3.67
Sh. Ch. Dalati Swynwyr	D	Sh. Ch. Bruce of Brent	Fressia of Hearts	Mr. and Mrs. N. Huntor Morgans	Mr. and Mrs. N. Huntor Morgans	17.7.68
Sh. Ch. Athelwood Diaperoxide	D	Nobleman of Tregwillym	Atalanth of Athelwood	Mr. and Mrs. B.J. Mullins	Mr. and Mrs. B.J. Mullins	26.3.68
Sh. Ch. Dalati Anwylyd	B	Sh. Ch. Diplomat of Hearts	Fressia of Heatts	Mr. and Mrs. N. Hunton Morgans	Mr. and Mrs. N. Hunton Morgans	3.5.67
Sh. Ch. Plattburn Pegasus	B	Plattburn Pen Rip	Plattburn Parasol	Mr. and Mrs. J.K. Burgess	Mr. and Mrs. J.K. Burgess	29.4.69
Sh. Ch. Plattburn Perchance	D	Plattburn Poacher	Emma of Glendry	Mr. and Mrs. J.K. Burgess	Mr. and Mrs. J.K. Burgess	4.1.69
Sh. Ch. Lily the Pink	B	Stokecourt Sam	Atlanta of Athelstone	Mr. and Mrs. B.J. Mullins	Mr. and Mrs. B.J. Mullins	12.9.69
Sh. Ch. Roger of Pencelli	D	Sh. Ch. Bruce of Brent	Sh. Ch. Marie of Pencelli	Harold Newman	Harold Newman	17.12.70
Sh. Ch. Tregwillym Golden Gem	B	Golden Shot of Tregwillym	Sh. Ch. Golden Tint Tregwillym	Mr. H.C. Payne	Mr. H.C. Payne	1.1.72
Sh. Ch. Plattburn Peewit	D	Plattburn Proclamation	Plattburn Peewee	Mr. and Mrs. J.K. Burgess	Mr. and Mrs. J.K. Burgess	10.8.71

Name	Sex	Sire	Dam	Owner	Breeder	Born
Sh. Ch. Plattburn Pinetree	B	Plattburn Proclamation	Sh. Ch. Plattburn Pegasus	Mr. and Mrs. J.K. Burgess	Mr. and Mrs. J.K. Burgess	1.12.70
Sh. Ch. Progress of Pencelli	D	Sh. Ch. Plattburn Progressor	Sh. Ch. Marie of Pencelli	Horold Newman	Harold Newman	17.8.71
Sh. Ch. Dalati Helwr	D	Sh. Ch. Bruce of Brent	Sh. Ch. Dalati Anwylyd	L.L. Ross	Mr. and Mrs. H. Hunton Morgans	10.3.71
Sh. Ch. Dalti Delwen	B	Sh. Ch. Athelwood Diaperoxide	Dalati Sidan	Mr. and Mrs. N Hunton Morgans	Mr. and Mrs. N. Hunton Morgans	22.8.72
Sh. Ch. Hillpark Pollyanna	B	Sportsman of Tregwillym	Polly Garter of Doonebridge	Mr. and Mrs. J. S. Walton	Mr. and Mrs. J. S. Walton	3.1.70
Sh. Ch. Hillpark Mr. Polly	D	Plattburn Proclamation	Polly Garter of Doonebridge	Mr. and Mrs. J. S. Walton	Mr. and Mrs. J.S. Walton	4.1.72

APPENDIX D

UNITED STATES – WELSH SPRINGER SPANIEL CHAMPIONS

UNITED STATES — WELSH SPRINGER SPANIEL CHAMPIONS

Date	Name	Sex	Sire	Dam	Owner	Breeder	Born
5-15-55	Ch. Holiday of Happy Hunting	D	Ch. Jester of Down-land (G.B)	Souvenir of Down-land	Happy Hunting Kennels	Mrs. Eleanor P. Howes	1-23-53
6-4-59	Ch. Dien Glynis of Randhaven	B	Ch. David of Happy Hunting	Randhaven's Geneth O'Rattle	H.R. and E.B. Randolph	H.R. and E.B. Randolph	12-24-57
3-16-60	Ch. Gwaint of Randhaven	D	Ch. David of Happy Hunting	Randhaven's Geneth O'Rattle	H.R. and E.B. Randolph	H.R. and E.B. Randolph	12-24-57
10-2-60	Ch. David of Happy Hunting	D	Ch. Jester of Down-land (G.B.)	Miss Timmy of Happy Hunting	H.R. and E.B. Randolph	Happy Hunting Kennels	6-15-56
10-2-60	Ch. Dere Nol of Randhaven	B	Ch. David of Happy Hunting	Randhaven's Geneth O'Rattle	Robert Gelfand	H.R. and E.B. Randolph	12-24-57
2-18-62	Ch. Trigger of Tregwillym	D	Tehran of Treg-willym	Teresa of Treg-willym	D. Lawrence Carswell	H.C. Payne (Wales)	8-13-56
7-18-63	Ch. Coch Pluen of Randhaven CD	D	Ch. David of Happy Hunting	Glannant Rattle	J.P. Parker	H.R. and E.B. Randolph	4-30-60
4-17-65	Ch. Tair of Rand-haven	B	Rhudd O'Randhaven	Showgirl of Treg-willym	H.R. and E.B. Randolph	H.R. and E.B. Randolph	7-1-61
5-12-65	Ch. Filicia's Dylan	D	Gameland of the Downs	Ch. Randhaven's D'LCar Gini	Nettie Carswell	Nettie Carswell	8-28-63
1-9-66	Ch. Randhaven's DL'Car Gini	B	Ch. Trigger of Tregwillym	Ch. Dien Glynis of Randhaven	Nettie Carswell	Nettie Carswell	9-17-61

3-9-69	B	Ch. Dilly	Gameland of the Downs	Ch. Randhaven's D'LCar Gini	Donna Kay Gatlin	Nettie Carswell	8-28-63
6-15-69	D	Ch. Cicero Gus-UD	Shadow of Story-land	Jewel of Mayfield	Mr. and Mrs. Charles Hatz	Stanley C. Spirala	5-10-68
5-31-70	B	Ch. Shadycreek's Patches	D'LCar's Mister Lucky	Ch. Dilly	D.K. Gatlin and F.A. Smith	Nettie Carswell and D.K. Gatlin	6-6-68
9-13-70	D	Ch. Aduno of Randhaven C.D.	Mikado's Tinker	Redhead Debutante	Betty June Siegel	E.B. Randolph	1-26-66
10-17-70	B	Ch. Llitith of Randhaven	Ch. Trigger of Treg-willym (G.B.)	Redhead Debutante	Nettie Carswell	E.B. Randolph	12-5-63
2-16-71	D	Ch. Bosn's First Mate	Coch Penion of Rand-haven C.D.	Bo Forte's Ballerina	Lawrence and Betty J. Siegel	Lawrence Siegel	2-8-70
2-20-71	D	Ch. Bosn's Dick Deadeye	Coch Penion of Rand-haven—C.D.	Bo Forte's Ballerina	Lawrence and Betty J. Siegel	Lawrence Siegel	2-8-70
3-27-71	D	Ch. DL'Car's Gottowin	Gary's Jethro of Randhaven	Iolanthe of Broomleaf	Nettie Carswell	D. Lawrence Carswell	6-25-68
9-6-71	B	Ch. Sylabru's Copper Ibitz	Ch. Filicia's Dylan	Iolanthe of Broomleaf	Sylvia Foreacre	D. Lawrence Carswell	11-12-69
3-25-72	D	Ch. DL'Car's Triggerleaf	DL'Car's Mister Lucky	Iolanthe of Broomleaf	D. Lawrence Carswell	D. Lawrence Carswell	6-1-67
4-16-72	D	Ch. Sylabru Cimri Aberystwyth	Ch. Filicia's Dylan	Ch. Sylabru's Copper Ibitz	Synthia and Sylvia Foreacre	Sylvia Foreacre	1-11-71

Date	Name	Sex	Sire	Dam	Owner	Breeder	Born
10-10-72	Ch. DL'Car's Gini Triggerboy	D	Gary's Jethro of Randhaven	Ch. Randhaven's DL'Car Gini	Nettie Carswell and Donna Gatlin	Nettie Carswell	8-20-68
2-13-73	Ch. Sylabru's Pocketful of Pennies	B	Ch. Filicia's Dylan	Tara-Fina of Bo Forte	Sylvia Foreacre	Byron E. Maine	3-18-71
4-29-73	Ch. Bachgen Dewr of Pencelli	D	Priory Major	Bonny Legend	Sylvia and Bruce Foreacre Jr.	H. Newman (Wales)	3-14-67
5-14-73	Ch. Pickwick's Brychan	D	Plattburn Pickwick	Ch. Plattburn Primrose	Richard L. Preston	Jane K. Seamans	4-15-71
7-8-73	Ch. Walter Gingham	D	Shadow of Story-land	Jewel of Mayfair	Bob Swonger and Glena Coffman	Stanley C. Spirala	5-10-68
7-14-73	Ch. Gwilyn of Brent	D	Sh. Ch. Plattburn Progressor (G.B.)	Rhiannon of Brent	Sylvia Foreacre	Mrs. D. Perkins (England)	6-5-71
11-25-7₃	Ch. Sylabru's Penny Candy	B	Ch. Sylabru's Cimri Aberystwyth	Ch. Sylabru's Pocket-full of Pennies	Richard L. Preston	Sylvia Foreacre	5-27-72
12-2-73	Ch. DL'Car's Prince of Wales	D	Ch. Filicia's Dylan	Tara-Fini of Bo Forte	Nettie Carswell	Byron E. Maine	3-18-71
3-10-74	Ch. Pencelli Rhyl	B	Sh. Ch. Roger of Pencelli (G.B.)	Freesia of Hearts	Cynthia Foreacre	T. Hubert Arthur (Wales)	4-13-72
4-28-74	Ch. Pickwick's Dylan	D	Plattburn Pickwick	Ch. Plattburn Primrose	Jane K. Seamans	Jane K. Seamans	4-8-72
5-4-74	Ch. Plattburn Primrose	B	Plattburn Proclamation	Plattburn Pretty Peeps	Jane K. Seamans	J. Kenneth Burgess (England)	7-2-69

5-26-74	D	Ch. Peter Dewi Sanf of DL'Car	Gary's Jethro of Randhaven	Iolanthe of Broomleaf	Nettie Carswell	D. Lawrence Carswell	6-26-68
12-1-74	B	Ch. Sylabru's Lollipop	Ch. Bachgen Dewr of Pencelli	Sylabru's Lady Brecon	Edith DuBois	Constance J. Schuyler	4-20-73
12-7-74	D	Ch. Wynfomeer's William the Welsh	Ch. DL'Car's Trigger-leaf	Bupers II	Edwin J. Cummings III	Louis Shoer	5-19-73
4-18-75	D	Ch. Dawn's Ethorp Two	Ch. Sylabru Cimri Aberystwyth	Sylabru's Penny Ante	D.F. & S.A. M. Spahr	D.F. & S.A. M. Spahr	5-15-74
4-18-75	D	Ch. Dawn's Ethorp Two	Ch. Sylabru's Cimri Aberystwyth	Sylabru's Penny Ante	D.F. & S.A. M. Spahr	D.F. & S.A. M. Spahr	5-15-74
4-27-75	D	Ch. Kyngsbree Aelwyn	Ch. Gwilym of Brent	Ch. Plattburn Primrose	Jane K. Seamans	Jane K. Seamans	5-21-73
5-3-75	B	Ch. Olympian Rhonda Redhead	Ch. Pickwick's Brychan	Ch. Sylabru's Penny Candy	Richard L. Preston	Richard L. Preston	3-8-74
6-8-75	D	Ch. Rickemshel Raynmaker	Ch. Walter Gingham	Heidi-chi's Bronwen of Ludlow	Richard L. Preston	Bob & Evelyn J. Swonger	12-1-72
7-13-75	B	Ch. Deckard's Holyhead	Ch. Filicia's Dylan	Tara-Fina of Bo Forte	Jane A. Pferd	Byron E. Maine	3-18-71
8-3-75	B	Ch. Olympian Brychan's Robyn	Ch. Pickwick's Brychan	Heidi-Chi's Bronwen of Ludlow	Sharon L. Merritt & Richard Preston	Richard Preston	3-29-74
9-27-75	D	Ch. Deckard's Sir Barnye	Sir Henry Cardiff	Krackton Rare Sequin	Kenneth D. McCullough	Jane A. Pferd	2-6-74
11-22-75	D	Ch. Randhaven Return of D'LCar	Ch. Filicia's Dylan	Tara-Fina of Bo Forte	Edna Randolph & Merle Bauer	Byron E. Maine	3-18-71
12-6-75	B	Ch. Pencelli Pandour	Sh. Ch. Roger of Pencelli (G.B.)	Paula Girl of Pencelli	Kenneth D. McCullough	H. Newman (Wales)	7-29-73

APPENDIX E

**WELSH SPRINGER SPANIELS
UNITED STATES—COMPANION DOGS**

WELSH SPRINGER SPANIELS

UNITED STATES—COMPANION DOGS

Date	Name	Sex	Sire	Dam	Owner	Born
3-30-56	Ace	D			Patrick Welch	
3-13-58	Duke	D			Patrick Welch	
10-28-67	Royal Lady of Llangollen	B	Gameland of the Downs	Tincian of Rand-haven	Ronald R. Brooks	
8-10-69	Ch. Aduno of Rand-haven	D	Mikado's Tinker	Redhead Debutante	Betty June Siegel	1-26-66
8-10-69	Coch Penion of Rand-haven	D	Mikado's Tinker	Redhead Debutante	Lawrence Siegel	1-26-66
10-19-69	Ch. Cicero Gus	D	Shadow of Story-land	Jewel of Mayfield	Mr. & Mrs. Charles Hatz	5-10-68
10-3-71	Ghost Inn's Matador	D	Nobleman of Treg-willym	Rona of Pencelli	Helen Mateer	
9-26-71	Ch. Sylabru's Copper Ibitz	B	Ch. Filicia's Dylan	Iolanthe of Broomleaf	Sylvia Foreacre	11-12-69
	Bo Forte's Ballerina	B	Ch. Coch Pluen of Randhaven	Bo Forte's Befana	Mrs. Charles Hatz	
5-10-75	Sharon Brent	B	Adonis of Brent	Ceinwen of Brent	Jean E. Paskiewicz	

WELSH SPRINGER SPANIELS

UNITED STATES—COMPANION DOGS EXCELLENT

Date	Name	Sex	Sire	Dam	Owner	Born
2-26-61	Ace	D			Patrick J. Welch	
4-7-61	Duke	D			Patrick J. Welch	
5-30-70	Ch. Cicero Gus	D	Shadow of Story-land	Jewel of Mayfield	Mr. & Mrs. Charles Hatz	5-10-68

UNITED STATES—UTILITY DOGS

5-16-71	Ch. Cicero Gus	D	Shadow of Story-land	Jewel of Mayfield	Mr. & Mrs. Charles Hatz	5-10-68

APPENDIX F

Points of the Welsh Springer

CHARACTERISTICS: The 'Welsh Spaniel' or 'Springer' is also known and referred to in Wales as a 'Starter.' 'He is of very ancient and pure origin, and is a distinct variety.

APPEARANCE: A symmetrical, compact, strong, merry, very active dog; not stilty; obviously built for endurance and hard work. A quick and active mover displaying plenty of push and drive.

HEAD AND SKULL Skull proportionate, of moderate length, slightly domed, with clearly defined stop and well-chiselled below the eyes. Muzzle of medium length, straight, fairly square; the nostrils well developed and flesh-coloured or dark. A short chubby head is objectionable.

EYES: Hazel or dark, medium size, not prominent, nor sunken, nor showing haw.

EARS: Set moderately low and hanging close to the cheeks, comparatively small and gradually narrowing towards the tip and shaped somewhat like a vine leaf, covered with setter-like feathering.

255

MOUTH: Jaw strong, neither under nor overshot.

NECK: Long and muscular, clean in throat, neatly set into long, sloping shoulders.

FOREQUARTERS: Forelegs of medium length, straight, well boned, moderately feathered.

BODY: Not long; strong and muscular with deep brisket, well-sprung ribs; length of body should be proprotionate to length of leg, and very well balanced; muscular loin slightly arched and well coupled up.

HINDQUARTERS: Strong and muscular, wide and fully developed with deep second thighs. Hind legs, hocks well let down; stifles moderately bent (neither twisted in nor out), moderately feathered.

FEET: Round, with thick pads. Firm and cat-like, not too large or spreading.

TAIL: Well set on and low, never carried above the level of the back; lightly feathered and lively in action.

COAT: Straight or flat, and thick, of a nice silky texture, never wiry nor wavy. A curly coat is most objectionable.

COLOUR: Rich red and white only.

SIZE: A dog not to exceed 19 inches in height at shoulder and a bitch 18 inches, approximately.

FAULTS: Coarse skull, light bone, long or curly coat, bad shoulders, poor movement.

APPENDIX G

AMERICAN KENNEL CLUB

Official Standard for the
Welsh Springer Spaniel

The "Welsh Spaniel" or "Springer" is also known and referred to in Wales as a "Starter." He is of very ancient and pure origin, and is a distinct variety which has been bred and preserved purely for working purposes.

Head:

Skull — Proportionate, of moderate length, slightly domed, clearly defined stop, well chiseled below the eyes.

Muzzle — Medium length, straight, fairly square; the nostrils well developed and flesh colored or dark.

Jaw — Strong, neither undershot nor overshot.

Eyes — Hazel or dark, medium size, not prominent, nor sunken, nor showing haw.

Ears — Set moderately low and hanging close to the cheeks, comparatively small, and gradually narrowing towards the tip, covered with nice setterlike feathering.

A short chubby head is objectionable.

Neck and Shoulders:
   Neck — Long and muscular, clean in throat, neatly set into long and sloping shoulders.

   Forelegs — Medium length, straight, well bones, moderately feathered.

Body: Not long; strong and muscular with deep brisket, well-sprung ribs; length of body should be proportionate to length of leg, and very well balanced; with muscular loin slightly arched and well coupled up.

   Quarters — Strong and muscular, wide and fully developed with deep second thighs.

   Hind Legs — Hocks well let down; stifies moderately bent (neither twisted in or out), moderately feathered.

   Feet — Round with thick pads.

   Stern — Well set on and low, never carried above the level of the back; lightly feathered and with lively action.

Coat: Straight or flat and thick, of a nice silky texture, never wiry nor wavy. A curly coat is most objectionable.
   Color — Dark rich red and white.

General Appearance: A symmetrical, compact, strong, merry, very active dog; not stilty, obviously built for endurance and activity.

DOG GLOSSARY

ABDOMEN (belly)—The part of the body between the chest and the pelvis.

ACTION—The way a dog walks, trots or runs. Its gait.

ANGULATION—The angles formed by the major bones at the joints.

ANAL GLANDS—Two glands on the sides of the anus that excrete a thick smelly substance.

ANUS—The outlet at the end of the rectum.

APPLE HEAD—Irregular roundedness of the top of the skull.

APRON—The longer hair below the neck on the chest. The frill.

BALANCED—All parts symetrically proportioned in relation to each other.

BARREL RIBS—All ribs in a line forming a chest like a barrel.

BEAUTY SPOT—Usually a round patch of colored hair on the topskull between the ears.

BEEFY—Overheavy hind quarters.

BENCH SHOW—Where dogs are on platforms for viewing when not in the ring.

B.O.B.—Best of Breed, the best dog of the breed in the show.

B.O.S.—Best of Opposite Sex to the Best of Breed.

B.I.S.—The animal judged to be best of all breeds at the show.

BIRD DOG—A sporting dog trained to hunt birds.

BITCH—A female.

BITCHY—A male dog with a female look or conformation.

BITE—The position of the upper and lower teeth when the mouth is closed.

BLAZE—White streak down the center of the head between the eyes.

BLOOM—The sheen of a coat in top condition.

BOW-LEGGED—Front legs sprung outward, hind legs too wide apart.

BRACE—Two dogs of the same breed well matched in color and markings.

BRISKET—Front of chest between forelegs, usually deep or shallow.

BROOD—A bitch kept for breeding. A brood bitch.
BULL-NECKED—An overdeveloped, heavy muscular neck.
BURR—An irregular formation on the inside of the ear.
BUTTERFLY NOSE—A dark nose, spotted with flesh color.

CANINES—The two upper and the two lower sharp-pointed teeth.
CAT-FOOTED—Round, compact feet, with arched toes.
C.D.—Companion Dog, a title gained with minimum scores in licensed obedience trials (U.S.A.) or a working trial (G.B.).
CHAMPION (CH.)—A title awarded to a dog who has defeated a specified number of dogs in specified competitions at a series of shows (U.S.A.), or a winner of three Challenge Certificates under three different judges (Great Britain).
CHALLENGE CERTIFICATE—An award for the best in each sex in a breed at a Championship Show in Great Britain. Known as a C.C.
CHARACTER—Expression, temperment, and general appearance typical of the breed.
CHOKE COLLAR—A chain collar that tightens when sharply pulled.
CLOSE-COUPLED—Comparatively short from the shoulders to the hips.
CONFORMATION—Form, structure, and shape relative to the breed standard.
COW-HOCKS—When hocks turn inward toward each other.
CRABBING—When the body of the dog moves at an angle to the line of forward movement.
CROWN—The highest part of the head or skull.
CRYPTORCHID—Male whose one or both testicles are retained in the abdominal cavity.
CULOTTE—The longer hair on the back of the thighs.

DAM—The female parent.
DEWCLAWS—Extra claws inside of legs, usually removed.
DISQUALIFICATION—A fault making the dog ineligible for showing.
DOCK—To shorten the tail by cutting.
DOG—The male parent. Used to designate both male and female.
DOMED—And evenly rounded top skull.
DRY-NECK—A neck with taut skin, neither loose nor wrinkled.
DUAL CHAMPION—A dog awarded show and field trial championships.
DUDLEY NOSE—Flesh colored.

EAR FRINGES—Long silky hair on edges.
ELBOW—The joint between the upper arm and the forearm.
ELBOWS OUT—Elbows not held close, turning out from the body.
EVEN BITE—Meeting of front teeth with no overlap of upper or lower teeth.
EXPRESSION—Appearance of the head as viewed from the front, particularly the eyes and the surrounding tissue.

FEATHERING—The long fringes of hair found on the legs, ears, tails, and body of the Welsh Springer Spaniel.
FETCH—The command and the act of retrieving game or an object.
FIELD CHAMPION—A title won by a gun dog as a result of competition in the field at a series of licensed field trials.
FLAT-SIDED—Ribs lacking sufficient roundedness.

FLEWS—Upper lips pendulous, particularly in the corners.

FLUSH—To force birds to take flight. To spring them.

FOREFACE—The muzzle in front of the eyes.

FRILL—The long hair on the chest.

FULL EYE—Round, slightly protruding eye.

FURROW—A slight indention down the center of the skull to the stop.

GAIT—The leg action of a dog as it moves.

GAY TAIL—The tail carried over the back line.

GAZEHOUND—A dog that hunts by sighting the game.

GROOM—To make a dog's coat neat.

GROUPS—The breeds as grouped in divisions for judging.

GUN DOG—A dog trained to find live game and to retrieve the game after it has been shot.

HACKLES—Hair on neck and back that raises in fright or anger.

HARE FOOT—A long, close-toed, narrow foot.

HANDLER—The person who exhibits the dog in the show ring or field.

HARD-MOUTHED—The dog that damages with his teeth the game he retrieves.

HAW—A third eyelid in the inside corner of the eye.

HEAT—Seasonal period of the female.

HEEL—Rear pad on foot. A command to keep close beside the handler.

HEIGHT—Measurement from the withers to the ground.

HOCK—The joint between the second thigh and the metatarsal.

HOUND—A dog used for hunting by scent or sight.

INBREEDING—The mating of closely related dogs.

INT. CH.—International Champion, a dog that has won the title in more than one country.

JOWLS—Flesh of lips and jaws.

LAYBACK—The angle of the shoulder blade with the vertical.

LEATHER—The flap of the ear.

LEGGY—A dog with extra long legs compared to the standard.

LINE BREEDING—The mating of dogs within the line or family, as, for example, a dog to his granddam or a bitch to her grandsire.

LITTER—The puppies of one whelping.

LOIN—The region between the last rib and the hindquarters.

LOW-SET—Base of tail not on straight line with back.

LOW-SET EARS—Ears attached to the side of the head.

LYMER—A hound of ancient times led on a liam or leash.

MATCH SHOW—A dog show at which no points are awarded.

MATE—To breed a dog and bitch.

MATRON—A bitch that has had a litter.

MUZZLE—The head in front of the eyes, the foreface.

NAILS—Horny extension on toes.

NOSE—The ability to detect by the means of scent.

OB. CH.—Obedience Champion, a dog that has won three Test C classes at Obedience Championship shows (Great Britain).

OCCIPUT—Upper, back point of skull.

OCCIPITAL PROTUBERANCE—A prominently raised occiput.

OUTCROSS—The mating of unrelated animals of the same breed.

OUT AT ELBOWS—Elbows turn out from the body when the dog is at rest or moving.

OVERSHOT—The front teeth of the upper jaw projecting some way over those in the lower jaw when the mouth is closed.

PADDING—Picking front feet up higher than necessary while in motion.

PADDLING—Moving with forefeet wide.

PADS—The tough soles on the underside of the feet.

PASTERN—The lower section of the leg between the knee and the foot.

PEDIGREE—The written record of a dog's descent of three or more generations.

POINT—The immovable stance of a dog indicating the presence of game.

POINTS—The record gained at recognized shows, which, after obtaining fifteen, leads to a championship (U.S.A.).

PROFESSIONAL HANDLER—A person licensed to show dogs for their owners for a fee.

PUPPY—A dog under twelve months of age.

PUREBRED—A dog whose sire and dam belong to the same breed, and are themselves of unmixed descent since recognition of the breed.

QUALITY—Combined breed characteristics that make the animal an outstanding specimen, both standing and while in motion.

QUARTERS—The hindquarters.

QUICK—Part of the nail containing blood vessels and nerves.

RANGY—Long-bodied, usually lacking in depth of the chest.

REGISTRATION—The recording of a dog's name, parentage, and ownership and the assignment of a number by the Kennel Club.

RUFF—Thick, longer hair growth around the neck.

SCENT—The odor left by an animal on the trail or through the air.

SH. CH.—Show Champion, a title gained by a gun dog that has been awarded three C.C.s, but has not obtained the necessary qualifying certificate at a Field Trial for full Championship status (G.B.).

SMOOTH COAT—Short haired coat with stiff hair lying close to body.

SNIPEY—A pointed, weak muzzle.

SOUNDNESS—Normal mental and physical health.

SPAYED—A female whose ovaries have been removed surgically.

SPREAD—An accentuated width between the forelegs.

STIFLE—The joint of the hind leg corresponding to a man's knee.

STOP—The indentation of the bone between the eyes where the nasal bone and skull meet.

STUD DOG—A male dog used for breeding purposes.

SWAYBACK—Concave curvature of the back line between the withers and the hipbones.

T.D.—Tracking Dog, a title won by a dog that has attained certain minimum scores in tracking tests (U.S.A.), or open T.D. Stakes at Working Trials (G.B.).

THIGH—The hindquarters from hip to stifle.

TICKED—Small isolated red areas on a white ground.

TRIM—To pluck or clip the coat.

TUCK-UP—A markedly shallow body depth at the loin.

TYPE—The characteristics that distinguish a breed, the embodiment of the essentials of the standard.

U.D.—Utility Dog, a title won by a dog that has attained certain minimum scores in a Utility class (U.S.A.) or a U.D. Stake at Working Trials (G.B.).

UNDERSHOT—When the lower teeth project some way beyond the upper teeth when the mouth is closed.

WHELPS—Unweaned puppies.

WINNERS—Awards given at American dog shows to the best dog and the best bitch competing in regular classes.

WITHERS—The highest point of the shoulder blades.

W.D.—Working dog, a title won by a dog that has attained certain minimum scores in working trials (G.B.).

W.T.CH.—Working trials champion, a title given to a dog that has two CH. Working Trial stakes (W.D., P.D., or T.D.) with more than a certain minimum score (G.B.).

BIBLIOGRAPHY

A Gentleman, *The Sportsman's Companion,* New York, 1783, Edited by Rodman, O.H.P., Outdoors, 1948.

Aelian on the Characteristics of Animals. Scholfield, A.F. (trans.). Harvard University Press, Cambridge 1959.

Alcock, Leslie. *Arthur's Britain.* St. Martin's Press, New York 1971.

Arkwright, William. *The Pointer and His Predecessors.* A.L. Humphreys, London, 1906.

Asdell, S.A. *Dog Breeding: Reproduction and Genetics.* Little, Brown & Co., Boston 1966.

Ash, Edward C. *The New Book of the Dog.* Cassell, Toronto 1938.

Bain, George. *The Method and Construction of Celtic Art.* Dover Publications, New York 1973.

Berners, Dame Juliana. *The Boke of St. Albans,* St. Albans 1486.

Bert, Edmund. *An Approved Treatise of Hawks and Hawking.* (1619) Quaritch London, 1891.

Blackmore, Howard L. *Hunting Weapons.* Walter and Co., New York 1972.

Birley, Anthony. *Life in Roman Britain,* G.P. Putman's Sons, New York, 1972.

264

Bowen, E.G. *Britain and the Western Seaway.* Praeger Publishers, New York 1972.

Brearly, Joan M. *Visualization of the Standards of Purebred Dogs of the United States.* Popular Dog Publishing Co., Philadelphia 1972.

Bruette, Dr. William A. *The Complete Dog Book.* Stewart Kidd Co., Cincinnati 1921.

Caius, Johannes. *Of Englishe Dogges.* Richards Johnes, London, 1576.

Chaucer, Geoffrey. *Prologue to the Wife of Bath's Tale.* Barron's Educational Series, Inc., Boston 1948.

Claudian, Vol. 2, Platnauer, M. (trans.). Harvard University Press. Cambridge, 1922.

Compton, Herbert. *The Twentieth Century Dog.* Grant Richards, London, 1904.

Cottrell, Leonard. *The Great Invasion.* Coward-McCann, Inc., New York 1966.

Cottrell, Leonard. *A Guide to Roman Britain.* Chilton Books, Philadelphia 1966.

Crampton, Patrick. *Stonehenge of the Kings.* The John Day Co., New York 1968.

Dahr, E. *"Studien uber Hunde aus primitiveu Steingutkulturen in Nordewrapa,"* Lunds University Press, Berlin 1937.

Dawkins, W. Boyd. *Cave Hunting.* MacMillan, London 1874.

Denny, Norman and Filmer-Sankey, Josephine. *The Bayeux Tapestry.* Atheneum, New York 1966.

Digby, George W. *The Devonshire Hunting Tapestries.* Her Majesty's Printing Office, London, 1971.

Edward, Duke of York. *Master of Game.* 1406 edited by W.A. and F. Baille-Grohman, Chatto & Windus London, 1909.

Ellis, Dorothy. *Illustrated Souvenir Guide Book of St. Mary's.* The Southern Publishing Co., Brighton 1960.

Ellis, T.P. *Welsh Tribal Law and Customs in the Middle Ages.* Calarendon Press, Oxford 1926.

Fiennes, Richard and Alice. *The Natural History of Dogs.* The Natural History Press, Garden City 1970.

Foster, I. Ll., Daniel, Glyn. *Prehistoric and Early Wales.* Routledge & Kegan Paul, London, 1965.

Frederick II of Hohenstaufen. *The Art of Falconary.* Translated and edited by C.A. Wood and F.M. Fyfe, Stanford University Press, Stanford 1961.

Giot, Pierre-Roland. *Brittany.* Praeger, New York 1960.

Goodall, C.S. & Gasow, Julia. *The New English Springer Spaniel.* Howell Book House, New York, 1974.

Hammond, B. & R.D. *Training and Hunting the Brittany Spaniel.* A.S. Barnes, New York, 1971.

Hooper, Dorothy Morland. *The Springer Spaniel.* Howell Book House, Inc., New York 1971.

Howard, M.M., Hodges H., & Pyddoke, E. *Ancient Britons.* How They Lived, Praeger, New York, 1970.

Hutchinson's Dog Encyclopedia. Edited by Walter Hutchinson, Hutchinson & Co., London, 1934.

Hywell Dda. *The Laws of (The Book of Blegywryd).* Richards, Melville (trans.). The University Press, Liverpool, 1954.

Jarry, Madeleine. *World Tapestry.* G.P. Putman's Sons, New York 1969.

Jesse, George R. *Researches into the History of the British Dog.* Hardwicke, London, 1866.

Jobé, Joseph (Editor). *Great Tapestries.* Edita, S.A. Lausanne, 1965.

Jones, Arthur F. and Rendd, John. *The Treasury of Dogs.* Golden Press, New York 1964.

Jones, E. Gwynne. *A Bibliography of the Dog.* The Library Association, London, 1971.

Klindt-Jensen, O. *Denmark.* Praeger Publishing. New York, 1957.

Latham, Symon. *Lathams Falconry.* Jackson, London, 1615.

Lee, Rawdon B. *A History and Description of the Modern Dogs of Great Britain and Ireland.* Vol II, Horace Cox, London 1906.

Leonard, Jonathan Norton. *The World of Gainsborough.* Time-Life Books, New York 1969.

Little, Clarence C. *The Inheritance of Coat Color in Dogs,* Comstock, Ithaca, 1957.

Lloyd, Alan. *The Making of the King, 1066.* Holt, Rinehart and Winston, New York 1966.

Lloyd, Sir John E. *A History of Wales.* Longmans, Green and Col, London 1967.

Lorenz, Konrad Z. *Man Meets Dog.* Penguin Books, Baltimore 1953.

Mac Kendrick, Paul. *The Iberian Stones Speak.* Funk and Wagnalls, New York 1969.

Markham, Gervase. *The Whole Arte of Fowling by Water and Land.* Math, London, 1621.

Masters, Robert U. *Dogs, What Dog for Me?* Sterling Publishing Co., New York 1966.

Maxwell, C. Bede. *The Truth About Sporting Dogs.* Howell Book House, Inc., New York 1972.

Mery, Fernand. *The Life, History and Magic of the Dog.* Grosset and Dunlap, New York 1970.

Minor Latin Poets. Duft, J.W. and A. (trans.). Harvard University Press. Cambridge, 1958.

Nicholas, A.K. *The Nicholas Guide to Dog Judging.* Howell Book House, New York, 1970.

Oppian, Colluthus, Typhiodorus, Mair A.W. (trans.). Harvard University Press. Cambridge, 1958.

Pequart, M & S.J., Boule, M., Vallois, H.V., *Teviec Station-Necropole Mesolithique du Morbihan, Archives de l'Institut de Paleontologie Humaine.* Paris, 1937.

Pfaffenberger, Clarence J. *The New Knowledge of Dog Behavior.* Howell Book House, Inc., New York 1972.

Phillips, C.A. and Cane, R. Claude. *The Sporting Spaniel.* "Our Dogs" Publishing Co., Manchester 1906.

Piggott, Stuart. *The Neolithic Cultures of the British Isles.* Cambridge University Press, Cambridge 1970.

Radcliffe, Talbot. *Spaniels for Sport.* Howell Book House, Inc., New York, 1970.

Rhys, John and Jones, David B. *The Welsh People.* T. Fisher, Unwin Ltd., London 1923.

Rivet, A.L.F. (editor). *The Roman Villa in Britain.* Praeger, New York, 1969.

Rutimeyer, W.H. *Die Fauna der Ptahlbauten der Schweiz.* Berlin, 1861.

Savory, Hubert N. *Spain and Portugal.* Praeger, New York 1968.

Schneider-Leyer, Dr. Erich. *Dogs of the World.* New York, 1970.

Skene, William F. *The Four Ancient Books of Wales.* Edmonston & Douglas, Edinburgh, 1868.

Smith, I.J. *The Welsh Springer Spaniel.* Welsh Springer Spaniel Club of America, New York 1966.

Smythe, R.H. *The Breeding and Rearing of Dogs.* Arco, New York, 1969.

Stenton, Sir Frank (Editor). *The Bayeux Tapestry.* Phaidon Publishers, Inc., London 1965.

Stetson, Joe. *Hunting With Flushing Dogs.* TFH Publications, Neptune City, 1965.

Stone, J.F.S. *Wessex Before the Celts.* Praeger Publishers, New York 1970.

Strabo, The Geograph of. Jones, Horace L. (trans.). Harvard University Press, Cambridge 1959.

The Mabinogion. Jones, Gwyn and Thomas (trans.). Everyman's Library, London 1973.

Thomas, Joseph B. *Hounds and Hunting Through the Ages.* Garden City Publishing Co., Inc., Garden City 1937.

Topsell, Edward. *The Historie of Four-Footed Beasts.* London 1607.

Turbervile, George. *The Noble Art of Venery.* 1576, Charendon Oxford, 1908.

Turbervile, George. *The Book of Faulconrie or Hauking.* Barker, London, 1575.

Ucko, P.J. & Rosenfeld, A. *Palaeolithic Cave Art.* McGraw-Hill, New York, 1973.

Viale, Mercedes. *Tapestries.* Paul Hamlyn, N.Y., 1969.

Waterhouse, Ellis. *Gainsborough.* Spring Brooks, London 1966.

Weigert, Roger-Armand. *French Tapestry.* C.T. Branford Co., Newton, 1956.

Welsh Springer Spaniel Yearbooks (1934, '35, '36, '37, '48, '49, '50, '67, '68, '69, '70, '71-'72, '73, '74-'75). Welsh Springer Spaniel Club of Great Britain. Dog Directory, Bracknell.

Whitney, Leon F. *This is the Cocker Spaniel.* Garden City Books, Garden City, 1894.

Williams, A.H. *An Introduction to the History of Wales.* University of Wales Press, Cardiff 1962.

Williams, Gwym. *An Introduction to Welsh Poetry.* Faber and Faber Limited, London 1962.

GUIDE TO FURTHER STUDY

General Care:
"Handbook of Dog Care," Ralston Purina Co., 1971.
The Complete Book of Dog Care, L.F. Whitney, D.V.M., Doubleday & Co., 1953.

Obedience Training:
Good Dog, Bad Dog, M. Siegal & M. Margolis, Holt, Rinehart and Winston, 1973.
Successful Dog Training, M.E. Pearsall, Howell Book House Inc., 1973.

Field Training:
Gun Dogs–Training and Field Trials, P.R.A. Moxon
Spaniels for Sport, T. Radcliffe, Howell Book House Inc., 1970.

Showing:
Dog Judging, A.K. Nicholas, Howell Book House, Inc., 1970.
Clipping and Grooming Your Spaniel and Setter, Stone and Migliorini, Avco Publishing Co., 1971.

Breeding:
Breeding and the Rearing of Dogs, R.H. Smythe, Arco Publishing Co., 1971.
The Springer Spaniel, D.M. Hooper, Howell Book House, Inc., 1971.

INDEX